The New Voices of Islam

There is a dramatic intellectual struggle between modernists and traditionalists for the legacy of the Islamic heritage that is now underway in the Muslim World. The outcome of this titanic struggle for winning hearts and minds will leave an indelible mark on the region and the global community for years to come. In this timely volume Mehran Kamrava has compiled a selection from some of the leading and most influential Muslim reformist thinkers whose voices have often been muted and marginalized. These essays introduce the reader to the nuances of the unfolding drama surrounding the issues of religion, politics and the public space across the Muslim World. They reflect on the state of present cultural and political malaise, the challenges of Western ascendancy, political authoritarianism, and the possible passages for liberation and salvation in an interdependent world. The essays reveal the richness as well as the limitations of these new attempts to synthesize Islam and modernity. This is a must read for all those interested in hearing the new voices and seeing the other face of Islam.

Manochehr Dorraj, Professor of Political Science, Texas Christian University

The New Voices of Islam is a fine collection which effectively answers the question: where are the reformist voices in Islam? Mehran Kamrava has done an excellent job in presenting the global diversity of Muslim thinking from North Africa to Southeast Asia, Europe to America.

John L. Esposito, University Professor and Founding Director of the Prince Alwaleed Bin Talal Center for Muslim–Christian Understanding, Georgetown University

This volume contains not the voices of Muslim governments and Islamist oppositions but the work of Muslim mavericks – refreshing in their originality, searing in their critiques, reassuring in their rationality. These voices deserve a wider audience in the West, and this book responds to that need. But also, and most especially, they deserve the attention of Muslims everywhere. Government repression and Islamist pressures unfortunately obstruct general access to such unconventional ideas in many Muslim states.

Robert D. Lee, Professor of Political Science, Colorado College

Western public concern about Islamic extremism is almost wholly uninformed by the views of the reforming intellectuals gathered together in Mehran Kamrava's very important book *The New Voices of Islam*. These men and women, living both within the Islamic world and in Europe and America, have been struggling for a modern, pluralist, tolerant and democratic transformation of the Muslim world years before the crises of 9/11 and 7/7. Their collective message deserves the widest exposure, particularly within western political circles where it has, sadly, gone unheeded.

David Waines, Emeritus Professor of Islamic Studies, Lancaster University

The New Voices of
ISLAM
Reforming Politics and Modernity
A Reader

Mehran Kamrava
Editor

Reprinted in 2009 by I.B.Tauris & Co. Ltd
6 Salem Road, London W2 4BU
175 Fifth Avenue, New York, NY 10010
www.ibtauris.com

First Published in 2006 by I.B.Tauris & Co. Ltd
Copyright © 2006 Mehran Kamrava

Library of Modern Middle East Studies 63

ISBN 10: 1 84511 274 1 (Hb)
ISBN 13: 978 1 84511 274 5 (Hb)

ISBN 10: 1 84511 275 X (Pb)
ISBN 13: 978 1 84511 275 2 (Pb)

A full CIP record for this book is available from the British Library

Typeset in Adobe Garamond Pro by A. & D. Worthington, Newmarket, Suffolk
Printed and bound in India by Thomson Press (India) Ltd

Contents

Credits

Grateful acknowledgment goes to Professors Leila Ahmed, Mohsen Kadivar, Muhammad Shahrour, and Amina Wadud for their kind permission to reprint their essays in this volume. I am also thankful to the following publishers for their permission to reproduce excerpts here from the sources below:

Mohammed Arkoun, "Present-Day Islam Between Its Tradition and Globalization," in Farhad Daftary (ed), *Intellectual Traditions in Islam* (London: I.B.Tauris, 2001), pp 179–221. Copyright, I.B.Tauris.

Tariq Ramadan, *Western Muslims and the Future of Islam* (Oxford: Oxford University Press, 2004), pp 31–61. Copyright, Oxford University Press.

Fethullah Gülen, "A Comparative Approach to Islam and Democracy," *SAIS Review*, vol. 21, no. 2 (summer–fall 2001), pp 133–8. Copyright, The Johns Hopkins University Press.

Mohamed Talbi, "Religious Liberty: A Muslim Perspective," in Leonard Swindler (ed), *Muslims in Dialogue: The Evolution of a Dialogue* (Lewiston, NY: The Edwin Mellon Press, 1992), pp 465–82. Copyright, The Edwin Mellon Press.

Nasr Abu Zaid with Esther R. Nelson, *Voices of an Exile: Reflections on Islam* (Westport, CT: Praeger, 2004), pp 165–80, 199–208. Copyright, Greenwood Publishing Group.

Leila Ahmed, "Women and the Advent of Islam," *Signs*, vol. 11, no. 4 (summer 1986), pp 665–91. Copyright, University of Chicago Press.

Amina Wadud, "A'ishah's Legacy: The Struggle for Women's Rights within Islam," *New Internationalist*, no. 345 (May 2002), pp 16–17. Copyright, New Internationalist.

For Melisa,
Dilara, and Kendra

CHAPTER I

Introduction: Reformist Islam in Comparative Perspective

Mehran Kamrava

Over the past two decades or so, at a time when the forces of "Islamic fundamentalism" have emerged as the dominant face of Islam in the West, a vibrant and highly influential discourse by a number of prominent Muslim thinkers is seeking to reform and reformulate some of the main premises of Islamic theology and jurisprudence. Throughout the Muslim world, from Indonesia and Malaysia in Southeast Asia to Algeria and Morocco in North Africa, there has emerged a group of highly articulate and influential public intellectuals whose ideas are inspired by reformist interpretations of Islam. Their voices might be faint and difficult to hear, drowned by the boisterous violence of self-righteous fundamentalists whose claims of exclusivity leave no room for discourse and debate. The intellectuals are men of letters—and in a few instances women—but they are not fighters and warriors. They are professors, writers, and essayists, gifted in the arts of letters and oratory, not in street battles and guerrilla tactics. Their disposition is to be moderate, their political passions tamed and reasoned.

It is little wonder that in the post-9/11 world, the voices of moderate Islam are all but impossible to hear. Political moderation itself is somewhat of a rare commodity today everywhere, whether in the lands of Islam or elsewhere, and perhaps at no other point in history has Islamic moderation in particular appeared so rare a phenomenon. Muslim moderates the world over are under attack and on the defensive. They are mistrusted and kept at bay by their own governments, are all too frequently accused of heresy and apostasy by the orthodox establishment in their countries and elsewhere, and are seldom fully understood and appreciated by their lay coreligionists. Moreover, the international milieu within which they are articulating their ideas—the most pronounced features of which today are blunt American unilateralism, the so-called "War on Terror," the occupation of Iraq by the US military, and recurrent acts of terrorism by Islamic fundamentalists—

hardly supports their calls for moderation, dialogue, and a broad rethinking of core Islamic precepts.

In its own small way, this book attempts to bring the voices of these reformist Muslim thinkers to a wider Western audience. What follows are the writings of some of the most astute and subtle thinkers belonging in the reformist camp of political Islam today. Their voices might indeed be faint and difficult to hear, but they are far from silenced and muzzled altogether. In fact, as part of a proud tradition of reformist Muslim thought that dates back to at least the late eighteenth century and even before,[1] today's reformists do not represent a novel or new phenomenon in Islam. What they do represent is a vision of Islam and its role in the human polity that is radically different from that advocated by orthodoxy, a vision whose very certainty and loudness has made it emerge in recent years as the dominant face of Islam. Noise ought not to be confused with dominance, and neither should relative silence be seen as irrelevance. Today, there are tectonic struggles within Islam over its very essence and its soul. This book presents the arguments of the protagonists on one side of this struggle, the reformist intellectuals.

For the purposes of this book, I have chosen to highlight 13 of the most renowned and influential Muslim reformist thinkers alive today. They include Leila Ahmed (Egypt and the United States), Nasr Abu Zaid (Egypt), Mohammed Arkoun (Algeria and France), Hasan Hanafi (Egypt), Fethullah Gülen (Turkey), Mohsen Kadivar (Iran), Fatima Mernissi (Morocco), Chandra Muzaffar (Malaysia), Tariq Ramadan (Switzerland), Muhammad Shahrour (Syria), Abdolkarim Soroush (Iran), Mohamed Talbi (Tunisia), and Amina Wadud (United States).

This is not, of course, by any means an exhaustive list. There are a number of highly influential reformist thinkers who are not included here because of space limitations. For example, there could have been chapters by Hüseyn Atay (Turkey), Rachid Ghannoushi (Tunisia), Mohammad Mojtahed Shabestari (Iran), Anwar Ibrahim (Malaysia), and Abdurrahman Wahid (Indonesia), among others.[2] The thinkers whose thoughts are represented here do, nevertheless, represent a broad cross-section of the reformist intellectual trend within Islam and have made significant contributions to the evolving discourse of reformism.

The inclusion of Arkoun, who has spent most of his adult life in France rather than in his birthplace of Algeria, and especially the Swiss-born Ramadan, who writes almost exclusively for Western audiences, demonstrates the global reach and impact of contemporary Islam far beyond the lands traditionally associated with it. Just as Islamic fundamentalism—the flip side of the reformism highlighted here—has emerged as a global phenomenon, so have attempts at presenting a reformist, modern interpretation of the religion assumed global dimensions. As Oliver Roy has argued, Islam has become "deterritorialized" and "globalized," and millions of Muslim migrants in Europe and North America have formed "imagined identities" with their religion at its center.[3] And, with them, so have the varieties of Islam—fundamentalist, reformist, and otherwise—become globalized.

Over the last few decades, a number of factors have converged to produce the rebirth of a highly vibrant discourse of Islamic reformism, one whose roots go deep into the history of the religion. This discourse is being articulated in an extremely hostile environment and faces what often seem like insurmountable political, cultural, and jurisprudential obstacles. Not coincidentally, some of its most skilled proponents reside in lands not traditionally associated with Islam. Despite these obstacles, the reformist discourse is here to stay and is bound to have lasting consequences for the tenor and direction of Islamic jurisprudence. It is far from certain, however, whether at any time in the near future this re-emerging discourse will become the dominant face of Islam, for it lacks the institutional support that would enable it to gain widespread acceptance and internalization. Nevertheless, the theoretical and jurisprudential groundwork has been laid, and is steadily gaining in depth. What is now needed are the appropriate forms of institutional support, political and otherwise, for the discourse to traverse from the halls of academia into neighborhood mosques and other mainstream venues.

The multiple faces of contemporary Islam

Reformist Muslim intellectuals represent only one strand of a complex and multi-layered phenomenon that collectively constitutes "Islam." At the outset, two basic yet important distinctions must be made, one between the "official" and "unofficial" or populist varieties of Islam—*al-Islam al-rasmi* and *al-Islam al-sha'bi* respectively—and the other between *Islam as religion* on the one hand and *belief in Islam* as manifestations of religiosity on the other. Broadly, official Islam refers to that version of the religion that is sanctioned and is at times even articulated by the state in an attempt to enhance its own legitimacy in relation to society and to limit its opponents. As James Bill and Robert Springborg maintain, "Muslim rulers have typically sought to cloak themselves in the legitimacy provided by al-Islam al-rasmi. In return for material favors and recognition of their status, the ulama [literally, "the holders of (religious) knowledge"] have generally facilitated that legitimization process by using their prerogatives accordingly" through "preaching Friday sermons that underscore obedience to authority, issuing *fatwas* ... supportive of government policies, and in general emphasizing the inseparability of Islam and government."[4] Fu'ad Zakariyya, a secular Egyptian thinker who is known for his criticisms of Muslim fundamentalists, labels this officially manipulated version of religion "Petro-Islam," one whose central aim is to "keep the Arabs (and other Muslims) retarded in the modern world, occupied with useless arguments and impossible goals, and irrationally concerned with matters that distract them from the real problems to which they ought to give attention."[5]

Not unlike other sources of legitimacy employed by non-democratic regimes, state-sanctioned interpretations of Islam are useful only when a variety of other material and non-material means of political legitimization also succeed in ensuring the public's political passivity. Throughout the Muslim world, and especially in the Middle East, official Islam succeeded in helping non-democratic governments maintain power so long as levels of state repression remained manageable and the continued growth of the national economy, fueled by rising oil prices, masked the corruption and inefficiency of the state apparatus and the incompetence and avarice of political leaders. Throughout the 1980s and the 1990s, however, recurrent bouts of economic recession, compounded by self-inflicted wounds and misadventures domestically and internationally—the most painful of which were the Iran–Iraq war of 1980–88, the Iraqi invasion of Kuwait, and the Algerian civil war beginning in 1992—began to crack the "ruling bargains" that once so successfully maintained otherwise unpopular states in power. By the early 1990s, as the American penetration of the Middle East became more pervasive, and, almost simultaneously, as the defensive impulse of the states involved drove them to unprecedented levels of repression, fewer people were willing to buy into governmental professions of religious piety and claims of Islamic legitimacy. Today, some two decades later, *al-Islam al-rasmi* is all but a dead force. Even the Iranian theocracy, the *Islamic* Republic, faces serious and far-reaching challenges to its interpretations of Islam from Iranians of all walks of life. For its part, the claim by the Saudi monarchy to be "the Custodian of Islam's Holiest Mosques" is taken no more seriously today than was Saddam Hussein's assertion in the 1980s that he was fighting the Iranians in defense of Islam when he decreed the addition of *Allahu Akbar* (God is Great) to the Iraqi flag.

The steady decline of official Islam was partly caused and reinforced by an inverse rise in the depth and popularity of non-official Islam among the various strata of society. It is here that the distinction between Islam the religion and religiosity as belief becomes important. Whereas religion may

Finally, I literally could not have worked on this project had it not been for the loving support of my wife Melisa and the nurturing environment she has fostered in our house. She has been a constant source of support and inspiration throughout work on the project, putting up with the many hours I spent behind the computer at all hours of the night, all the while taking care of our beautiful daughters Dilara and Kendra. For all the love and joy they have given me, it is to my three ladies that I dedicate this book.

Acknowledgements

The idea for this book was originally proposed to me in November 2003 by I.B.Tauris's Turi Munthe, who believed passionately that the voices of reformist Muslim intellectuals deserved a wider hearing in English than had hitherto been the case. Although I was in the midst of another project at the time, it was hard to resist Turi's enthusiasm for the project. By the time I was able to turn my full attention to this project in late 2004, Turi had moved on to greener pastures. I was fortunate to then be working with Alex Wright, who shared Turi's contagious enthusiasm for the topic and who was a tremendous help through the different stages of work on it. I am thankful to both individuals for their help and advice throughout and also for their confidence in my ability to give greater voice to the Muslim intellectuals whose works are highlighted here.

At the University of California Press, Naomi Schneider was equally supportive, and her keen insights into the topic were instrumental in shaping the manuscript into its present form. I am grateful for her enthusiastic support of my work on this volume and for her astute recommendations throughout.

Throughout the work on the project, I have been extremely fortunate to work with a number of highly talented research assistants. Bojana Kocijan contacted many of the intellectuals around the world and was instrumental in collecting valuable research materials. Holta Turner continued the collection of materials and did much of the tedious word processing. Mohamed Galal, among other things, collected most of the data related to Kuwait, Saudi Arabia, and Egypt. I am grateful for their collective efforts, and I am convinced that the final product would have been seriously delayed had it not been for their hard work.

Colleagues Manochehr Dorraj, Mahmood Monshipouri, Gabriel Raymond, Greg Truex, and Nathan Weinberg kindly read and commented on earlier versions of my introductory chapter, all at very hectic times in the academic calendar. I am most thankful to all five for their invaluable input and suggestions.

be defined as "a coherent corpus of belief and dogmas collectively managed by a body of legitimate holders of knowledge," religiosity refers to the "self-formulation and self-expression of a personal faith."[6] Beginning in the 1970s and lasting up to the present day, levels of religiosity have risen in depth and intensity among the Muslim masses all over the world. Observers of Islamic societies today cannot help but be impressed by the depth and the degree to which Islam has re-emerged as an integral part of the average person's identity.[7] This is especially the case among the very urban classes who looked for definitions of the self in largely non-religious terms a mere two or three decade ago.[8] Headscarves, beards, the *hijab*, and other indicators of religiosity have re-emerged in such secular political environments as Indonesia, Malaysia, Turkey, Syria, Egypt, and Tunisia. This newly found piety owes as much to the people's pervasive distaste for and opposition to the political establishment, and the secularism for which it stands, as to their reinvigorated devotion to religion *per se*. Whatever its cause and genesis, religiosity has seen a steady resurgence throughout the cultures and societies of Muslim lands.

Some data can shed more light on this deepening sense of religiosity in Muslim societies. In Kuwait, the number of mosques increased from 650 in 1995 to 900 in 2000, and then to 1,150 in 2005, an increase of nearly 180 percent over a decade.[9] There was a similar increase in the number of mosques in Saudi Arabia, jumping from 35,376 in 1995 to 50,538 in 2004, a rise of 42 percent.[10] The number of Saudi charitable organizations specializing in the memorization of the Qur'an also rose dramatically, jumping from 4,386 in 1995 to 111,484 in 2004.[11] Other types of religious establishments experienced similar growths throughout the Muslim world. Prior to the eruption of major scandals in the early 1990s, for example, there was a major increase in the numbers and the influence of "Islamic investment companies," which were often greatly favored over government-owned and controlled banks.[12] In Egypt, despite severe government controls and restrictions, the number of learning institutions under the control of the Al-Azhar mosque-university rose from 600 in 1982 to 5,080 in 1995, with another 1,500 slated for construction in the near future.[13] Today, the total number of students in the elementary, middle, and high schools related to the Al-Azhar is reported to be in excess of 1,140,000.[14] There has been a similar explosion in the publication and sale of popular religious books—the so-called "Islamic books"—commonly sold on the sidewalks of Cairo and other major cities of the Muslim world, whose sales frequently reach into six figures.[15]

In the broadest of terms, this rise in levels of religiosity tends to take one of four forms: popular Islam, politically activist Islam, intellectual Islam, and Islamic fundamentalism. These categories are neither mutually exclusive of one another nor do they exist as neatly packaged, separate phenomena in the real world as they can be delineated on paper.[16] In fact, they often have a strong symbiotic, mutually reinforcing relationship with one another. Growing piety and observance of religious rites and dictates (popular Islam) has facilitated the rise and popularity of the latest attempts to turn Islam into both a political means and a political end in itself (political Islam). This politicization of Islam, occurring in stifling and repressive political environments in which dogma thrives and civil discourse suffers, has often manifested itself in extremist and violent forms (fundamentalist Islam). Nevertheless, it has also found expression in learned and scholarly circles, not just among the traditional ulama but also among university professors, writers and essayists, and other members of the intelligentsia (intellectual Islam).

Among the different varieties of religiosity, intellectual Islam is the one likely to have the most resonating consequences for Islamic jurisprudence in both the near and the distant future. We are, I will argue below, some distance away from an "Islamic reformation." Nevertheless, the evolving intellectual discourses surrounding Islamic jurisprudence (*fiqh*), especially as they are currently taking shape, go to the heart of what Islam the religion is all about. Clearly, the intellectual skills and the willpower profoundly and fundamentally to rethink and redefine Islam are in no short supply. What mitigates the transition from thought into practice, or acceptance and internalization, is the larger context within which both the intellectuals and their potential audiences find themselves. For their part, the intellectuals themselves do not speak with a single voice, as we will see presently, and are divided internally between those generally considered "conservative" and others who are more "reformist" and liberal. Before examining the arguments and the internal divisions of intellectual Islam, brief mention must be made of political Islam and its fundamentalist variety.

"Political Islam"—the synthesis of Islam and politics whereby Islam becomes a medium for the expression and practice of politics—is now more than a century old. As far back as the 1860s, a generation of thinkers in Ottoman lands—e.g. Ziya Pasha, Namık Kemal, and Rifa'a Badawi Rafi' al-Tahtawi—sought to articulate nationalist and modernist ideas imported from Europe through the prism of Islam. "They set high values on the social morality of Islam, and tried to justify the adoption of western institutions in Islamic terms, as being not the introduction of something new but a return to the true spirit of Islam."[17] Jamal al-Din al-Afghani (1839–97), also called Asadabadi, and then his disciple Muhammad Abduh (1849–1905), saw in Islam the potential to foster the creation of independent, modern nations, free of colonial domination and based on rationality, progress, and modernity.[18] The Iranian Constitutional Revolution of 1905–11 gave religiously inspired intellectuals and the clergy the opportunity to put many such ideas into practice, albeit only temporarily and with fleeting success.[19] The early decades of the 1900s saw a new breed of Islamic political activism with the establishment of the Muslim Brotherhood (al-Akhwan al-Muslimin) in Egypt in 1928, ultimately overshadowed by the repressive secularism of the nationalist interlude lasting from the 1950s to the mid-1970s, and then revived and radicalized in the late 1970s. The dramatic expansion in the number of university students throughout the Muslim world beginning in the 1950s—many of whom had experienced government repression first-hand and then faced few opportunities for advancement upon graduation—only swelled the ranks of the Islamists.[20] Lionized by the success of the Iranian revolution, political Islam became thoroughly revolutionized by the 1980s, a force not only to be reckoned with but indeed *the* force dominating either the political landscape itself or the challenge to it.

For all the noise and drama it caused throughout the 1980s and the early 1990s, by the start of the new millennium political scientists began writing about "the failure of political Islam" and foretold of a major transformation to its inner logic and its goals.[21] This failure arose from political Islam's inability to formulate viable political concepts, articulate and express them in canonical texts, and then to successfully implement and put them into practice.[22] Unable to replicate the example of the Iranian revolutionary state elsewhere, which had quickly proven to be not that exemplary anyway, political Islam steadily morphed into one of two varieties. One variety opted for pragmatic incrementalism, seeking to change the political system from within by participating in existing political venues. At the same time, it also set out to prepare the social and cultural groundwork for its eventual political victory through emphasizing the need for greater social morality, ethical living, and piety.

When the opportunity presented itself, even if temporarily, Islamist political parties and organizations formed and willingly took part in state-sponsored elections: the Muslim Brotherhood in Egypt in 2005,[23] the Islamic Action Front in Jordan in 2003, the Islamic Salvation Front in Algeria in 1990 and 1991, and the Refah Party in Turkey in 1995. Tunisia's Movement for Islamic Tendency even went so far as to change its name to al-Nahda (Renaissance) in 1989, assuming that dropping the reference to Islam would enable it to take part in the country's legislative elections scheduled for that April. The name change, however, turned out to be of no avail.[24]

Although they made few political inroads through state-sanctioned procedures and institutions, throughout the 1980s and the 1990s Islamists grew increasingly influential within the burgeoning professional associations. In the absence of viable venues for political participation, many Islamists directed their efforts and energies through various middle-class shelters that were—or acted in lieu of—civil society organizations, the most important and viable of which were professional associations.[25] Through these professional associations, Islamists created "new models of political leadership and community which stand in sharp contrast to the policies and practices of state elites," appealed directly and through grassroots efforts to the ideological sensibilities of urban professionals, and advocated the re-establishment of once-popular statist social contracts between the state and society.[26] Not surprisingly, throughout the 1980s and the 1990s, all over the Muslim world associations belonging to engineers, physicians, dentists, and attorneys swelled their ranks with Islamist professionals.

Participatory politics is not, of course, a hallmark of the political systems found in the Muslim world, and, by the late 1990s, most Islamist parties and professional associations were at best either simply banned or at worst had their leaders thrown into prison. The much-anticipated democratization of Muslim-majority countries did not come about, and, in fact, many of the countries seeming to move in democratic directions in the late 1980s and the early 1990s instead experienced authoritarian contractions within less than a decade. It was within this context of reinvigorated authoritarianisms at home, coupled with mounting political and economic frustrations among almost all echelons of society, and the increasing depth and bluntness of American hegemony regionally and globally, that political Islam gave steady rise to its fundamentalist stepchild throughout the 1980s. And, in turn, as "pax-Americana" became a more firmly entrenched feature of global politics, by the mid-1990s Islamic fundamentalism had acquired a decidedly anti-American face.

Whereas political Islam is generally willing to work within the restrictive political parameters set by the state, Islamic fundamentalism wholly rejects the legitimacy of existing states and has no patience for gradualism and incremental change. In fact, many of the most extremist religious organizations were specifically a product of—or experienced political ascendance in relation to—comparatively moderate Islamist ventures that appeared to have reached tactical and strategic deadlocks. Algeria's Islamic Salvation Front (FIS), for example, was avidly committed to non-violent political action, and many of its leaders, such as Abbasi Madani and Malek Bennabi, are generally considered to be moderate political activists.[27] Following the 1992 military coup and the cancellation of the parliamentary elections, however, in the first round of which the FIS had emerged victorious, "armed Islamist groups began to mushroom and entered in violent confrontations with the regime."[28] In Palestine, a similar phenomenon led to the growth of the Islamic Jihad organization out of the Palestinian Muslim Brotherhood and the Mujama (Islamic Congress), which were seen as gradualist and uncomfortably close to the Israeli establishment.[29] And, in Egypt, the increasing political marginalization of the Muslim Brotherhood by the state has only added fuel to the radicalism and violence of the Islamic Group (*Jama'at Islami*). As one observer has noted, "the Brotherhood views revolutionary groups as offshoots of its movement and ideology that have mistakenly taken up violence," the blame for which, it maintains, goes directly to the government.[30]

By and large, Muslim fundamentalists everywhere adhere to a number of common, and at the same time inflexible, ideological propositions. To begin with, they have embraced and operationalized an instrumentalist conception of *Jihad*, whereby what others may see as "a moral struggle for self-betterment" is instead viewed as a holy war against the enemies of Islam, one in which every Muslim is duty-bound to engage.[31] Along with their passionate hatred of secular society, their conception of *Jihad* in militaristic, violent terms bestows them with a sense of power, the quest for which is a dominant feature of their goals and their discourse.[32] They also tend to be fanatically obsessed with the notion of *tawhid*, the absolute oneness of God, to the point of considering the veneration of imams and saints, and at times even the Prophet Muhammad himself, as *shirk* (polytheism).[33] At the same time, they advocate emulating the life of the Prophet and his Companions (*aslaf*). They zealously promote the five pillars (*fara'id*) of Islam—declaration of faith, prayer, pilgrimage to Mecca, almsgiving, and fasting—and call for the immediate implementation of the *Sharia*. Lastly, they categorically reject the dogma of *taqlid* and instead call for *ijtihad*.[34]

The fundamentalists' rejection of *taqlid* and advocacy of *ijtihad* needs to be clarified. *Taqlid* literally means imitation, and refers to adherence to legal precedent as set by the various theological schools of Islam. *Ijtihad*, on the other hand, means independent reasoning, calling on the believer to "draw independent conclusions and judgments on legal and other issues."[35] Fundamentalists, it is important to note, embrace a decidedly different interpretation of *ijtihad* than do reformist intellectuals. Both groups call for *ijtihad* based on the Qur'an and, especially in the case of the fundamentalists, the *sunna* (traditions) of the Prophet. The fundamentalists, however, have a very literalist interpretation of the Qur'an, as if the sacred text remains frozen in time and place. Their *ijtihad*, therefore, seeks to revive an original Islam that is unencumbered by centuries of what they perceive as misguided interpretation. The reformists, on the other hand, embrace a dynamic and context-driven approach to *ijtihad*, calling for interpreting the text based on changing and evolving circumstances. For the reformists, the "gates of *ijtihad*" remain wide open; for the fundamentalists, the gates are open only so long as they determine who and what enters through.

"The Al-Qaeda phenomenon"—which is global in scope and has in turn elicited a global reaction—is bound to have demographic, strategic, and doctrinal consequences for Islamic fundamentalist movements world-wide. Precisely what these consequences are remains to be seen. Within less than a decade or so, Islamic fundamentalism has already undergone major changes in its composition, direction, and its goals. For one thing, it is no longer geographically limited to "the Muslim world," extending from the Middle East—which still continues to be its epicenter—to Southeast Asia, Africa, Europe, and North America. Moreover, the Muslims drawn into its orbit no longer fit into a single profile: Palestinian suicide bombers, often recruited by friends and relatives, are generally believed to be well-adjusted socially and seldom give any prior indication of the carnage they are about to unleash;[36] Chechen rebels rely extensively on the wives of dead fighters, called "Black Widows," for suicide bombings; Al-Qaeda's core cadre and its foot soldiers remain "Afghan Arabs" with middle-class backgrounds, cut off from their families and the communities they leave behind, now immersed in their new cause;[37] the March 2004 Madrid train bombings were blamed on marginalized migrants from North Africa; the London bombings in July 2005 were the work of British-born Muslims. (Of the four suicide bombers involved in the London attacks, three were born in England to Pakistani parents, and a fourth, born in Jamaica, had lived there since the age of five months and had converted to Islam when he was 15 years old.) Does all this mean an expansion in the scope and reach of Islamic fundamentalism? Only time will tell.

Similarly, at the time of writing, the American occupation of Iraq and the "War on Terror" remain in full force and, even with the inevitable change of presidents at the White House, do not show signs of changing direction. Clearly, the political vacuum and chaos caused by the collapse of the Iraqi state in 2003 enabled Al-Qaeda to expand its activities and its reach beyond Afghanistan. What ultimately happens to Iraq, and more broadly what the United States and its allies do in the coming years and decades, are bound to have important consequences for the future direction f Islamic fundamentalism. Just as consequential will be the domes. es of states with large Muslim populations, which today are found not o n Southeast Asia and the Middle East but in Europe as well.

Pervasive authoritarianism in the Muslim world and global A n heavy-handedness may keep fundamentalist varieties of Islam alive s a political force for some time to come. On a deeper, jurisprudentia level, however, the future prospects of Islamic fundamentalism do not seem terribly bright. Fundamentalist Islam's increasing turn to violence bespeaks of its theoretical and jurisprudential bankruptcy in face of the realities of the modern world. It suffers from a basic inability to present viable solutions to the complex social, economic, and political problems arising out of processes of modernity. Instead, it advocates either jurisprudential retrenchment in archaic notions of religiosity, or physically and militarily lashing out at the symbols and manifestations of modernity, or both. It offers neither new ideas nor new solutions, calling on believers to instead regress into some utopian ideal that is found only in a mythical past.

In the short run, Islamic fundamentalism may have captured the *hearts* of many of the dispossessed and oppressed masses in the Muslim world. But, given the competition it faces from another, more learned variety of the religion, it is doubtful whether it can also capture the *minds* of most Muslims in the long run.

A final variety of Islam found in the Muslim world may be called "intellectual Islam." This is the Islam of the learned person. It is philosophically rich and is painstakingly constructed, and is steeped in dialogue and discourse. Whereas popular Islam tends to be ritualistic, and fundamentalist Islam is impetuous and impatient, intellectual Islam deals on the plane of ideas and interpretation (*tafsir*), is preoccupied with philosophical "disputations" revolving around Islamic theology (*kalam*), and pays premium attention to intellectual prowess (*'aql*) and independent reasoning (*ijtihad*). Its primary arenas of activity are universities and seminaries rather than mosques, party cells or headquarters, or street rallies. It is formulated and expressed through books and essays, not the pulpit, and certainly not through the barrel of a gun.

Intellectual Islam has been a historically salient feature of the religion dating as far back as the earliest years of its appearance. Intellectual debate and discourse among the learned elite have never been absent from Islam, even if overtly suppressed or controlled by the caliphate for prolonged periods of time. It is true, of course, that this intellectual vibrancy—which initially revolved around such profound issues as the question of succession to the Prophet and the conquest and conversion of non-Arabs to the faith[38]—gradually subsided as central state authority solidified its hold over the ulama. Nevertheless, Muslim scholars continued to make significant contributions to the study of history, grammar, poetry, and, later on, through translations of mostly Greek texts, to philosophy, medicine, astronomy, and astrology.[39] Despite lacking court patronage or, at least in the early years, the institutional framework within which to engage in their intellectual endeavors—*madrasas* not having appeared until the eleventh century[40]—numerous Muslim philosophers engaged in in-depth studies of the Qur'an and the *hadith*. The significant contributions to Islamic thought of the likes of al-Kindi (805–73), al-Farabi (870–950), Ibn Sina (Avicenna) (980–1037), Ibn Rushd (Averroës) (1126–98), and Ibn Taymiyya (1263-1328) were frequently complemented with the works of less well-known, more popular thinkers whose writings appealed to wider audiences.[41]

By the time it reached the peak of its power in the sixteenth century, the Ottoman caliphate was able to ensure its institutional and political dominance over a good number of the ulama, thereby greatly reducing the religious thinkers' independence and the scope of their scholarly and intellectual freedom.[42] It was not until after the steady erosion of Ottoman power in the late nineteenth century, largely as a result of European colonial encroachment, that a new breed of Muslim scholars emerged and advocated the pursuit of social and political objectives through the prism of religion. Al-Afghani and Abduh were precisely two such figures, with the former calling for a pan-Islamism of sorts and the latter advocating Islamic reformism as the most effective ways of resisting European colonialism.

Beginning at around the same time, and steadily gathering pace as the twentieth century wore on, the ulama lost more and more of their legitimacy to be the sole interpreters of Islam, a function they increasingly had to share with secularly educated intellectuals. This development owed its genesis to several factors. At a time of profound and rapid social and political change, a vast majority of the ulama remained steeped in "defensive conservatism."[43] The establishment and growth of the modern state was key in undermining many of the social roles and functions of the clerical classes, and especially in breaking their monopoly over the field of education. "The educational institutions under their control lost resources, students, and influence and in many places were simply taken over by the states, which were increasingly dominated by secularist modernizers."[44] The most venerable centers of Islamic learning—the traditional university-mosques of Al-Azhar, al-Qarawiyyin, Az-Zaytuna, or the Shi'a seminaries of Najaf and Qom—found themselves in uneven competition for resources and students, and therefore prestige, with the modern, secular universities of Cairo, Istanbul, Aligarh, Algiers, and Tehran.[45] Not surprisingly, an overwhelming majority of influential Muslim thinkers in the twentieth century—whether or not politically active—came from non-clerical backgrounds.[46] Especially by the final decades of the century, some of the most important contributions to Islamic thought were being made by intellectuals with secular backgrounds.

Intellectual Islam has its own internal divisions. Two broad and fluid strands can be discerned, one of which may be classified as conservative and another as reformist, or, alternatively, as "neo-traditionalist" and "modernist" respectively.[47] In very general terms, conservative Muslim intellectuals are somewhat reticent to strike a philosophical and practical balance between the various tenets of *fiqh* and modernity. They tend to be "strongly loyal to the traditional practices and past consensus, finding in them a wisdom which is not to be lightly rejected. There should be no unseemly rush to abandon them."[48]

On the whole, these conservative intellectuals tend to eschew political activism and are often quietist. Their reluctance to synchronize Islam with modernity may be rooted in their training in and their attachment to more traditional methods of *ijtihad*, as is often the case with the graduates of institutions such as the Al-Azhar and other similar seminaries. While they do include a number of prominent academic figures, most Islamist thinkers in this category come from traditional ulama backgrounds. As such, they

> are generally better placed to draw on the wealth of the past, both traditions of learning and popular customs, with which the more modern groups are less in touch, and they may be in more effective contact with the masses of their society. They are likely to have a reasonable appreciation of modern innovations and may not be so mesmerized, positively or negatively, by the West as the others often are. They may, therefore, be more appropriately selective in their borrowing.[49]

The conservative intellectuals' preference for more traditionalist interpretations of Islam may also be due to their attraction to Sufism, as is the case, for example, with Seyyed Hossein Nasr, the US-based academic from Iran.[50] A few others are disenchanted with the consequences of modernity, much in the same way as the post-modernist thinkers of Europe, and critique modern society through the perspective of religion. They are not quite as preoccupied with "authenticity" in the same way that ultra-conservatives and fundamentalists are,[51] though they remain deeply critical of the West and the modernity to which it has given rise. "[Western] civilization does not have the answers for the planet," writes Akbar Ahmed, the Muslim scholar of Pakistani descent who for years has lived in the West. "Indeed in its arsenal of nuclear weapons, its greedy destruction of the environment, its insatiable devouring of world resources, its philosophy of consumerism at all costs, it is set to terminate life on Earth in the near future unless it can change its ways fundamentally." [52] "On the threshold of the twenty-first century, what can Islamic civilization contribute to the world," asks Ahmed rhetorically?

> The answer is, a great deal. Its notion of a balance between *din*, religion, and *dunya*, the world, is a worthy one. It can provide a corrective and a check to the materialism that characterizes much of contemporary civilization, offering instead compassion, piety and a sense of humility. [53]

Other Muslim intellectuals who present post-modernist critiques of Western civilization and offer ostensibly Islamic solutions include the Iranian Reza Davari Ardekai and the Pakistani-born Ziauddin Sardar. Davari, a philosophy professor at the University of Tehran, advocates the eradication of "the tree of modernity" and instead calls for the establishment of "a virtuous society" that is "grounded in the axioms of guardianship and prophecy." [54] Sardar, for his part, sees the balance and equilibrium that Islam has been able to establish between the three basic aspects of civilization—materialism, rationalism, and spiritualism—as the key reason why it ought to be adopted and internalized. [55] "In Islam," he writes, "the most significant indicator of man's nobility, besides righteousness, is the use of moderation and balance in material dealings, reasoned pursuits and spiritual quests." [56]

On the other side of the spectrum, reformist Muslim intellectuals are not necessarily any less critical of the offerings of Western civilization. However, their frame of reference, and the way in which they frame the issue, is slightly different. Basically, whereas conservative intellectuals advocate Islamizing modernity, reformist intellectuals, although they would never admit it, call for the modernization of Islam. For the conservatives, the "gates of *ijtihad*" continue to remain open. But they are not quite willing to throw the gates wide open to innovative interpretations and commentaries of the Qur'an and the *hadith* as applicable to prevailing contemporary—i.e. modern— circumstances. For the reformists, on the other hand, interpretation and innovative *ijtihad* are the cornerstones of a "dynamic theology" (*fiqh-e puya* in Persian), which is the essence of true Islam.

Before exploring the key themes that are at the center of the reformist Muslim discourse, it is important to point out that the two categories of "conservative" and "reformist" are fluid and in certain instances interchangeable. A Muslim intellectual may be an avid advocate of active and innovative *ijtihad* but continue to uphold certain Islamic values that are

"traditional" and "conservative." Yusuf al-Qaradawi, for example, is generally regarded as one of the main contemporary figures within the reformist
intellectual fold of Islam. At the same time, however, he condones female
circumcision, unequal treatment of women in the domestic sphere and in
relation to inheritance laws, and Palestinian suicide bombings against Israeli
targets.[57] Similarly, few of the Iranian thinkers who have been instrumental
in giving birth to the vibrant reformist discourse in the country have had
much to say on the issues of women's rights and their equality with men.[58]
This silence could well be part of a calculated move to selectively pick the
jurisprudential fights that need to be fought. But it could also be a conscious
choice driven by preference. The ultimate outcome is that the distinction
between conservative and reformist thinkers, at least insofar as the issue of
women is concerned, is blurred.[59] Nevertheless, despite possible overlappings
on specific issues, the two groups have articulated different discourses, one
aimed at defending the core principles of Islam against perceived threats
generated through the forces of modernity, and another designed to ensure
the religion's resilience through built-in adaptability and flexibility.

A question of interpretation

The central goal that reformist Muslim thinkers have set for themselves is
to reformulate and reinterpret popular notions of Islam in ways that are
consistent with and supportive of the tenets of modern life. As one observer
has noted:

> moderate Muslim thinkers still struggle with the concept of modernity and
> the need to integrate the Muslim world. To them a Muslim has to coexist
> with modernity—and, nowadays, with the more problematic set of concepts
> grouped under the umbrella of "post-modernism." The problems of the world
> are the problems of every Muslim. To these thinkers, the emphasis on *asala*
> (authenticity) is only an attempt to ignore the conditions created by the modern
> world.[60]

To maintain that "Islamic political thought in the twentieth century has
... become a discourse of crisis"[61] may be somewhat of an exaggeration. It
is clear, nonetheless, that reformist Muslim thought has found itself in a
largely reactive mode, having to respond to predicaments and developments
in whose appearance and consequences it has so far played no significant
role. The central goal of the reformists is to make Islam relevant by articulating a jurisprudence that addresses contemporary—i.e. modern—concerns
and issues. Islam is not the problem, they maintain, and neither is modernity. The problem is with mutually exclusive interpretations of Islam and
modernity. Such interpretations, they claim, are fundamentally wrong.

The primary focus of the reformist intellectuals is the Qur'an, which is itself seen as a highly dynamic and progressive text. What is essential to a proper understanding of Islam is not the letter of the text but instead the spirit of the Qur'an and the Prophetic tradition. They maintain that there is no single, valid interpretation of the Qur'an or the *hadith*. The key is *ijtihad*, and, more specifically, original *ijtihad*. In the words of the late US-based Pakistani academic Fazlur Rahman (1919–88), the formulation of "an adequate hermeneutical method" is "imperative" to a proper understanding of Islam.[62] Literally every single Muslim reformist thinker has a deep and abiding conviction of the need for continuous *ijtihad* based on changing and evolving circumstances. The position of Khurshid Ahmad (b. 1932), the Pakistani Islamist leader, is typical of the overall reformist approach to *ijtihad*:

> God has revealed only broad principles and has endowed man with the freedom to apply them in every age in a way suited to the spirit and conditions of that age. It is through the *Ijtihad* that people of every age try to implement and apply divine guidance to the problems of their time.[63]

The exercise of *ijtihad* even takes priority over the literal dictates of the Qur'an, which must be historically contextualized in order to be properly understood and implemented. As the Sudanese-born Abdullahi Ahmed An-Na'im (b. 1946) maintains:

> there is strong and clear precedent from the earliest times of Islam that policy considerations may justify applying a rule derived from *ijtihad* even if that requires overriding clear and definite texts of the Qur'an and the Sunna. ... I would also argue that contemporary Muslims have the competence to reformulate *usul al-fiqh* (principles of jurisprudence) and exercise *ijtihad* even in matters governed by clear and definite texts of the Qur'an and Sunna as long as the outcome of such *ijtihad* is consistent with the essential message of Islam.[64]

It isn't just the original context in which the Qur'an was revealed or the Prophetic traditions occurred that must be taken into account. What is equally important, as the Egyptian philosopher Hasan Hanafi points out, is the predicament and preferences of the person doing the interpreting as well. "The interpreter is not a neutral person," he warns. "There is no interpreter without a commitment to something. The absence of commitment is a negative commitment, a commitment for nothing, for non-commitment. ... The interpreter lives between text and reality."[65] Accordingly, Hanafi proposes "a theory of interpretation which permits reading reality in the texts and the texts in reality for a new hermeneutics departing from holy scriptures."[66]

Charles Kurzman aptly calls this the "interpreted *Shariah:*" "the position that all interpretation of Islamic sources is humanly interpreted, and therefore fallible, and therefore unworthy of imposing upon others."[67] The emerging reformist discourse, relying heavily on Qur'anic exegesis and hermeneutics, is dynamic: "I must necessarily move in the same direction as that indicator ordains (in the Qur'an): continuous liberation, continuous moderation, continuous justice, in a form which brings me as close as possible—through acknowledging the situation I am in today—to what the Law-Giver intended."[68] This conclusion, reached by Mohamed Talbi after a searching analysis of the position of women in the Qur'an, widely echoes that of other reformist thinkers.

There are four broad themes that can be teased out of the emerging Muslim reformist discourse. First is a deep and abiding conviction in Islam as faith and a system of belief. In its current manifestation, the discourse of reformist Muslim intellectuals does not seek to instrumentalize Islam for purposes of achieving modernity in a manner palatable to the masses at large. Islam is not a means to an end; it is an end in itself. It simply needs to be re-thought and reformulated. The reformists' reliance on and endless references to the Qur'an bespeaks of the text's cultural centrality to them.[69] Their engagement with it is not simply academic and intellectual: it is also profoundly personal and emotional. Commenting on the writings of the Tunisian academic Mohamed Talbi, Derek Hopwood has noted:

> There is no ambiguity for him. His faith is absolute, and his attachment to coherent and satisfying views of modern man is also total and firm. He is one of those rare intellectuals who has worked openly to gain a satisfactory balance between a living faith and an uncompromisingly modern vision. For him faith is the free choice of the individual which does not conflict with, or constrain, reason. God has given man entire freedom in this.[70]

A second theme running through the reformist discourse is democratic pluralism. Pluralism, the reformist discourse's proponents maintain, is a salient feature of the spirit of the Qur'an as well as the *Sharia* and the *hadith*. What is necessary is a project of deconstruction whereby the barnacles of historical *Sharia* and *ijtihad* are removed and the true spirit of Islam is thus revealed. The writings of the authors assembled here all demonstrate a deep level of commitment to civil liberties and democracy *through the prism of Islam.* As Abdulaziz Sachedina argues, "the Koranic provisions about civil society allow a legitimate juridical judgment concerning inclusive political, civil, and social participation in the political community."[71] After "a meticulous sifting of the Koranic exegetical materials, both classical and contemporary,"[72] Sachedina comes to the following conclusion:

The challenge for Muslims today, as ever, is to tap the tradition of Koranic pluralism to develop a culture of restoration, of just intrareligious and inter-religious relationships in a world of cultural and religious diversity. Without restoring the principle of coexistence, Muslims will not be able to recapture the spirit of early civil society under the Prophet.[73]

A similarly dynamic contextualization of Islamic law finds it equally support-ive of broader notions of civil rights. An-Na'im, for example, maintains that "an alternative formulation of Islamic public law which would eliminate ... limitations on human rights is both desirable and possible."[74]

By the same token that Shari'a as a practical legal system could not have disre-garded the conception of human rights prevailing at the time purported to apply in the seventh century, modern Islamic law cannot disregard the present conception of human rights if it is to be applied today.[75]

Related to the topic of civil liberties and democratic pluralism is a third theme within the reformist Islamic discourse, namely Islam's relations with other great faiths. Over the last few decades, many prominent figures within the Islamic reformist movement have made significant theoretical as well as practical contributions to interfaith dialogue. At the theoretical level, many have tackled the difficult subjects of a person's right to convert away from Islam—which has traditionally been punishable by death—and the question of *jizyah*, the tax initially imposed on non-Muslims living in the Muslim community (see Kadivar's chapter in this book). The scholar Abdur Rahman I. Doi (1933–99), for example, who spent most of his professional life designing and upgrading Islamic curricula in various African universi-ties, suggests that while the payment of the *jizyah* is obligatory in an Islamic state, it is merely a symbolic gesture.[76] Interfaith relations and dialogue form a major strand in the thought of Mohamed Talbi, who maintains that Islam's built-in emphasis on pluralism fosters mutual respect and dialogue, including especially dialogue with other faiths.[77]

These important theoretical contributions have occurred parallel to a series of practical steps in the last three to four decades aimed at furthering interfaith dialogue. Perhaps the most significant step was taken in the 1981 adoption of the Universal Islamic Declaration of Human Rights, whose article XIII states:

Every person has the right to freedom of conscience and worship in accordance with his religious beliefs.

Similarly, article 1(a) of the Cairo Declaration of Human Rights in Islam, which was adopted at the 1990 meeting of the Organization of the Islamic Conference in Cairo, declares:

All human beings form one family whose members are united by submission to God and descent from Adam. All men are equal in terms of basic human dignity and basic obligations and responsibilities, without any discrimination on the grounds of race, color, language, sex, religious belief, political affiliation, social status or other considerations. True faith is the guarantee for enhancing such dignity along the path to human perfection.

There have been other recent initiatives aimed at furthering interfaith dialogue between Islam and other religions, including numerous conferences on the subject, discussions of Muslim–Christian relations within the British Commonwealth in 2000, and the December 2001 drafting of an Arab Muslim–Christian Covenant in Cairo.[78]

Concern with interfaith dialogue and Islam's relationship with democracy and human rights form part of a larger, fourth concern that underlines the reformist Islamist discourse, namely coming to grips with the phenomenon of modernity. The impulse here is more than to simply "embrace modernity ... on distinctly 'Islamic' terms."[79] Instead, the approach is deeper, more subtle, and has been internalized by its articulators. As Laith Kubba observes, it is the "intrinsic merits" of modernity that concern reformist Muslim thinkers. "Aware of the Islamic civilization's great and many contributions to the world, this approach seeks to take advantage of the best that humanity has to offer, precisely for the sake of pursuing such high Islamic ideals and virtues as truth, justice, charity, brotherhood, and peace."[80] These theorists advocate a "paradigm shift in Islamic thinking" and "consider a 'weak' form of cultural relativism acceptable."[81]

At the same time, no one advocates the wholesale adoption of "modernity" and all that it entails. Hasan Hanafi's warning that a binary distinction between "authenticity" and "modernity" is misleading is echoed by many other like-minded thinkers.[82] The two are linked, and the wholesale adoption of one without consideration of the other is fraught with danger. Modernity does have "a darker side," reformist Muslim intellectuals warn, one which religion can help to mollify through its spiritual nourishment. "Religion can lend its support to ameliorate the crises of meaning, disempowerment, and perplexity that accompany the process of modernization."[83] As the Iranian thinker Mojtahed Shabestari has argued, this important role ascribed to religion is not the same as the political management of society. What is key, rather, is society's embracing of religion, in this case Islam, as a larger social and philosophical blueprint for self-fulfillment.[84] What society needs is moderation and balance—balance between a dynamic *fiqh* that nourishes the soul and makes humanity what it is, and a modernity that ensures progress and advancement.

Whither reformist Islam?

The discourse of reformism currently being articulated by Muslim intellectuals owes its genesis to four primary sources: the emergence of a larger "global discourse of rights," a dramatic rise in educational opportunities for the Muslim masses and the concomitant breakdown of the monopoly of the traditional ulama over religious interpretation; increasing international communication and easier access to global cultural trends; and "the failure of Islamic regimes to provide an attractive alternative to the dominant global institutions."[85] Despite the best efforts of many authoritarian states throughout the Muslim world to combat these trends—to suppress the voices of dissent and democracy, limit access to international communications and global cultural trends, dictate and control educational curricula, and enhance their own fragile and artificial sources of legitimacy—none can be easily reversed. Moreover, beginning in the final decades of the nineteenth century and picking up pace throughout the twentieth century, the powers and authority of the old-style ulama eroded as educational opportunities spread to new social classes on the one hand, and, on the other hand, as the ulama failed to provide viable political, social, and cultural alternatives to the most pressing needs of the urban masses.[86] Conversely, devout, self-taught Muslim intellectuals—responsible for a "spectacularly wild growth of interpretations"[87]—steadily emerged as the primary force behind a deepening discourse of religious reformism. By the time the twentieth century drew to a close, reformist Islam, articulated by thinkers and intellectuals with mostly secular educational backgrounds, had emerged as a formidable force to be reckoned with.

Not surprisingly, literally all of the articulators of reformist Islam advocate original *ijtihad* based on the Qur'an. As Charles Kurzman has observed,

> Autodidacts are, in a literal sense, practicing theology without a licence. When secularly educated elites engage in religious discourses, they do so as competitors, as often as allies, with seminary graduates. ... One way to read the theological work of such figures is as an attempt to reconcile the modern values they learned in secular schools with the religious values they assimilated outside of school. Indeed, more than one critic has assailed these authors on such grounds.[88]

These autodidacts are thinkers as well as intellectuals, students of their contemporary societies and their religious traditions and, at the same time, also committed to transforming both.[89] Through their writings and speeches, which are at once steeped in Islamic learning and committed to its reform and transformation, they have emerged as public intellectuals. They are not mere academics isolated in their ivory towers. They have public profiles and, as such, command the public's attention, if not always respect.

With deep religious convictions, these "new interpreters of Islam" have access to new means of getting their message across, chief among which is the Internet. As Jon Anderson has noted, through the Internet, Muslim reformists are able to

> put into circulation views that previously circulated only in narrow circles and bring additional techniques for interpreting Islam, drawn first from those that facilitate access to the Internet. This extends the process ... [of] massification of education in the contemporary Muslim world, which has given wider access to both the texts of Islam and to a wider range of interpretation that developed in mosque-university (*madrasa*) and religious lodge (*zawiya*). Born in the world of higher education, the Internet facilitates and links specific new interpreters lodged within or enabled by it to form an extended discursive space, marked by new techniques not only for interpretation but also for creating a public that lies between, draws on, and links previously discrete discourses.[90]

Does all of this mean that we are currently witnessing the unfolding of an "Islamic reformation"? The notion of a reformation in Islam has long been a staple of both Western and Islamic scholarship on the religion.[91] Since the late 1800s, a number of Muslim intellectuals have openly called for a reformation of Islam along the same lines that occurred in the Christian Church, most recently by the Iranian academic Hashem Aghajari, who was subsequently sentenced to death by the country's conservative religious establishment.[92] At the same time, a number of Western academics studying Islam hold the view that an Islamic reformation has indeed already begun. In support of their arguments, they point to the depth and vibrancy of the reformist discourse and the dramatically transformative context within which it is being formed. Perhaps the most compelling argument in this regard is made by the anthropologist Dale Eickelman, who writes:

> Years hence, if my suspicion is correct, we will look back on the latter half of the 20th century as a time of change as profound for the Muslim world as the protestant reformation was for Christendom. Like the printing press in the 16th century, the combination of mass education and mass communications is transforming this world, a broad geographic crescent stretching from North Africa through Central Asia, the Indian subcontinent, and across the Indonesian archipelago. In unprecedentedly large numbers, the faithful—whether in the vast cosmopolitan city of Istanbul or in Oman's tiny, remote al-Hamra Oasis—are examining and debating the fundamentals of Muslim belief and practice in ways that their less self-conscious predecessors would never have imagined. This highly deliberate examination of the faith is what constitutes the Islamic Reformation.[93]

According to Eickelman, what is occurring in the Muslim world is nothing short of a great transformation, spurred by the dramatic rise of education, the breakdown of traditional authorities, and the spread of the means of communication. "No one group or type of leader in contemporary Muslim societies possesses a monopoly on the management of the sacred," he writes.

> Without fanfare, the idea of Islam as dialogue and civil debate is gaining ground. This new sense of public space is emerging throughout Muslim-majority states and Muslim communities elsewhere. It is shaped by increasingly open contests over the use of the symbolic language of Islam.[94]

Eickelman reminds us that Martin Luther's ideas did not get hold until years after he had nailed his 95 Theses to the door of the Wittenberg church in 1517. An Islamic reformation, he claims, could not be too far in the offing.[95]

Eickelman may well be right in his prediction. The discourse of Islamic reformism shows no signs of abating and, indeed, appears to be globalizing. But before this discourse can lead to a reformation in Islam in the same way that occurred in Christianity—albeit with characteristics unique to Islam, its tradition, and its environment—it has to overcome at least four fundamental obstacles. These obstacles are not inherent in Islam itself but instead revolve around the overall context within which Islam and its reformist discourse find themselves. They include: the difficulty accessing various institutional means through which they can get their message across to intended audiences; an international environment that seriously undermines their message; opposition from the traditional, orthodox religious establishment; and, opposition from the state.

Perhaps the most difficult obstacle that the reformist discourse faces is lack of access to various institutional means through which it can establish viable means of communication and nexus with the larger Muslim masses, especially in the urban areas. Throughout the Muslim world, mosques and other religious institutions are either under the direct control of the state or are controlled and supervised by clerics with conservative, often orthodox, worldviews. In the Sunni-majority countries of the Arab world, the state keeps a close eye on the Grand Mufti and ensures his political compliance, while simultaneously supervising the content of the curriculum at various religious educational institutions and the sermons delivered at the state-controlled mosques.[96] In Shi'a Iran, the state's control of religious matters is more complete and direct, with local state agencies even choosing and coordinating the content of the weekly sermons delivered by the provincial Friday Prayer Imams. Throughout the Muslim world, despite the widespread availability of satellite television and the Internet, the religious content of the state-run or state-supervised media, especially in radio and television programming and in the printed media, are also heavily controlled by the state, usually through a cabinet-level ministry specifically devoted to religious affairs. Although it would be inaccurate to imply that the traditional ulama throughout the Muslim world are under the thumb of the state at all times, the purview of their activities and their own preferences severely limit the extent to which they could engage in anything as bold as heralding sustained doctrinal change in Islam without direct state prodding or support. For the foreseeable future at least, the ulama remain, as they have long been, "the custodians of change," [97] a change that does not appear to be forthcoming anytime in the near future.

The only venues open to the reformist intellectuals, therefore, remain limited to publications and lecture halls, neither of which, under ordinary circumstances, necessarily affords them the social reach necessary to effect meaningful change to Islamic doctrine or practice. In a few instances, reformist doctrines have become the guiding principles of grassroots organizations and efforts, as in the so-called "Gülen schools" that Fethullah Gülen has established in Turkey and in numerous other Muslim countries.[98] How resonant and socially meaningful such efforts end up becoming remains to be seen, although their significance is bound to be limited for now given the larger hostile environment within which they operate.

The hostility that reformist Muslim thinkers face can at times be threatening to their very lives and livelihood. The story of Professor Nasr Hamid Abu Zaid is only one of the more dramatic examples of the perils that intellectuals of his disposition can face.[99] If not threatened by death or beatings from militant fundamentalists, reformist intellectuals often have to contend with the prospects of prolonged unemployment or even imprisonment at the hands of the state. Throughout the Muslim world, there are indeed few reformist Muslim intellectuals who have not lost their jobs or have not been put on trial and imprisoned, often on trumped-up charges: Hashem Aghajari, Mohsen Kadivar, Mohammad Mojtahed Shabestari, and Abdolkarim Soroush in Iran; Anwar Ibrahim in Malaysia; Rachid Ghannouchi in Tunisia; and countless others.

Despite their moderation and reformism, Muslim intellectuals are still often viewed as threatening by the state. Calls for accountability, pluralism, and democracy, even if based on the Qur'an, are very much unwelcome in non-democracies. Authoritarianism breeds suspicion and mistrust. The best that the reformist Muslim intellectuals can hope to get from the state is benign neglect. For its part, if the state does not actively suppress their activities, it does not help them either. Regardless of whether the political system in question is ostensibly secular or religious, the political will to lend institutional support to the discourse of modernity proposed by the intelligentsia is conspicuously absent. It is simply not part and parcel of the "ruling bargain." The state, in fact, already has a rocky and at best tenuous relationship with the influential and conservative religious establishment, one marked by frequent clashes, near constant tensions, and, at best, grudging acceptance. Insofar as moderate, reformist religious intellectuals are concerned, the state has neither the resources nor, more importantly, the political will to help facilitate the advancement of their agendas. After all, their advocacy of political accountability and representation is as threatening to the authoritarian state and its modus operandi as are the radical fundamentalists' calls for the state's violent overthrow.

This hostile environment is not limited to the domestic arena. Inhospitable domestic arenas have often compelled these intellectuals to seek shelter and refuge in Western academia. Since 9/11, however, the Western embrace has been less than welcoming. Witness, for example, what happened to Tariq Ramadan. A respected scholar of Islam from Switzerland, his work visa was abruptly revoked in July 2004 by the US State Department weeks before he and his family had relocated to the United States to take up an endowed professorship at Notre Dame University. No explanation other than vague references to US "national security interests" was ever given. The ideological zeal with which the Bush administration's "War on Terror" has unfolded, meanwhile, has made Islam the religion fair game for popular ridicule. At a time when "the trouble with Islam" [100] is seen to lie in its teachings rather than in their interpretations, those calling for dialogue and understanding are side-stepped and marginalized, "collateral damage" [101] in the global war on terror and the missionary zeal of an empire on the march. In the "clash of fundamentalisms" that is now underway,[102] moderation has been one of the biggest losers.

Not all hope for reformist Islam is lost, however. Despite the myriad of restrictions and obstacles it faces, reformist Islam has proven itself to be remarkably resilient. More than a mere intellectual exercise, it is part of a long tradition of original *ijtihad* with deep roots in Islamic thought. In its current manifestation, it is part of a larger discourse of rights emerging nearly simultaneously on a global scale. History has taught us two crucial lessons. First, religion is an inalienable part of the constitution of Muslim societies the world over, both classical and contemporary. Even the most thorough campaigns to eradicate religion altogether as a cultural and political force—as Mustafa Kemal Atatürk tried in Turkey, for example—have met with at best limited success. Second, neither democracy nor modernity can be indefinitely delayed or combated. The forces of science and industry—the driving powers behind modernity—cannot be stopped at national boundaries. Cultural modernity may lag behind scientific modernity, but they both move in parallel, albeit uneven, trajectories. Neither religion nor modernity can be ignored or eradicated, and the striking of a synthesis between the two, while often resisted or greatly resented, is inevitable. All that is needed is the political will and the institutional means to make such inevitability a reality. Neither authoritarianism nor an empire's "war on terror" are ever-lasting; both religion and modernity are. The necessary ingredients for a synthesis between the two are all there. All that is needed is the right context.

This volume

The authors whose works appear in this volume represent the most active and influential reformist thinkers in the contemporary Muslim world. While some are better known internationally than others, in one way or another all are contributing significantly to the deepening discourse of Islamic modernity. All thinkers emphasize the need to place the "unchangeable principles of Islam" within the appropriate historical context, from which a dynamic conception of the religion and its fundamental compatibility with political pluralism and what is today called "modernity" can be acquired. It is not Islam in itself that needs to be reformed, they maintain, but rather our understanding and our historical operationalization of it that needs changing.

The book begins with a wide-ranging examination by Mohammed Arkoun of the multiple, and often contradictory, forces operating on Islam in the contemporary world. Arkoun, who is himself one of the main architects of the evolving discourse of reformist Islam, offers a historical overview of the causes of and the need for the emergence of the modernist discourse. Chapter 3, by Tariq Ramadan, offers another broad overview, this time of some of Islam's core principles and notions—*Sharia, maslaha, fatwa, ijtihad,* and *tawhid*—both in relation to the history of Islam in general and the growing presence of Islam in the West in particular. Ramadan also discusses some of the doctrinal controversies that have historically divided the different schools of thought in Islam, all the while calling for a dynamic approach to Islam, for ways to "change the old paradigms" and to rediscover "new ways," while making sure that the essence and spirit of the religion remain intact.

Chapters 4 to 8 examine the multi-faceted and complex relationship between Islam and democracy. In Chapter 4, Fethullah Gülen places Islam in a comparative and historical context. In Chapters 5 and 6, by Mohamed Talbi and Mohsen Kadivar respectively, extensive references to the Qur'an— and in Kadivar's case to the *hadith*—are offered to demonstrate the Holy Book's emphasis on spiritual uplifting and inclusiveness, especially insofar as peoples of other faiths are concerned. Muhammad Shahrour's discussion of the same topic in Chapter 7 is somewhat more personal, reflecting on some of his experiences following the publication of his highly influential and controversial book, *The Book and the Qur'an: A Contemporary Reading*. Nasr Abu Zaid's discussion of the essence and spirit of the Qur'an in Chapter 8 is necessarily even more personal and political, given the extremely difficult circumstances he has faced in recent years because of his writings and his views.

Chapters 9, 10, and 11 feature works by three Muslim feminist intellectuals, namely Leila Ahmed, originally from Egypt and currently living and working in the United States, Amina Wadud, from the United States, and Fatima Mernissi, from Morocco. Ahmed presents a piercing analysis of the role and position of women in the earliest days of Islam and how Islam changed, in many fundamental ways, the basis on which gender relations prior to its rise were based. Ahmed's conclusions go to the heart of Islam's dealings with women: there is a basic tension, she maintains, between the pragmatic treatment of women in Islam—both by the Prophet Muhammad and as sanctioned in the Qur'an—and its highly egalitarian spirit and ethics. Wadud develops this point further, arguing that the message and practice of Islam, properly contextualized and understood, is liberatory and highly egalitarian in relation to both men and women. Mernissi, for her part, maintains that despite the best efforts of Islamic fundamentalists to keep women segregated and in socially inferior positions, the processes of social change that are underway in the Muslim world, and especially advances in education and therefore access to formal and informal sources of power, are bound to erode the fundamentalists' segregationist agenda. Originally published nearly 20 years ago, the central thesis of Mernissi's essay is perhaps more valid today than when it was first articulated.

In Chapter 12, Chandra Muzaffar emphasizes a slightly different perspective on Islamic hermeneutics. Concerned primarily with the notion of justice as embedded in the Qur'an, Muzaffar examines the internal threats to justice from within the Islamic community as well as the global dispositions and obstacles that perpetuate discrimination and injustice.

Chapters 13 and 14 offer a more philosophical perspective on the essential compatibility of Islam with science, freedom, and democracy. Chapter 13, by Hasan Hanafi, presents an Islamic approach to "facts" and "values," arguing that contrary to the Western philosophical tradition, Islam, and more specifically the Qur'an, does not recognize a separation between the two. The book ends with a chapter by Abdolkarim Soroush, who offers a detailed discussion of the basic philosophical compatibility of Islamic rationality with freedom and democracy.

Collectively, these intellectuals and their writings represent the most influential aspects of the unfolding discourse of Islamic reformism. Their advocacy of a dynamic, progressive, and contextualized hermeneutics of the Qur'an and the *hadith* faces countless obstacles from multiple sources and directions. Nevertheless, their voices and the discourse to which they have given rise are gaining in strength and momentum. Islamic reformation may not be upon us yet. But all indications are that it cannot be too far in coming.

CHAPTER 2

Present-Day Islam Between Its Tradition and Globalization

Mohammed Arkoun

Mohammad Arkoun is arguably one of the most influential voices of moderate Islam today. Born in Algeria in 1928, he moved to Paris to pursue graduate studies at the Sorbonne, obtaining a PhD degree in 1956. Having held several academic positions in France and elsewhere in Europe and in the United States, Arkoun is currently Emeritus Professor of the History of Islamic Thought at the Sorbonne. He is also a Senior Research Fellow and a member of the Board of Governors of the Institute of Ismaili Studies in London. A powerful advocate of Islamic modernity and humanism, he is the author of a number of books in French, Arabic, and English.

Over the years, Arkoun has produced a rich body of literature on a wide variety of topics dealing with Islam, using the findings and methods of semiotics, structuralism, discourse analysis, post-structuralism, and structural anthropology. This has at times left Arkoun open to the criticism that there is no unifying theme in his writings. Nevertheless, Arkoun's principal concern is to critique traditions—both Western and Islamic—and, in the process, to articulate a new philosophical and jurisprudential framework for understanding and practicing Islam. Towards this end, the topics he has written about range from the relationship between "the church and the state," the importance of constructing a new hermeneutics of Islam, Islam's relationship with other religions, and Sufism, to name a few. In the essay that follows, Arkoun presents a wide-ranging, critical overview of the history, current predicament, and the future of Islam in the age of globalization. The essay originally appeared in Mohammed Arkoun, "Present-Day Islam Between Its Tradition and Globalization," in Farhad Daftary (ed), Intellectual Traditions in Islam (London: I.B.Tauris, 2001), pp 179–221.

The title of this essay announces three major fields of inquiry and critical analysis: *present-day Islam*; the *living tradition* dating back to the emergence of the *Islamic fact* in 610–32 and 661; and globalization. My objective in including under the same critical scrutiny themes as complex as these is to set apart, in every possible manner, the *implicits* that are lived but unthought in each of these three areas of individual existence and historical action from the *explicits* that are problematized, thought for the first time or rethought, in the perspectives opened up by the new phenomenon of globalization.

For methodological and epistemological reasons which will become apparent in the course of the exposition, I will begin by defining the new context created by the forces of globalization and then tackle the questions of present-day Islam and Islamic tradition.

What is globalization?

Until the years 1960–70, human thought had known a particular idea of the world, or worlds in the plural. This idea itself nourished a large number of representations whose spiritual, artistic, and scientific productivity varied according to their cultural environments and historical conjunctures. It is thus that with Copernicus, Galileo, and Kepler, one passed "from the closed world to an infinite universe." What has long been called international relations by no means covers the concept of globalization, the active forces and the realities of which all individuals and societies are discovering or experiencing at the present time.

Globalization upsets all the known cultural, religious, philosophical, and politico-juridical traditions; even modernity that issued from the reason of the Enlightenment does not escape from it. That is why, since the 1980s, various analysts, thinkers, and researchers, particularly in the United States, speak of *post-modernity*. I prefer to avoid this term, which refers to a concept badly and little elaborated and which keeps us in the linear historical trajectory inaugurated in Western Europe during the seventeenth and eighteenth centuries. Globalization forces the Europeans themselves to speak of the limits and perverse effects of the reason of the Enlightenment, which has allowed, among other things, the construction of the secular, democratic, and liberal nation-state, the progress of scientific research, and the transition from the solidarities of clan, blood, and confession to the contractual solidarities regulated by the state of law. With the resolute march towards European union, one crosses a new historical stage in the organization and widening of the spaces of citizenship, which is at the same time the basis and object of democratic life. The nation-state is in the process of accomplishing its mission in Europe by putting in place civil societies, sufficiently emancipated juridically, to act as effective and necessary partners of the states of law. However, crossing this historical stage proves as difficult and uncertain as that which led absolute monarchies of divine law to become constitutional monarchies and democratic republics. The problems arise, in effect, from diverse European cultures and visions of the world linked to the slow and difficult ascent of nation-states, which reveal their provincial limits, their exclusion of other cultures of the world, their xenophobia, and their latent violence, always ready to be exercised against the foreigner, however near geographically (as was the case in the Franco-German wars).

The economic, monetary, and technological forces of globalization have achieved a primacy and priority in the process of history, while snatching from abstract idealism the spiritual, philosophical, ethical, political, and juridical values, whose bases or concrete material components are increasingly better explicated. However, political idealism continues to seek refuge in nationalist discourse, as can be noted in the resistance to the progress of the European Union which began as no more than a simple community formed to regulate the production of coal and steel. The claims of national specificity, authenticity, and exception curb the advances towards the revision of national historiographies, intellectual frames of interpretation, and re-appropriation of values. The example thus given by the "old" nations to their former colonies, which became "emerging nations" without transition, provides dangerous "arguments" to the party-nation-states which assumed power in these countries during the years 1950–70 in conditions that are known to us, and which are leading programs of "national construction" in the new context created by globalization. This remark must be retained for a better evaluation of the role of Islam and its tradition in the mounting tensions between these party-nation-states and societies whose democratic structure and legitimate aspirations towards democratization are not really taken into consideration.

Since the dissolution of the Soviet Union as a geopolitical power, the United States exercises a hegemonic control over all the forces of globalization. The Europeans, including Russia and its former satellites, rather than nourishing rivalries, seek alliances, contracts, and collaboration with the United States. Thus the burden of this hegemony makes itself felt more upon peoples and nations in the process of emancipation and unification. "The right of peoples to self-determination," which nourished so many illusions about national emancipation in the context of the Cold War, has become an ideological insanity in the face of intolerable civil wars that tear apart so many societies long seized in the grip of totalitarian nationalisms and projected suddenly into the savage liberalism of *McWorld* (which I discuss in the next section). The latter invented a new concept, "humanitarian aid for peoples in danger of genocide," which is as vague and illusory as its predecessor. But the economic and monetary forces of globalization do not today concern themselves with humanitarian aid any more than the bourgeois

capitalist conquerors of the nineteenth century worried about the emancipation of their own womenfolk, the working classes, or, *a fortiori*, the colonized peoples. Humanitarian aid, the rights of peoples, human rights, and
democratic sermons form part of the panoply of political slogans, adapted
to every geopolitical conjuncture by those who contrive to their advantage
the operations of globalization. It is thus that the nationalist elites—who
believed that they were giving real content to these slogans by engaging,
in the years 1960–70, with the politics of economic development in the
frame of "cooperation" and "development aid"—generated, with their statist and economic partners of the West, the riposte of the so-called Islamic
Revolution (see what follows on *Jihad* versus *McWorld*), supported by
marginalized social strata which were badly integrated in enclaves of modernity too narrow, and dispossessed (even in the case of rural villagers and
forcibly sedentarized nomads) of their languages, cultures, ecological equi-
libria, customary codes, and traditional solidarities—just as the European
peasantry had been dispossessed under mounting pressures of industrializa-
tion, but in its case with long transitions and effectively integrated institutions. Globalization deploys on a planetary scale the strategies of market
conquest and multiplication of consumers and their loyalties without any
regard for the cultural regression, intellectual misery, political oppression,
social tragedy and individual enslavement brought about by this "unequal
exchange" which for so long has been denounced in vain. We know how
the strategies of globalization bring about, on the one hand, *interstate* agree-
ments and diplomacy for the flow of goods in exchange for the importation
of raw materials, and, on the other hand, the media which denounce the
totalitarian, fanatical, and regressive policies of those very states recognized
officially as respectable partners and interlocutors.

Let us note here an important political notion rarely highlighted by
analysts and almost never included in the themes of electoral campaigns in
the most advanced democratic regimes. It concerns the systematic ignorance
in which citizens are kept about everything pertaining to interstate diplomacy. That which is called popular sovereignty is unable to exercise any type
of control over diplomatic relations, which lie in the exclusive competence of
the heads of states and their ministers for foreign affairs. Thus the responsibilities incurred in conflicts such as those of Algeria, Rwanda, Zaire, Iran,
Sudan, Bosnia, etc., are not only dissimulated to those citizens most capable
of undertaking juridical, historical, and ethical analysis, but are knowingly
distorted by the easy indignation generated against the crimes, assassina-
tions, and destruction stigmatized every day by the media. On this level, the
most pertinent analyses and the most legitimate critiques are brushed aside

with repeated appeals to the "reason" of state security against the "chattering" of idealist intellectuals.

This functioning of democracy is accepted particularly by civil societies as they are inclined in the first place to defend the "social gains" which are in themselves brought about by globalization. This accounts for the development within the European Union of the notion and practice of strikes by proxy—the strike by every sector or professional category, supported unconditionally by all the workers who feel equally threatened with losing the advantages gained, and above all their jobs. One is far from the simplistic frontiers charted by class conflict, but the selfishness of civil societies, necessarily supported by their states, replaces that of the former classes, and it exacerbates the situation of those very people who are at the same time exploited and excluded by the forces of globalization, especially when delocalization is involved. One thus finds, once again, a relation comparable to that between the colonizing nation-states and the peoples colonized until 1945.

It must be admitted that in the current state of the world, the relentless march of globalization generates more ruptures, tensions, contradictions, and collective conflicts than did the exportation of fragments of material modernity to colonies in the nineteenth and twentieth centuries. Neither the researchers and theoreticians with the highest competence and know-how, nor the expanding armies of managers of large multi-national firms, nor the politicians who monopolize the use of "legal violence" (as Max Weber would say) integrate into their analyses, expectations, and strategies of development the real problems, the needs and hopes of those peoples who are deprived of adequate representation, as well as possibilities of direct expression and emancipation. The philosophical implications of this global process of change, which relate as much to scientific research as to technological innovation and economic expansion, are not even evoked as one of the decisive parameters which ought to inform decisions at all levels and in every sphere of activity. This is because philosophical thought itself is hardly mobilized by the urgent need to rethink the essential connections which bind together philosophy and democracy. I refer here to the very suggestive report entitled *Philosophie et démocratie dans le monde*, compiled by Roger Pol Droit at the request of UNESCO, on the present state of the teaching of philosophy in member countries. Rare are the countries which have introduced or maintained any serious teaching of philosophy at the high-school level. In the Islamic context, the rich philosophical tradition that was developed from the eighth century until the death of Ibn Rushd (Averroës) in 1198 has, since the thirteenth century, been lost. Here is how

Droit defines the traits of "the common space" fundamental to philosophy and democracy: both bring about a "founding relationship" with the following features:

1. *Speech*: for a thought exists only when it is stated, expounded, submitted to discussion, criticism and arguments of others; this remark applies to philosophical thought as well as political positions in a democracy.

2. *Equality*: for one does not ask others "by what right" they intervene in the debate; one does not require by any means that they be provided with any authority or authorization; it is sufficient that they should speak and argue. [I modify Droit's remark as follows: In the perspective of globalization, it is no longer only the citizens of one particular nation who take part in the political debate; for the first time, and in philosophy since the ancient Greeks, the entire human race is concerned as much with the political as with the philosophical debate on the subject, notably the founding conditions of political legitimacy in local regimes and the *governance*—in English, governability of the inhabited planet.]

3. *Doubt*: since immediate certitudes have wavered, in order to ensure that the research of the true as well as general discussion of the subject is open, it is necessary for one to be no longer in a universe of answers and beliefs, but of questions and research.

4. *Self-institution*: for no external decision comes to create the philosophical stage or the democratic community, no authority legitimates it "from outside," nothing guarantees it "from above;" they receive their power only from themselves and are not subjected to any authority whose source they would not be.[1]

I shall return to the critical examination of these definitions when I compare the status of the theologico-political implied by R.P. Droit to that of the philosophico-political which is inseparable from our modernity. This comparison is indispensable for demonstrating the incoherencies, anachronisms, and illusions of the contemporary Islamic discourse on Islam and democracy. But first I will put forward three preliminary remarks:

1. On February 25, 1795, the French Revolution was defined by Joseph Lakanal as this "educative Utopia" aiming "to put an end to the inequalities of development affecting the citizen's" capacity to judge.[2] In fact, philosophical teaching organized by the Republic was and still is offered in public and private establishments subsidized by the state. This French tradition may have been able to generate a taste for theoretical speculations, yet one cannot say that political thought in France and the current traits of French-style democracy are more marked than elsewhere by a philosophical attitude as just defined. The original harm comes, without doubt, from the tight

control exercised by the secular republican state in the French sense, ever since the foundation of technical schools and high schools. In the seventeenth century, Benedict Spinoza defended rather the right for all men "to teach [philosophy] publicly, at their own expense and at the peril of their reputation." [3]

2. In the perspective of *political reason*, called upon to manage all the processes of globalization in the real, constant interest of every *person-individual-citizen*, it becomes necessary for the society and the regime, where this reason is called upon, to deploy its existence and redefine the conditions for a concretely universalizable philosophical attitude. It is in this sense that I shall examine the contribution that critical thought can make to this project in concrete Islamic contexts.

3. The concept of person-individual-citizen which I have just introduced deserves to be elaborated in the perspectives opened up by anthropology for the exploration and critical analysis of all cultures, and no longer only the "great" cultures which, at various times in history, exercised or still exercise a hegemony. In other words, the classical philosophical attitude is no longer sufficient for rethinking, with all the *descriptive* and *explicative adequacy* required by globalization, the status of the *person*, the *individual* and the *citizen* in a political, juridical, and cultural space—a space which is no longer only that of the nation-states and still less that of religious communities such as the *Ummah* which the Islamist movements are trying to set up as a universal model of historical action.

It is to be feared that the call to philosophy, cultural anthropology and critical history of cultures, beyond all the hegemonic frames of realization of human existence, will draw little attention, even less than in the context of the nation-state, from the economic, monetary, and political establishments, from official representatives in large international conferences, and from the variegated protagonists who contribute to the accelerated pace of globalization. All these actors are generally little prepared to accord a just place to the philosophical implications of the responsibilities that they prefer to exercise as *effective* experts. One follows in them less the historical project of promoting and extending democratic values to all peoples and societies in the world than the conquest of new markets for consumer goods which no longer find enough buyers in glutted markets.

Even if one were to agree to a philosophical and anthropological examination of the problems raised by the expansion of *McWorld*, it would still be necessary in the first place to work towards an indispensable intellectual overtaking of the frame of thought inherited from classical metaphysics. The latter has long remained a prisoner of recurrent interferences, in spite of efforts at distinction which are always invalidated by polemical tensions between theological themes and philosophical categories. What sociologists call the "return of the religious" contributes, even in the most secularized societies, to the obstruction of efforts to elucidate the stakes peculiar to a theology and a philosophy that can be cultivated without polemics, without mimetic rivalry, in accordance with the new scientific spirit and new cognitive systems proposed by biology, linguistics, semiology, psychology, socio-anthropology, and the study of historical problems. In other words, the process of economic, technological, and monetary globalization is being deployed in a climate of "disposable thought," where the crises in the study of man and society stand in sharp contrast to the spectacular advances of technological knowledge which are readily appropriated by the desire for power and profit.

All this shows the need to express clearly the philosophical attitude and the type of cognitive activity which must accompany present-day globalization as a concrete historical practice. Without minimizing, and much less ignoring, either the Greek references of philosophical thought or their journey and expansion in the European historical sphere, one will recognize the distances separating positions linked to precise socio-cultural and political spaces and those related to visions of the world too hastily proclaimed universal. Grammarians, logicians, and linguists have long reflected upon this tension: from the famous *disputatio* (*munazara*) between the grammarian al-Sirafi and the logician Matta b. Yunus in tenth-century Baghdad, to the enlightening analysis of E. Benveniste of the Aristotelian categories articulated in Greek and the linguistic categories, one will grasp the idea that a universalizable philosophical attitude is precisely that which cultivates systematically the aporia of tension between the local and the global. The implantation in the local of the sense of the universal is inscribed, in a more or less insistent manner, in every linguistic experience. This tension has been cultivated as a speculative theme, like the humanism of the lettered which nourished beautiful literary compositions until World War II. Only modern social and cultural anthropology furnishes the concrete data peculiar to every socio-cultural construction in a precise time and space, while situating every local type in a global context of political, social, cultural, and religious facts. It so happens that, as philosophy and anthropology continue to be taught and practiced as distinct and specialized disciplines, the many incursions of philosophers into anthropology remain incidental and cursory, while anthropologists are not always able to go beyond the ethnographic stage of their scientific practice.[4] We also cover here the important question of the reform of education systems in order to adapt them everywhere to the exigencies of globalization.

Is present-day Islam impervious to globalization?

An American political scientist, Benjamin R. Barber, has recently promoted the Qur'anic and Islamic concept of *Jihad* to the rank of a polar figure of contemporary history, dialectically linked to *McWorld*, that is to say, to ongoing globalization, viewed from the perspective of the United States and Western Europe.[5] The author is not at all interested in *Jihad* in order to denounce the expansion of Islam through "holy war," or to propose a new theory of "just war," a theological concept elaborated long ago by St Augustine and raised again in the early 1990s by Presidents Bush and Mitterrand during the Gulf War. He considers, correctly, that the violence which tears apart many societies called Muslim (I prefer to use, in contra-distinction to the custom of all Islamic studies and political science litera-ture, the expression "societies molded by the Islamic fact," which I shall explain later) is a manifestation of not only serious internal crises, but the protest common to all societies, including those of the West, against the blind forces of globalization called *McWorld*, characterized by its market economy, monetary system, technology, media, and revolution in informat-ics, which affect work and leisure, genetic engineering, etc. This protest opposes the structural violence spread in the world by incomprehensible, anonymous decision makers with ethically irresponsible, murderous, physi-cal violence; it is a radical rejection in the name of traditional and religious values, not exclusive of the means of effective action obtained by material modernity. *Jihad* and *McWorld* convey much irrational and semantic disorder which remains to be analyzed within the critical and cognitive perspectives defined above; they confront each other with very unequal weapons, but with different objectives, both succeeding in perverting the democratic proj-ect of emancipation of the human condition. In order to defend democracy, Barber forces the opposition between *Jihad* and *McWorld*: the first wants to resuscitate the obscure forces of the pre-modern world such as "religious mysteries, hierarchic communities, suffocating traditions, historical torpor," whereas the second goes beyond modernity by insisting upon the promotion of the market over the rights and spiritual aspirations of mankind.

In qualifying negatively the two poles, the political scientist stays in the epistemological frame of the reason of the Enlightenment, whereas global-ization obliges us to revise the cognitive systems bequeathed by all types of reason which respect the rules of critical historical epistemology. Thus the qualifications applied to the pre-modern world are pertinent if one sticks to the discourse of contemporary fundamentalist movements, but historically incorrect if one refers to the humanist culture (*adab*) of the urban milieux of the Islamic world in the ninth to eleventh centuries. The reason at work in this culture anticipated many critiques and cognitive postures, which developed much later the humanism of the Renaissance and subsequently amplified the reason of the Enlightenment in Europe. The latter instrumentalized the Persians, Turks, and the Muslims in general, not for enlarging significantly their cognitive field, but in the first place to lead its battle against the main enemy of that time: clericalism. The colonial nineteenth century developed a historiography, ethnography, sociology, and psychology, largely marked by an epistemology which present-day anthropology depicts as an ideology of domination. The argumentation of *Jihad* vs. *McWorld*, although seductive in its resolute option for a universalizable humanist democracy, cannot be retained for the project of a critical history of thought in the Mediterranean space, encompassing the stakes-of-meaning and the wills-to-power which became manifested there since the first emergence of the Islamic fact in Arabia in 610–32. Present-day Islam, in effect, needs to go beyond the sterile and often dangerous protestations of *Jihad* to integrate at the same time the positive gains of modernity and the new opportunities of political, economic, social, and cultural emancipation opened up by globalization—the latter to be understood as an extension of the historical project of modernity and also a correction of its errors and injustices.

If modernity is an incomplete project consisting of a determination to push back ever further the limits of the human condition, it must orient globalization towards a better integration of values made discordant by the systematic opposition between the visions of traditional religions and the ideological categorizations of secular religions. As a result of this conflict, the secular voices of the prophets, saints, theologians, philosophers, artists, poets, and heroes have been relentlessly marginalized, disqualified, and driven back to a past relegated to erudite historiography or to definitive oblivion. Our societies produce great captains of industry, bankers who work in secrecy, sports champions and stars who generate ephemeral enthusiasm, and highly specialized scientific researchers; but these people have neither the time nor the sources of inspiration necessary for generating intellectual and spiritual values to mobilize at the level where the economic system of production and exchange engages the ecological future of the planet and the quality of human life. I have deliberately refrained from mentioning politicians here because everywhere they continue to disappoint the people they are supposed to lead—not to mention the corrupt and corrupting leaders, bloodthirsty tyrants and oppressors, obscurantists and absolutists, who enjoy the honors and consideration due to "heads of state."

In these observations there is neither a desire to moralize nor nostalgia for a past to be compared with the present in developed or developing societies; they are meant, rather, to define with precision the new functions which the irresistible forces of *McWorld* assign to present-day Islam. The latter continues to guarantee to the social masses, excluded from the liberties and comforts reserved for limited privileged groups, a hope mixed with the traditional expectation of eternal salvation, the possibility of attaining moral dignity in intimate encounter with the Just and Merciful God of the Qur'an, a belief in a promise of imminent justice to be accomplished by their charismatic leader, a "modern" substitute for the ancient Imam-Mahdi. Or it demands obedience to the divine injunction to eliminate by a just and holy war (*Jihad*) all the "Pharaohs" who sow disorder and corruption on earth.

The historian-sociologist-anthropologist will not enumerate, as I have just done, all these psycho-socio-political components of what one no longer calls *hope*, but representations of the social *imaginaire*. For the politico-religious vocabulary familiar to the believers of yesterday and today, one substitutes that of the critical analyst for whom *societies produce religions* like ideologies which, once systematized in normative codes, act in their turn upon societies. This epistemological postulate doubtless allows one to deconstruct a joint psychological configuration of the rational, the *imaginaire*, and the remembered truths, which are for the most part memorized but not written and are confused in the expressions of belief and conduct. However, insofar as such explicative analysis does not reach the actors to the point of provoking in each of them a better reconstruction controlled by the psychological configuration bound to religious systems through *beliefs* and *non-beliefs*, the "scientific" theory of religion will merely act as a mental, cultural, and political frontier in societies where it is erected implicitly (as in secular republics) or explicitly as a doctrine of state (as in socialist and popular atheistic republics). One understands, consequently, why the liberal secular state loses in philosophical flexibility that which it gains in juridical neutrality, whereas the religious state despises both. The exclusion in French public establishments of all teaching of the comparative history of religions and theological thought illustrates clearly what I mean by philosophical and scientific flexibility. It is significant that this question of philosophical and political essence is not yet being discussed within the European Union with a view to proposing new academic programs to reflect, simultaneously, the needs of multi-cultural societies and the exigencies of scientific knowledge adapted to the progress of globalization.

But the perverse effects of the latter must not distract us from the historical advances founded upon the positive experience of intellectual modernity. If the great religions and philosophies have long taught that man is spirit, one must not forget that spiritualism, ontologism, transcendentalism, theologism, essentialism, and substantialism are as much rationalizing derivatives or dangerous *imaginaires* as those of present-day globalization, on the real nature of mankind. Drawing on contemporary Islam, I shall attempt to show that the work prescribed by the historical conjuncture of globalization consists in going philosophically, ethically, juridically, and institutionally beyond all the systems of beliefs and non-beliefs inherited variously from the past, towards a better mastery of powers available to man for changing man.

Rethinking Islam: facing its traditions

Raising the Islamic concept of *Jihad* to the rank of a historical figure of resistance to *McWorld* cannot be the basis of present-day Islam if it is to fulfill, as it claims, the role of an alternative model to that of the West for producing more just regimes and better-integrated societies. The claim of the West to remain the unique model of reference for all contemporary regimes and societies is equally not acceptable so long as the conditions defined above are not strictly fulfilled to the point of creating, among all the observers and actors of our world, the feeling of a restraining *debt-of-meaning*. Now, one can contract a *debt-of-meaning* only towards the social actors who, like the prophets, saints, heroes, thinkers, and artists, are able to demonstrate in their behavior, and articulate in a discourse accessible to the greatest number, the existential paradigms which encourage free emulation by others. In the democratic and secular Western milieu, the individual, protected by the state of law coupled with a welfare state, tends to be his or her own model, increasingly incapable of recognizing a debt-of-meaning to a religion, philosophy, nation, community, hero-liberator, thinker, or poet. In Muslim contexts, the *debt-of-meaning* towards the Qur'an as the word of God, towards the Prophet as the messenger of God, and towards the "pious forefathers" (*al-salaf al-salih*) who have ensured the faithful collection and transmission of the founding messages of all truths, of all valid thoughts and all correct norms, continues to play a role so preponderant that there remains no place for the adoption of, or even the mere respect for, an idea, institution, innovation, or personality that cannot be integrated into the system of identification and evaluation through which the *debt-of-meaning* is perpetuated.

The social and political dialectic which has prevailed since independence from colonial rule has, despite the interlude of the years 1950–60, reinforced the psychological configuration postulated by this *debt-of-meaning*. The politics of traditionalization and the celebration of Islam as a component of national identities have thwarted the possibilities of modernizing tools of thought and institutions for the benefit of a religion which is cut off from both its historical origins and contemporary scientific contexts. It is not rare, therefore, to encounter "intellectuals," academics, and managers of large enterprises, banks, and complex administrations, who shelter from all critical intervention in the "sacred" and sacralizing domain of founding texts and beliefs of this *debt-of-meaning* without which social order would collapse.

The critical analyst will explain that all discourse is the bearer of the will-to-power because it seeks to share with others the proposition of meaning that every interlocutor articulates. The more my proposition infringes upon the sphere of meaning already occupied by other social actors, the more the conflict will become rough and lead to violence; and if I enter the mythical and symbolic sphere of their foundational accounts, then a "holy," "sacred," "just," "legitimate" war becomes inevitable. Consequently, even the most secular republics have their foundational accounts, their symbolic politics, their "places of memory" constructed by historiography, which are officially and periodically celebrated. It is in these collective representations sacralized by time that national identity takes root; it is here that the "values" which legitimize patriotic fervor, supreme sacrifices, and heroic conduct take shape. I deliberately use this ethico-political vocabulary, from which sermons and official discourses are woven, to recall that at this level of production and consumption of meaning, the interferences between the religious and the political, the sacred and the profane, the spiritual and the temporal, are so constant, so inseminating, that it is misleading to stick to the juridical and institutional theme of the separation between church and state.

This deconstructive analysis of current terminology also shows another piece of evidence, hardly familiar even to cultivated minds, about what is called truth in the functional trilogy of *violence, sacred,* and *truth*. In the ordinary sense, truth is an immediate sentiment of perfect equivalence between words and deeds, between a statement and its objective referents, or more generally between current language and the empirical experience which everyone has of reality. Religions and metaphysics represent this truth as unique, intangible, transcendent, and divine. But for the critical analyst, truth is defined as the sum of the *effects of meaning* which authorizes for every individual or collective subject the system of connotations represented

in its language; it is the totality of representations retained in the living tradition of a group, confessional community, or nation which is more or less unified by a common political and cultural history.

These two definitions of truth draw an increasingly distinct mental cleavage between two postures of reason itself: the *classical metaphysical posture*, amply described by historians of philosophy, continues to resist the rise of the *new posture* of the so-called exact sciences, the biological and social sciences, which are themselves put in disarray by the information revolution. Historians have clearly distinguished between several postures of reason in past epochs which continue to coexist in contemporary discourse without the knowledge of their authors. Clerics, essayists, ideologues, sermonizers, and experts, highly specialized experts in activities which do not require know-how grounded in historical culture, express themselves on general problems without regard for the postures of reason and cognitive systems which they use. One finds in them a confusion between theological attitudes and philosophical reasoning, between ideological argument for the invocation of a belief and the historical fact, an ingenious striving to find in the founding religious texts (Bible, Gospels, Qur'an) or the medieval exegeses consecrated as orthodox, teachings on human rights, social justice, democracy, human dignity, etc. Inversely, the pressing needs for ethical principles to regulate, in however small a measure, the confusion and anguish brought about by discoveries in the life-sciences, force us to speak again about the status of the individual, the spiritual vocation of being human, and the inalienable values which underpin the ethics of conviction and responsibility. One thus perceives that the reason of the Enlightenment has opened up horizons which it had practically abandoned or badly explored, and that theological reason seeks to regain credibility in a context of a generalized crisis of thought. On the other hand, rather than harnessing itself to the conquest of an epistemological status adapted to the pressing challenges of history at the threshold of the third millennium, the reason which claims to be post-modern even indulges in a do-it-yourself kind of individualism and militantism.

All this distances us from the definition of present-day Islam. To approach the latter, I want to break as radically as possible from the epistemological attitude and the so-called scientific practice which treats Islam as a domain apart from the history of religions, cultures, and civilizations. One cannot deal with present-day Islam by simply repeating the linear chronological account of its historical spread, the theologico-juridical frames of its articulation as a *system of beliefs and non-beliefs* fixed by God, dedicated to the pious observance of the faithful, and the no less conformist and repeti-

tive transcriptions of the Islamicists which have been adopted by political scientists to describe present-day Islam. It has been shown to what extent Islam is subjected, like all living traditions of thought, culture, and beliefs, to the irresistible hurricane of globalization. There is no need to reinforce ritual expressions extended to an impressive number of the faithful; no need to mobilize and inspire armies of young militants, ready for all sacrifice; no need to retain the attention of all the political strategists who are themselves surrounded by experts more or less sagacious, or by charlatans. The fact remains that the historical test through which Islam has been passing as a religion since the 1970s has already created an irreversible situation which affects all living religions, and beyond religions, the conditions of production, transmission, and consumption of meaning in human societies. One understands, therefore, why I have devoted such a long preamble to the question of the metamorphoses of meaning and of what continues to be called *the truth* under the pressures of globalization.

To encompass the historical situation of what I call present-day Islam, chronology has its importance. Innumerable works, dating back to the nineteenth century, have dealt with Islamic modernity, modern Islam, and Islam facing modernity. Under these titles, the authors are interested, in fact, in the intellectuals and researchers who have tried to apply to the history of societies shaped by the *Islamic fact* decontextualized fragments of modernity from the classical age as they were translated especially in the historiographical and philological works of the nineteenth century. The Orientalists then praised the relative successes of their pupils such as Taha Hussein, Zaki Mubarak, Bishr Faris, Salama Musa, and others, who reproduced their methodologies. But Islam and its tradition have been very little affected by those initial, modest essays, even when they gave rise to violent condemnations on the part of the guardians of an obscurantist orthodoxy; the examples of Taha Hussein and 'Ali Abdel Raziq are repeated today by other authors with writings no less soothing. Present-day Islam would not have turned to fundamentalist excesses at the end of the twentieth century if modernity, even of a historicist and philological kind, had really succeeded in penetrating the frames of traditional thought as it did for Christianity. With the advent of the Muslim Brotherhood movement in the 1930s, intellectual modernists rushed to make concessions to apologetic tendencies such as those manifested in the writings of al-Aqqad, Hussein Haykal, and even Taha Hussein.

After 1945, the political movements of liberation were able to harness to their advantage the mobilizing power of Islam, while maintaining a general secular and social orientation, because of the presence of militants inspired by communism, or converts to the political philosophy of the Third French Republic such as Bourguiba, Ferhat Abbas, and their disciples. The nationalistic fever, the priority unanimously accorded to political freedom, and the geopolitical strategies used by the two superpowers of the time (the United States and the Soviet Union) to attract the emerging nation-states to their spheres of influence, succeeded in maintaining Islamic militancy in a subsidiary role. One had to wait for the great defeat of the Arab armies in 1967, the failure and death of Gamal Abdel Nasser in 1970, the first symptoms of the demise of Soviet hegemony, the demographic growth which upset the social frames of knowledge and political expression, the revelation of the limits of oil as a weapon, the fallout of the euphoria generated by the independence that had been so dearly achieved, and the subsequent erosion of ill-founded legitimacies, for there to emerge on the scene what is today called *radical Islam, Islamic radicalism, political Islam, Muslim rage* (these are typical titles of books or articles on the subject) which assumed power spectacularly in Iran in 1979, and has since then pursued a devastating struggle, ill-adapted to the magnitude and the real scope of the challenges of modernity complicated by those of globalization, as has been demonstrated.

Present-day Islam is witnessing the end of secular messianic ideologies and the certitudes of a conquering science;[6] it also witnesses the disarray of the legitimacies constructed by and for the nation-states and the concomitant awakening of peoples, ethno-cultural minorities, and regional communities long marginalized and oppressed by centralizing religious or secular states. It refuses nevertheless to record the numerous, repeated disappointments which the *internal* history of all societies called Muslim has inflicted upon the Utopia of a "revealed divine law" (*Sharia*), which continues to be proclaimed and imposed by clerics while political regimes are lacking in legitimacy and there is an upsurge of populist Islam claiming to be "revolutionary." To understand the reactivation in contemporary Islamic contexts of a contradiction common to all great religions, we must pause here to reflect on the internal history of the Islamic Utopia and the sociology of its current expressions. But how can one proceed without repeating the many expositions which rehash relentlessly the frozen data, lacking critical objectives or explicative intentions?

If one aims to be exhaustive, informative, explicative, and critical, one would require a proper frame for further research in a domain as vast and complex as the map of the world. One can obtain an idea of this complexity and its extent by going through the chronological and genealogical survey of the dynasties in the land of Islam, recently published by C.E. Bosworth.[7] The author enumerates some 186 dynasties scattered over the globe from the Philippines to Morocco and from Central Asia to South Africa. I do not mean, of course, that it is sufficient to go through the chronological history of the dynasties from their origins to our days in order to understand present-day Islam. I propose, rather, to begin with a sociology of contemporary expressions of this Islam to show how, in every socio-cultural and political context, the history of Islam has been solicited and interpreted according to the needs of ongoing struggles. This procedure allows us to distinguish clearly the imaginary productions of contemporary societies, with their manipulations of a multi-dimensional object which all the actors confusedly call Islam, from the critical, scientific knowledge of the different domains (spiritual, ritual, theological, juridical, political, artistic, etc.) which make up the historical realization of the same object. There is no question here of conflicts, in the manner of defensive or apologetic theologies, between an ideally constructed "true Islam" and an imaginary Islam manipulated by actors and therefore *false*. The objective of our analysis remains scientific in both cases. In effect, religions, like all great mobilizing ideologies, structure the *imaginaire* of all social groups and thereby contribute to what C. Castoriadis has aptly described as "the imaginary production of society." In the case of present-day Islam, the projection of its "values" and salutary hopes towards an inaugurating age, not just as part of an Islamic era but of a universalizable *existential paradigm*, takes on a psycho-social and political significance in the horizons opened up by the liberation struggles of the years 1950–60. The strong recurrence of the paradigm of historical action put in place already by the Qur'an, together with the teachings and normative conduct of the Prophet, are in themselves a fact which lead us to think about the links between religious and political hope in the historical evolution of societies.

To bring together all these data, I shall now introduce the concept of the dialectic of the local and the global, richly illustrated in the works of Clifford Geertz,[8] which from 1967 inaugurated, in contrast to the writings of the Islamicists, an anthropological problematic that has been insufficiently exploited.

The dialectic of the local and the global

The Islamic fact emerged in the most circumscribed locale: the modest city of Mecca, which after ten years was replaced by the yet more humble agglomeration of Yathrib/Medina. Receiving support, successively, in these two centers, a Meccan, Muhammad ibn Abdullah, with some disciples, was able to activate the most pertinent elements of a social, political, and cultural dialectic which was sufficiently intense to generate an existential paradigm whose expansion raised the unrelenting hostility of some, and the fervent adhesion and inexhaustible hope of others. The Christian fact began in the same manner with Jesus of Nazareth. The passage of the two religions from the local to the global recognized neither the same rhythms nor the same vicissitudes; but in both cases, the same distinction asserts itself between a *prophetic moment* and an *imperial moment*. I reserve the case of Judaism which also inaugurated a prophetic function, but was not linked to an independent state before the creation of the state of Israel.

I call the *prophetic moment* the conjunction of a local historical dialectic with a discourse of mythical structure which transfigures ordinary actors and channels in educative spiritual tensions between man who is called to the exercise of a responsible freedom, and a God who is given to interiorize as a living counterpart, transcendent, demanding judge, merciful, protector, benefactor, etc.

This definition has no theological objective; it is programmatic in the sense that it introduces tools of analysis and understanding for the linguist, historian, psychologist, psycho-socio-linguist, and anthropologist for the purpose of interpreting mythical accounts and identifying the evolving structures of the social *imaginaire*. I have demonstrated elsewhere,[9] with the example of Sura 18 of the Qur'an, how three ancient accounts—the Seven Sleepers or the "People of the Cave" (*ahl al-kahf*), the Epic of Gilgamesh, and the Romance of Alexander—illustrate the following three equally programmatic definitions of language, myth, and scientific activity:

> Language is in the first instance a categorization, a creation of objects and relations between these objects (E. Benveniste).

> Myth is an ideological palace constructed with the rubble of an ancient social discourse (C. Levi-Strauss).

> Scientific activity is not a blind accumulation of truths; science is selective and seeks truths which matter most, either by their intrinsic interest or as tools for confronting the world (W. Van O. Quine).

The type of thought and the epistemological engagement of reason required by these definitions remain inaccessible to all those who have not made the methodological and conceptual journey peculiar to every discipline invoked. The difference between a *mental object* created by language and a *physical object*, whose existence does not depend either on the perception or the name given to it, remains *unthinkable* for all those who perceive, think, and express themselves in the cognitive frame established by this verse of the Bible and reiterated in the Qur'an: "God taught Adam all the names." Naming possesses not only a power of existentiation (*ijad*) of the named objects, but also an ontological guarantee included in the names taught by God. This onto-psycho-linguistic mechanism is a main characteristic of what I call the *prophetic discourse* as embodied in its linguistic manifestations in the Hebrew Bible, the discourse of Jesus of Nazareth articulated in Aramaic and later transcribed in Greek, and the Qur'an, together with their respective expansions in living traditions. The reconquest of the *prophetic discourse* as *linguistic fact* contextualized by the historian-anthropologist is in itself an educative operation that is difficult to achieve, even politically impossible in certain cases, because of the pressures exercised by religious orthodoxy, which is the basis of the legitimacy of power and of the representations which the community of the faithful itself gives to the founding moment of its religion. In the case of Islam, the work of misrepresentation is seen in the transfiguration of the historical actor Muhammad into the prophet-mediator of the "Word of God," which is conceived as transcendent, normative, and immutable Revelation, uncreated according to the "orthodox" position that eliminated the Mu'tazili theory of the created Qur'an.

These observations have nothing theoretical or speculative about them; they result from my personal experience with the most diverse Jewish, Christian, and Muslim groups. The most patient pedagogical procedures and the most simplified explanations come up against either the opposition of the dogmatic minds, or an *unthinkable* linked to two diametrically opposite formations but leading to the same psycho-linguistic blockage. The "orthodox" religious formation uses a strategy of refusal to rid itself of all the attitudes of thought which would compromise the ideal knowledge of what, without any critical examination, is called faith. In the democratic context, where every citizen is perfectly entitled to his own "different" view, particularly when it is connected to the sacred region of faith, we are witnessing, in Europe notably, an intellectually exasperating and dangerous use of this strategy of refusal. No less exasperating and dangerous is the attitude of minds trained in the *culture*—which is termed modern and secular—of *unbelief,* the dogmatic cult of "the death of God," the rejection not only of the dogmas and catechisms perpetuated by all types of "church," but more seriously of the religious dimensions of all the cultures manifested in history. In this connection, the word of Voltaire is still very enlightening today: to those who were already worried about the void, nay the ruins, caused by the success of the battles fought by the reason of the Enlightenment, he would reply, "I deliver you from a ferocious beast and you are asking me with what I shall replace it!" Assuredly, the reason worrying about its autonomy in relation to external dogmas could not fight against an all-powerful and obscurantist clericalism and at the same time construct values of substitution. But it is a historical fact that the nation-state, representative democracy, universal suffrage, and political philosophy managed by the state, are today showing their exhaustion, just as religious regimes did prior to modern revolutions.

One understands in these circumstances why the rare, innovating works on the major questions handed down by the prophetic discourse and its diverse articulations, piously collected and transmitted in every community under the name of a *living tradition*, do not have any *target public* capable of understanding it and making any contributions to it through fruitful debates. Look at the electoral campaigns in democratic societies: the problem of the production, management, and functions of meaning and of the effects of meaning are never on the agenda. To say that the average elector would not understand anything of it is incorrect and unjust; the blinding and more frightening socio-cultural truth is that in their great majority, the "representatives" of the people themselves do not have any interest in engaging in such debates. In the case of societies which claim affinity to "Islam," researchers, thinkers, writers, and artists who would think of transgressing, however little, into the orthodox living tradition, are simply forbidden to delve into religious questions. I know a significant number of "intellectuals" and colleagues who contribute to the maintenance of such taboos.

Considering everything that has been said so far, it will be noted that the prophetic moment does not escape the burden of history; it represents the stage of emergence, the socio-political and linguistic construction of a *system of beliefs and non-beliefs* not yet fixed in ritual, ethical, juridical, and institutional codes which will intervene in the subsequent stage of the *imperial moment* when a state apparatus brings religion under its control. In the early Qur'anic stage, the relationship between men who hear the call and God is expressed in the context of an oral culture, outside the intervention of clerics who exercise a power of interpretation in favor of, or in opposition to, the state. Besides, what will later become the *Mushaf* or *Closed Official Corpus* and the orthodox collections of *hadith*, set up equally in the *Closed Official Corpus*, exist and function in this stage only as a form of oral statement open to the questioning and immediate reactions of the actors. I insist upon these historical data, which the normative discourse of belief will efface very quickly by projecting on the prophetic moment of the inaugurating age all the operations of sacralization and mythologization effected during the imperial moment.

I call the *imperial moment* the period of formation and rapid expansion of the caliphal state which institutionally lasted from 661 to 1258, despite the political vicissitudes it witnessed from the intervention of the Buyids (932), and then the Saljuqs (1040). The caliphal state is characterized by the construction and maintenance of a politico-religious legitimacy accepted by the Sunnis, but rejected by the Kharijis and the various Shi'a branches. The entire Muslim historiography, following Orientalist scholarship since the nineteenth century, has maintained these political and doctrinal facts without burdening itself with the problems raised by the passage from the prophetic moment to the imperial moment; and of the mythical construction of the former by the latter, on the one hand, and by the constant dialectic between the stakes-of-meaning and the wills-to-power engaged in theologico-political debates and confrontations for power in all the spaces administered by the caliphal state, on the other. I am not overlooking the contribution of modern historians to the critical analysis of ancient texts, particularly since the Orientalists are more open to the inquiries of the social sciences. But the fact remains that the prejudice of rationality continues to prevail over considerations of the role of the *imaginaire* in the construction of legitimacies, the formation and expansion of orthodoxies, the representations of religious truth, and the discursive strategies of Islamic thought to cover with a sacred divine veil the ethical, juridical, political, and economic norms which bring into relief all the activities and profane struggles of the social actors.

It is thus that past and present historical writings, reinforced by the literature of political science, have imposed a rigid, immutable, artificially sacralized image of a hypostatic Islam which ignores the local, historical, sociological, psychological, linguistic, and mythological factors and assigns a legal status of divine essence to all thoughts, initiatives, and productions of men in society. One rarely finds in the most critical writings—in the sense of the social sciences—about this Islam, written with a capital letter, the concepts of state control over religion, sacralization, transcendentalization, spiritualization, ontologization, and mythologization of religion. All this has made it necessary today for the analyst to undertake the reverse process of de-sacralization, etc.—in other words, *unveiling, deconstruction, de-historicization*; laying bare the reality which has been constructed by and for the social *imaginaire*, under the cover of a discourse formally critical and rationalized such as that of the *usul al-din* and *usul al-fiqh*; a critique of *hadith* (the "authentic" collections including the *asbab al-nuzul*), and more generally the *akhbar*, the history of the Qur'anic text and Qur'anic exegesis, the elaboration of juridical norms (*istinbat al-ahkam*), the putting in "historical" form of the Sira of the Prophet, Ali, the Imams, etc. That is the entire history of Islamic thought and the imperial context where it fulfilled, *simultaneously,* functions of ideation and ideologization/mythologization—a history that must be rewritten for two main reasons: to acquire a better descriptive and explicative understanding of a domain that is still badly included in the tasks of theoretization undertaken by the social sciences; and to respond to the vital intellectual and cultural needs of all societies which today depend on false representations and illusory beliefs conveyed by the state-controlled and ritualized Islam, dangerously manipulated in the new contexts of flourishing populism and the disintegration of popular as well as urban cultural codes.

Present-day Islam provides neither the educative and cultural resources nor the political and sociological liberties which are indispensable for dealing successfully with the immense edifice of the "orthodox" Islams bequeathed by the imperial moment; the great historical ruptures with their exhaustive traditions and geopolitical and geohistoric environments (the Mediterranean world and modern Europe); and the increasingly more decisive challenges of science and technology, and of economies linked to the revolution in information technology. The long historical period which extends from the thirteenth to the end of the eighteenth century is described by historians in terms of *decadence, lethargy,* and the *retreat of underdeveloped societies,* in contrast to the European societies which, from the same thirteenth century, commence an irresistible, uninterrupted march towards modernity with its still ongoing developments under the name of globalization. If we come back to our dialectic of the local and the global, one can speak of the revenge of the local upon the global after the gradual weakening and final demise of the caliphal state. Doubtless, one must take into account what is called the Ottoman Empire. In the frame of analysis which I have chosen—the dialectic of the local and the global, of the stakes-of-meaning and wills-to-power in the Mediterranean world, including the most dynamic part of Europe, from the fifteenth to eighteenth centuries—one can speak of a shrinking of the intellectual and cultural horizons of scholarly Islam, of its ritualization, its immersion in symbolic and customary local codes with, notably, the wide proliferation of religious brotherhoods to compensate for local deficiencies in different political centers which are too far away or too weak to exercise an effective control upon all ethno-cultural groups and regions. The depredation of meaning and intellectual diligence, the insignificance of literary creativity and scientific innovation, the disappearance of doctrinal pluralism and the humanist attitude (philosophical *adab* of the tenth century), are linked to several facts which dominated the Ottoman period: the imposition of a single official juridical school (the Hanafi) throughout the empire, the total elimination of philosophy, the widespread emergence

Sanctions and defences

Sanctions against market abuse

3.1   The Financial Services Authority ('FSA') has authority to impose sanctions for market abuse that are intended to complement the existing criminal law relating to insider dealing and market manipulation. It is possible, however, that there is overlap between the provisions, and market participants could find themselves subject to the provisions of a mainstream Financial Services and Markets Act 2000 ('FSMA 2000') offence as well as an offence legislated against outside of this Act. In addition, it is the FSA that has the authority to decide on the most appropriate way forward when investigating market abuse, regulatory sanctions or a criminal prosecution.

3.2   The statutory definition of market abuse has been referred to in Chapters 1 and 2. As we have seen, the power to impose penalties is contained within the FSMA 2000, s 123 and the actual conduct amounting to an abuse is captured by the three conditions under the FSMA 2000, s 118(2)(a), (b), (c): misuse of information, false or misleading impressions and distortion.

3.3   A penalty may be imposed if any person is engaged in market abuse or has required or encouraged another to take or refrain from a course of action. The actual amount of the fine will be of such amount as the FSA considers appropriate under the particular circumstances. As we saw in the Chapter 2, the imposition of a penalty will not render a transaction void or unenforceable. The core element of proof is the concept of behaviour by the alleged miscreant in that he has failed to maintain appropriate standards of conduct as determined by the regular user or the FSA equivalent to the 'man on the Clapham omnibus'.

3.4   The first category of behaviour sanctioned – against misuse of information – is subject to a number of tests that relate to whether the information, subject to the misuse, is generally available. The FSMA 2000 creates four areas for defence associated with the information:

- if the dealing was subject to a legal or regulatory requirement;
- if the decision to deal was taken before the information was available;
- if normal dealing in the information would not constitute market abuse (although it may be front running); and
- if an equity position has been developed (subject to the caveat that it is for the benefit of the offeror in a take-over bid).

3.5 Creating a false impression is an offence when it is likely to give a regular market user a false impression about the supply of, demand for, price of or value of an investment. There must be a real likelihood that the conduct will have this effect. The knowledge of the participant creating the effect is crucial if a prosecution is to succeed as it must be proven that he knew, or could reasonably be expected to know, that his actions would cause the effect achieved (ie inflate or depress the market).

It will not amount to market abuse under this limb where the primary rationale for the action taken is:

- in pursuit of a legitimate commercial venture;
- a required transaction reporting activity; or
- a permitted cross-trade or price maintenance operation.

3.6 Distortion of the market will be complete when a regular user considers that a certain course of conduct will have the effect of impeding the natural forces of supply and demand on the market. This is a fairly vague activity that will be hard to pinpoint at times. This may lead to challenges as mentioned previously under the concept of legal clarity and legitimate expectation and, more specifically, if one is acting in accordance with agreed rules of conduct.

3.7 There are two statutory exceptions that exist within the FSMA 2000. It will not be market abuse if, first, the behaviour does not amount to market abuse in the opinion of the FSA and, second, if the behaviour conforms with a rule that stipulates a range of conduct that will not be determined to be market abuse. There are also the defences that the party subject to the alleged offence took all reasonable steps to avoid engaging in market abuse or that he did not believe that his behaviour amounted to market abuse.

3.8 The first of these – the subjective view of the FSA in determining behaviour as an abuse of the market – is contained within the FSMA 2000, s 122(2):

> 'Otherwise, the Code in force under section 119 at the time when particular behaviour occurs may be relied on so far as it indicates whether or not that behaviour should be taken to amount to market abuse.'

What this means is that in circumstances other than when a Code (eg the City Code) gives a specific defence, a Code may still be relied upon to indicate that the behaviour did not amount to market abuse.

3.9   If the FSA determines guilt of market abuse it may impose a financial penalty. A penalty may not be imposed when in response to a representation made under the defence that all reasonable precautions were exercised or the participant believed, on reasonable grounds, that the behaviour was not abusive. In this case the FSA may choose not to impose a financial penalty but may instead publish a statement to the effect that a certain party has engaged in market abuse.

3.10   The FSA is not obliged to follow this course of action; it is an option (FSMA 2000, s 123(3)) and the exercise of this discretion is most likely to be seen in cases of inadvertence. Those matters that more closely straddle the civil and criminal divide would be far less suitable for condemnation alone, and this course of action is most unlikely to be taken in cases where there is a clear intent that amounts to market abuse that can also be determined as a criminal market manipulation.

3.11   The issuing of a notice is triggered by representations made to the FSA by a person in response to a warning notice. It is important to remember that this does not exhaust the range of sanctions available to the FSA for market abuse as there is also the power to apply for an injunction to restrain the market abuse: see the FSMA 200, s 381. The FSA also has the power to require restitution without making an application before the courts (FSMA 2000, s 384); the person concerned can apply to have the matter reviewed by the Tribunal.

3.12   The general power to order restitution is not restricted to cases of market abuse and applies to any authorised person committing any offence under the FSMA 2000, as well as insider dealing and money laundering under the FSMA 2000, s 402. Under s 383 of the Act the FSA may apply to the court for a restitution order against persons who have engaged in market abuse. It is for the court to decide on the appropriate level of restitution and the recipients.

3.13   Whilst it is difficult to speculate about the level of fines that the FSA may impose, there are guidelines in the Enforcement Manual and a number of factors will be taken into consideration. The seriousness of the abuse, the degree of culpability and intention, the frequency of the offending, the impact on the market that the conduct had, the gain or loss made by the participant and the cost to other market participants will all be relevant. The FSA will also look at the pattern of trading by the firm or individual to establish whether the offence is a singular event or part of a series. The FSA does not propose to implement a fines tariff for cases of market abuse, as each case will be dealt with on an individual basis.

3.14   It will also be a factor when determining sanctions to take into account the conduct of the firm or individual in assisting with the process of an investigation and responding to any findings. There are 13 examples, cited in Consultation Paper 65, Chapter 16, p 5, of factors that will be taken into consideration by the FSA; these should be viewed as an exemplar and not an exhaustive list.

Financial crimes under section 6

3.15 Under the FSMA 2000, s 6 the FSA is charged with reducing financial crime. The contextual parameters for this preventative role are, in association with other enforcement agencies, to reduce the opportunities for financial participants to be the conduits for crime. This is principally manifest in the offences legislated against outside of the FSMA 2000; that is money laundering. However, there is a recognition that the financial sector is vulnerable to infiltration by organised crime groups through a number of activities. To this end, s 6 specifically mentions fraud or dishonesty and handling of stolen goods in addition to the more obvious market abuse offences.

3.16 It is not proposed that this chapter will attempt an extensive commentary on the provisions of the relevant legislation relating to handling stolen goods and fraud (deception), but for the purposes of completeness there will be a brief overview of the provisions, sanctions and defences. In particular readers will be directed towards areas of further reading.

3.17 Handling of stolen goods is most likely to manifest itself in the guise of money laundering; this is dealt with in para **1.28**, but it should be remembered that handling money or items that represent the money obtained from criminal acts will also be handling of stolen goods if it is done for the purposes of dishonestly receiving or assisting in the retention, removal, disposal or realisation by or for the benefit of another person. This offence is triable either way. It is punishable with imprisonment of up to six months and/or a fine up to the statutory maximum if dealt with at the magistrate's court. It is punishable with 14 years' imprisonment and/or an unlimited fine on indictment.

3.18 Goods may be stolen goods not only if obtained by the conventional channel of theft but also if obtained by a deception or wrongful credit. The requisite element of proof for the prosecution to discharge is that the defendant handled the goods knowing or believing them to be stolen. The blurring of a distinction between the elements of knowledge and belief is succinctly put by Professor Smith who holds that 'this seems to be merely a distinction between two sources of D's knowledge or belief: if D had direct evidence, he knows, if he has circumstantial evidence, he believes'[1]. There is no statutory defence to handling. A related, but separate, offence has newly been created under the Theft Act 1968, s 24A in that a person who dishonestly retains a wrongful credit is liable on indictment to ten years' imprisonment and/or an unlimited fine. This offence may be dealt with

of a subservient scholastic class which glossed indefinitely over some classical manuals selected to serve their orthodoxy, the absence of doctrinal
disputations (*munazara*) between scholars belonging to different schools,
and the obliviousness to currents of fruitful thought as well as significant
works and authors of the classical period. On the other hand, the Ottoman
state always favored certain works and institutions, such as architecture and
the army, which were more directly linked to the glory of the empire, the
deployment of its power, and the maintenance of its legitimacy. One will
note, however, an instance of resistance by the ulama who refused to grant
to the sultans the coveted title of caliph.

Can one then speak of a "renaissance" (*Nahda*) as have the "Arabs"—the
Arabic-speaking domain of the Ottoman Empire—who suffered a rehabili-
tated domination afterwards, notably in Algeria, to extol the Turks as the
"protectors of Islam" against the colonizing enterprises of Christian Europe?
This question has introduced a huge problem of historical knowledge: we are,
in effect, far from an objective definition of the role and place of the Ottoman
period in the wider perspective of a global history of peoples, cultures, religions, and hegemonies in the Mediterranean space. This objective implies
the renunciation by European peoples and nation-states of a unilateral, self-
centered historiography which mentions the Muslims in general and the
Turks in particular as negative forces opposed to their expansion. Similarly,
the colonized peoples and the party-nation-states which have taken charge
of them after independence must cease to write and teach their history in
terms of moralizing, apologetic, and militant categories, which explain their
historical stagnation in relation to modern Europe and all their present-day
difficulties as a product of savage colonial domination, thus dispensing with
the need to examine much older structural mechanisms.

There was a renaissance from the nineteenth century, to the extent that
there was a reactivation of the intellectual field, an opening up of cultural
creativity and sensibility to the material progress of civilization on account
of a mode of knowledge ignored until then in Islamic contexts. The scientific curiosity for the classical period (the *imperial moment*) welcomes for
the first time the methods of philology and the frame of historicist inquiry;
one is interested in the critical edition of ancient texts after the manner of
the European Renaissance of Graeco-Latin texts. The modern political and
juridical institutions are subjected to scrutiny, but not to the point of trigger-
ing a current of critical revision of the methodological and cognitive foundations of Islamic thought. Albert Hourani rightly designated this period as
the *liberal age*.[10] But from the perspective of present-day Islamist discourse
and the return to a disguised locality under the pretext of universality, the

Nahda and even the Salafi thought were more charged with hope, with overtures to intellectual political and juridical modernity, than the Arab Socialist Revolution of Nasser which was too aligned to a communism without critical Marxists, or the present-day Islamic Revolution in Iran which is too dominated by clerics closer to *populist* religion than to an intellectually demanding spirituality.

Many will reject this proposition because it seems to neglect the colonial domination which weighed until 1945 over all societies with Islamic references. This point is important, because it allows us to measure the responsibility of "organic" intellectuals who, in order to benefit from the privileges of the new *Nomenklatura*, supported ideologies which were as much foreign to the Islamic tradition—considered obsolete and without political relevance—as to the customary and cultural codes of the rural and nomadic worlds. The "proletariat" were the only driving force of a revolution which one can today only denounce for its horrors without relegating it to the camp of absolute evil, that is, colonialism and imperialism. This politico-Manichaean division, which has long affected the social link in post-war Europe, is being raised again today with more *anti-intellectual* radicalism by the militants of the Islamic Revolution. That is because the sociological bases of the socialist-communist ideology of the years 1950–70 have been considerably enlarged since then by population explosions, while the uprooting of rural populations and nomads has led to the expansion of cities which were conceived at the beginning of the century, or even in the nineteenth century, for more limited urban classes. The rapid development of a populist social force is explained by the conjugation of these factors, to which must be added the system of education conceived and imposed by party-nation-states.

The separation between the sciences of the engineer and the sciences of man and society has been more radical and even more harmful than in the model systems of the West. If engineers trained in the new faculties of sciences commit themselves more readily to Islamist movements, it is because they are even more deprived than their peers at the faculties of law and social sciences of the tools of thought which are indispensable for receiving or producing the reasoning of a historian, sociologist, linguist, psychologist, or anthropologist. These domains of reality are lived and interpreted through the categories of beliefs and non-beliefs taught by religion, with the ideological re-appropriation effected by scholarly discourse, which is itself modelled by the official discourse of national construction (the ministers of education work with their colleagues at the ministries of interior, "national orientation," religious affairs, and information in the line fixed by the party-state). Thus the *populist* ideological Maquis find themselves spread in all strata and sectors of society; but it is in the great urban centers that they manifest themselves with the greatest political potency and social pressure. That certain regimes succeed better than others in regulating, diverting, and containing these forces of protest and change is undeniable; the fact remains that populism is a structural, sociological phenomenon generated during the course of the years 1960–80 in all societies of the former Third World. This fact conditions the demagogical discourse of the states, weighs upon the manipulation of religious "values," and reduces the chances of diffusion of critical and disalienating modes of thought.

I have remarked on the scientific distances, the psychological postures, the objectives of meaning and power, which separate present-day Islam from the historical Islams which the critical historian tries to reconstruct. The most valuable lesson of this brief journey concerns not only Islam and its faithful; it also touches the *status of meaning* and of *what makes meaning* in human society. One will recognize, however, an important difference between, on the one hand, the situation of Islam as a *model of historical action* and those Muslims who lay claim to it today, and, on the other hand, modernity, its producers, and its users. In the first case, at least since the thirteenth century, generations of social actors allowed an immense *unthought* to accumulate, generating *unthinkables* which have become more and more burdensome to handle today; in the second, one makes perilous jumps beyond the values, stakes, works, signs, and symbols which one has not taken the time to evaluate and integrate into the successive "paradigms" which only political battles have made to prevail. These paradigms are from then on possessed of philosophical contingence and political arbitrariness; they go even as far as favoring the consumption of what Pierre Bourdieu has recently called "discardable thought." Will one take the time to rethink it and eventually reintegrate it in the more complete, legible, and enriching map of the cultures of the world? In other words, modernity has also generated unthoughts and unthinkables by putting the quest for meaning at the service of the will-to-power, whereas it ought to be careful not to bind human destiny to short-lived *effects of meaning*. Julia Kristeva spoke of "the destructive genesis of meaning" at a time when semiotics cultivated the ambition of introducing more effective cognitive strategies for better mastering the conditions of production and consumption of meaning.

Having said all this, it is necessary to elaborate further the concept to avoid reinforcing the idea, already too widespread, that Islam is a substantial entity which generates itself from its founding texts and imposes its brand upon societies and cultures which have accepted it. Present-day Islam, like classical Islam and the nascent Islam of the Qur'an and the actions of Muhammad, is the evolving and changing product of social actors so diverse and under historical conditions so complex through time and space, that we prefer to speak of a hypostasized Islam of texts and believers rather than one molded doctrinally and ideologically by concrete forces. Today these forces are termed populism, the uprooting of rural populations and nomads, the disintegration of urban mercantile and cultured milieux—in the sense of the learned written culture[11]—under the combined pressures of demography, the influx of unemployed rural populations, the destruction of cultural codes and systems of traditional solidarity, party-nation-states more concerned with monopolizing legal violence than constructing modern legitimacies, social and economic disparities between islets of supra-modernity; the middle classes maintained below their most legitimate ambitions, and the masses doomed to uncertainty, frustration, exclusion, and unemployment, that is, to the constitutive situations of the *imaginaire* of revolt. I speak of revolt rather than revolution because I prefer to reserve this latter concept for popular uprisings supported and legitimized by an ideology heralding imminent and lasting emancipation. That was the case of the Qur'anic discourse which accompanied the concrete organizing action of Muhammad while opening horizons of meaning which would allow future generations—particularly those who produced classical Islam under the great Abbasid caliphs—to construct the ideal sacred figure of the mediating-prophet and of a founding Revelation as the indispensable reference for the actions and conduct of the faithful.

The Qur'anic discourse has neither the same cognitive status nor the same discursive strategies as that which I call the *prophetic discourse*. The latter is not to be confused with the sayings of the Prophet collected in the great "closed official corpus" of *hadith*; for in the orthodox belief the *hadith* cannot be identified with the Qur'anic discourse which is divine. The *prophetic discourse* is that which is memorized, perceived, meditated, commented upon, and put to advantage in a vast semantic expansion through sacralization, transfiguration, mythologization, transcendentalization, and ontologization of the interpreting community in the course of centuries. It is the product of the collective *imaginaire* of various social groups; in return, it nourishes, galvanizes, stirs up, and inflames this very same *imaginaire* which believers call faith. By its enunciation, every believer liberates himself from his ordinary individual self, and from profane time and space, to make himself a contemporary of the Prophet, a witness to the descent of the Word of God; the pious ancients transfigured like the Prophet as models of faithfulness, transmitters by word and action of all the teachings which come to inflate the living tradition and enrich the efficacy of the prophetic discourse. The latter is a homogenous space of articulation of a necessarily true intangible meaning, which applies to all times and places but is itself independent of time and place. It combines the citations of the Qur'anic verses, the *hadith*, the edifying accounts of the lives and deeds of other recognized prophets, and saints who have attained proximity to God with the intercession of the Prophet, and the founder-imams of schools acknowledged as orthodox. It excludes, on the other hand, all other human discourses which are not authentically derived from the source-foundation-discourse. The recurrence of this discourse in the most diverse socio-cultural milieux and diverse historical conjunctures is explained by its mythical structure, paradigmatic nature, and its power of intercession, purification, and spiritual elevation of the believer. This definition applies, of course, to all monotheistic religious traditions which link all their discursive productions, and their conducts orientated towards salvation, to their foundational sacred texts (Bible, Gospels, Qur'an)[12] and to their expansion in the living tradition, through complex mechanisms of integration, selection, and rejection.

The revolutionary secularist discourse in the English, American, and French Revolutions of the age of the Enlightenment breaks totally with the postulates and religious representations of the prophetic discourse; but it retains with the latter several common traits. It also presents itself as the founder of a new departure of existential code; it sets up a principle of hope for all mankind, paradigms, and definitions which inform and govern all productions of human existence. At the same time, it detaches ethics, law, and spirituality from explicit references to a living God, revealing Himself to men in history; and it confers to a sovereign and responsible reason the task of defining and evaluating all legitimacies. The rupture with the metaphysical vision of spiritual theologies is therefore not total: there is a substitution of a secularist spiritual power for the power of divine law—it is in this sense that I speak of secularist (laic) discourse. The rivalry between the two discourses has continued until our day; and although the second has had a shorter life span and fewer instances of application than the first, one must recognize that the existential fecundity and promises of emancipation of both have not yet been exhausted. The destiny reserved by history to the Bolshevik Revolution of October 1917 confirms *a contrario* the validity of the comparative analysis which I have outlined here for better evaluating the status of what is called today, since the rise of Khomeini to power, the Islamic Revolution. One cannot, in fact, speak of present-day Islam without reflecting on the significance, scope, and limits of this great event.[13]

Before examining the case of the Islamic Revolution, it is useful to insist upon the ideological derivatives of the two discourses I have just presented as two existential codes which are, at the same time, discontinuous, rival, and intricate. The passage from prophetic discourse to theological, juridical, and political codifications is comparable to the passage of the revolutionary discourse of the Enlightenment to the philosophical, juridical, and institutional codifications which still function in the democratic societies of the West. The believers speak of degradation of the divine Revelation in the perverse usages which men make of it in societies; the laic citizens speak of crises, corruption and infidelity to the principles of 1789 (in the French case). It is a fact that the Christian empires of Byzantium and the West, the Muslim empires under the caliphate and then the Ottoman sultanate developed oppressive clerical systems which obliterated the emancipatory visions of the prophetic discourse and action. There is progress and a new departure of code with the reason of the Enlightenment because it liberated the intellectual field from false knowledge, as well as arbitrary political and juridical orders, accumulated by the clerical institutions of all religions. But in its turn, this liberating reason quickly exhausted its ethical and spiritual ethos by becoming conquering, dominating, and dogmatic. Particularly in France, the anti-clerical struggle, which was so necessary and fruitful but also violent and radical, engendered a secularist religion that reveals its dogmatism and incapacity to manage cultural pluralism after two centuries of rich and powerful experiences.

Present-day Islam is engaged in demonstrating the intellectual and cultural limits of the revolutionary discourse initiated and nourished by the *Aufklarung*. I do not mean to say that present-day Islamic thought launches intellectual challenges, hitherto unknown, to the reason of the Enlightenment. The Christian counterpart has already made the most of all types and degrees of resistance, rejection, and claims which can emanate from a religion of the Book before the rise of modernity in Europe. In any case, the Islamic thought of today is too unprepared in the face of modernity to serve as a fruitful dialectical partner in the ongoing debate on the functions of religion in the context of globalization. The challenge of present-day Islam to the societies of the West resides essentially in its semiological and sociological presence, which is visible enough to bring forth reactions of fear and rejection in populations reputed to be educated by the Enlightenment. It is a fact that in France the declaration of the rights of man and of the citizen was not followed by women's right to vote until 1945!

Can it be said that the Islamic Revolution, which sustains the political audacities and claims of *Jihad* vs. *McWorld*, has introduced new elements to enrich the typology just outlined by a third type? In the absence of any intellectual challenge on the part of Islamic thought, there would thus exist a historical challenge of paradigmatic scope which would imply stakes-of-meaning not only for the reason of the Enlightenment but, more decisively, for a new, emerging reason.

This question returns under a more programmatic form, but always with a radical and comprehensive critical intention, as I have already said, on the irreversible situation created for Islam and its tradition by the historical test of the 1970s. This time, Islam will not be able to elude, as it did with the excuse of liberation struggles, the major intellectual revolution which bears upon the conditions of production, transmission, and consumption of meaning in human societies. At this point in our analytical and critical journey, it is necessary to introduce the problems raised by the attitude of present-day Islam towards its tradition.

The approach of tradition in the Islamic context

For this part of the exposition, I shall content myself with resuming a long study which I devoted to tradition in 1984 and which was published in 1985 under a title resembling the one I have adopted here by integrating the new data of globalization and taking into account *Jihad* as an ongoing figure of history.[14] One may notice that the critical and constructive objective of my earlier reflections imposes itself with more pertinence and urgency in the present-day context of political and social tensions culminating in the Algerian Civil War.

At this juncture, I would like to introduce some key notions by defining more clearly concepts which have become indispensable tools for any serious contribution to the project of a critique of the Islamic reason, which I have been developing for some 40-odd years.[15] I distinguish between two frames of the cognitive activity of this reason, corresponding to two moments in the history of thought: *the frame of the intermediate civilization* as S.D. Goitein has defined it,[16] and *the frame of modernity* as presented historically and philosophically by F. Braudel and J. Habermas.[17] In the first frame, we have the closed sphere of a reason which is at once theocentric and logocentric but whose sovereignty is exercised in the limits fixed by God; in the second, the open sphere of modernity, an incomplete project in which reason remains logocentric but arrogates to itself a sovereignty whose limits are fixed or raised by its own decisions alone. Between the two frames, there is neither a chronological partition nor an impervious cognitive partition. It is, therefore, very important to be able to identify in the first frame certain postures already anticipated by pre-modern reason, which will be fully deployed only subsequently; inversely, the postures peculiar to pre-modern reason continue to resist all the disappointments raised by modern critical analysis. One witnesses even the failure of this latter before political progress and the social expansion of an aggressive, obscurantist religion because it ignores even the elementary critical preoccupations of pre-modern reason.

To illustrate these quick historical glimpses, it would be appropriate to resume here the analysis of concepts which I have often used elsewhere in the perspective of a critique of religious reason on the basis of the Islamic example. I shall mention the following concepts and say a few words about the first: *Qur'anic fact and Islamic fact, societies of the Book/books; holy, sacred, sacrilege, sacrifice; orthodoxy and heresy; exegesis, interpretation and critique of discourses; existential; myth, mythify, mythologize, mystify; ideation, ideologization and critical relation.*

The concept of the *Qur'anic fact* has been generally understood by my readers as the expression of a fideistic view to preserve the dogma of the divine authenticity of the Qur'an from the reach of modern critique; one can, on the other hand, concentrate upon the *Islamic fact* which is more directly the product of the ideological strategies of social actors. This common misunderstanding informs us more about the cognitive system of the readers who close themselves in positivist historicism than the epistemological posture which I am trying to apply in a new critique of religious reason from beyond the example of the Qur'an and its theological expansions. Lately, Malek Bennabi has used the expression *phénomène coranique* (Qur'anic phenomenon) in an apologetic perspective which assures great success for his book in the Islamist circles of today. That is why the conquest of a critical operational concept regarding the Qur'an is doomed to failure, for opposite reasons, from the Islamic side as well as from the side of the historians, guardians, and administrators of the positivist historicist orthodoxy.

By the Qur'anic fact I mean the historical manifestation, at a time and in a precise socio-cultural milieu, of an oral discourse which accompanied, for a period of 20 years, the concrete historical action of a social actor called Muhammad ibn Abdullah. One sees that this concept aims not to defend or discard the religious dimension of the discourse, but to fix the attention, within a first methodological time-period, on the linguistic, cultural, and social conditions of articulation of the discourse by an interlocutor and of its reception by various, explicitly targeted addressees. There is in it a project of investigation which claims to be simultaneously linguistic, semiotic, sociological, psychological, and anthropological. All these dimensions are, in fact, present in all units of the discourse which exegetical literature and modern philology have tried to identify. Separating these dimensions, under the pretext of respecting the independence of various disciplines as they are defined by university scholars, amounts to imposing a first choice-reducing agent which is no less dangerous than that of the theologians, jurists and, even more so, the fundamentalist militants of today who only know the arbitrary projections of the oral discourse into text (the famous *Mushaf*, which I call the *Closed Official Corpus*).

The linguistic and historical jump from the stage of the oral discourse, articulated in changing situations in the course of 20 years, to that of *Closed Official Corpus* has been considered until now neither by the literature on the juridical objectives of the discourse (the *asbab al-nuzul*, circumstances of the Revelation), nor by the historicist and applied philological scholarship which shares with traditional exegesis the reading of the discourse as a sacralized and transfigured text as believers do. I have never come across the concept, however essential, of the *Closed Official Corpus* in the works of any of the most eminent "modern" Qur'an scholars. The traditional term *Mushaf* is unanimously accepted without commentaries, other than those of textual philology. Under the circumstances, one understands that the concept of the *Qur'anic fact* is not only disdained but interpreted in a "scientifically" disqualifying sense.

The concept of oral discourse, transformed into written discourse and then consigned to a *Closed Official Corpus* by a long series of complex manipulations—which philological inquiry clarified within the limits of its own problematics—is all the more fruitful as it allows us to open up a site of theoretical analysis where all the founding religious texts, and in the first place the Bible and the Gospels, can be taken into account. And one will no longer aim to inquire separately about the authenticity of textual fragments, or even words in a given corpus, which was the object of philological critique. What is at stake in the passage from the oral discourse to a *Closed Official Corpus* (one will note that I never say just "corpus" because then I would be disregarding, as with the term *Mushaf,* all the problems relating to the notions of corpus, official and closure) is the cognitive status of meaning produced at the linguistic and historical stage of the oral discourse, taking into account all the real situations of discourse and the effects of meaning constructed by the successive exegeses in ideologically difficult contexts, and particularly the exclusive status of a *Closed Official Corpus* resulting in an irreversible fact which can be dated to the orthodox *Commentary* of al-Tabari (d. 923).

Islam and its tradition have until now encountered modernity as a cultural aggression (*al-ghazw al-fikri*), not as a historical phenomenon local and universal at the same time. It remains to be explained why the intellectual, scientific, cultural, and economic advances of the area molded by the Islamic fact from the seventh to the thirteenth centuries have given way to the set of regressive forces which have detached the southern and eastern shores of the Mediterranean from all the historical activities of modernity to the point that at the end of the current century, the rejection of the West has assumed the dimensions of a pole of contemporary history and the rank of a symbolical figure dialectically opposed to the rival figure of *McWorld* in the new historical stage opened by the failure of international communism and the triumph of unbridled libertarianism. Although *McWorld* and *Jihad* translate the eternal dialectic of the dominators and the dominated, they are now united in fettering the very spirit to works which alienate and destroy it.

While sharing the arguments of B.R. Barber on the subject of political, economic, and juridical strategies of *McWorld* and the phantasmical proclamations of *Jihad*, I would like to go further than him by taking into account the stakes-of-meaning and culture engaged in the irrational, suicidal confrontation of the two monsters of our contemporary history. I find a theoretical advantage in reflecting upon present-day Islam facing its tradition no longer only from within this tradition, which has been tried too often since at least the *Ihya 'ulum al-din* of al-Ghazali, but from the forces which subvert, for the first time in its history and in an irreversible manner, this very interior, this resistant nucleus upon which *Jihad* is believed to lean, and even to seize many tools of *McWorld*, while declaring them to be satanical in its dialectical opposite. In this confrontation with unequal arms, Islam-*Jihad*, like yesterday's nationalist discourse of liberation, presents itself as an innocent victim and a savior-depository of divine law and promise before an atheistic, materialistic, dominating, and radically immoral West. The colonized peoples were promised only civil liberties and social justice in the frame of scientific socialism perfected in popular democracies, the inheritors of the revolution of the Enlightenment. In the confrontation between *Jihad* and *McWorld*, one returns to the Manichaean struggle between light and darkness after the apparent defeats and irremediable disqualifications of theologies, theocracies, empires, and monarchies, as much as that of modern revolutions founded upon the secular cult of sovereign reason.

Who will take charge of all these sites in ruin? Who will inaugurate the new history after the proclaimed end of a certain history? Will it be religious reason, purified of the errancy, false hopes, and oppressive violence of the scientific atheistic reason, at last re-enthroned as in Iran, Afghanistan, and the Sudan, in its rank and functions of the "vicar of God on earth" (*khalifat Allah fī'l-ara*)? That is the ambition set into motion by *Jihad*. Or will the reason of the Enlightenment, correcting its excesses, contradictions, false knowledge, and theoretical dogmatism, restart on bases more solid and principles better mastered? That is the thesis of the more or less competent and convinced defenders of post-modern reason. But once again, thought as it is exercised in contemporary Islamic contexts is too caught up in semantic disorder, as generated and widely perpetrated by the conjugated violence of *Jihad* and *McWorld*, too handicapped by the unthoughts accumulated since the sixteenth century, to contribute to the great open debate on a world scale, other than through the violence of the poor and the excluded, and the support extended to *McWorld* by a greater number of consumers. Participation in the debate at the more essential level of intellectual responsibility is, to a large degree, conditioned by the orientations of philosophical thought within the crisis which molds *McWorld*.

How do we think about this crisis that includes the radical changes which science and technology impose on all societies as well as the problems peculiar to societies dominated by Islam, be it dogmatic and ritualistic, conservative and traditionalist, or liberal within the non-transgressible limits fixed and supervised by the managers of orthodoxy? The politics of religion pursued in a large number of societies called Muslim make too many concessions to the forces of traditionalism, while favoring the adoption of all the benefits of material civilization. This results in dangerous mental cleavages, increasing backwardness in the systems of education, fruitless self-censorship, and the impoverishment of creativity in various domains of intellectual and cultural life. Whereas divisions, contradictions, and conflicts, individual and collective, become the common lot of numerous populations, there remain few workers capable of assuming the indispensable tasks of an emancipation which is always aspired, always deferred and sometimes openly rejected (I think of the condition of women and the rights of children). Who is concerned with mastering the frames and tools of thought of the hegemonic powers that set all the agendas of historical outcome, as well as the modes of interpretation of the various epochs, so as to avoid being trapped again by false knowledge, false conscience, mental objects (such as the East, the West, Islam, development, the rights of man, the right to self-determination, etc.), constructed by and for the centers of homologation of "true" knowledge and meaning which support their wills-to-power? Where are the institutions for training researchers and teachers who would widen the fields of investigation of the human and social sciences, and radicalize their critical questioning of the problems bequeathed to us by the unknown, mutilated, and unthought pasts and presents, which blur or smash our visions of the future?

I have long shared the prevailing opinion which reclaims the elaboration of a "modern theology" of Islam, after the manner of what the Catholics and Protestants have continued to do in the Western milieu since the beginning of what historians call the "modernist crisis." The collapse of all ideologies, added to the challenges posed by experimental sciences to the political, juridical, ethical, and philosophical reason, have surely increased the demand for solutions in the direction of traditional theologies; but these remain too imprisoned by medievalist cognitive frames and tools to assume with any success the delicate tasks imposed by the ongoing exit of the religious *imaginaires*. With regard to Islam, the discourse of *Jihad* has practically reduced to silence, or struck with derision, every voice which attempts to reactivate theological, philosophical, ethical, and juridical thinking, capable of integrating in the same critical movement all the tasks prescribed by the specific historical development which I have called the exhaustive Islamic tradition. A historical outline is necessary here to render more intelligibly these observations on the adventures of meaning in Islamic contexts.

1. The system of thought elaborated in the Islamic context during the phase of emergence and the classical period (661–1258) is totally closed in the antique and medieval cognitive, or pre-modern, space.

2. The long period which extends from the thirteenth to the beginning of the nineteenth century has long been passed over in silence, superficially evoked in school textbooks under the headings of decadence, lethargy, oblivion, conservatism, and return to popular superstitions. The Turks can pride themselves on the initial success of a vast empire, but they are obliged to lower the tone in view of the irresistible rise of Europe after the defeat of Lepanto in 1571. Now, it was during this crucial historical phase that were programmed the factors, politically, sociologically and culturally important, of the crises, tensions, explosions, state formations, and ruptures which characterize the contemporary evolution of all the societies subjected to hasty, arbitrary, and uncontrollable reconstructions. It was then, in effect, that two major ruptures were accomplished in these societies which prescribe specific tasks for us today: the internal rupture of Islamic thought with regard to doctrinal pluralism, ethno-cultural cosmopolitism, and incipient humanism, which constituted the richness of the classical period; and the rupture

with the outside, that is to say with Europe, where the great changes and constitutive discoveries of modernity occurred.

3. When the intellectual and cultural movement of the *Nahda* engaged in the work of reactivation of the precious legacy of the classical period under the names of *Turath*, the golden age of Islamic civilization, the two ruptures just mentioned had already created a profound gulf between the revolutionary, euphoric Europe of the Enlightenment and the societies which could no longer benefit either from the tools bequeathed by classical thought, or still less from those proposed in the nineteenth to twentieth centuries (1850–1940) in Europe by the practitioners of historicist historiography and the philological reading of the major texts. Thus the promising efforts of three generations of intellectuals, researchers, writers, and artists have instigated since the 1920s a rejection leading to more radical political battles during the wars of liberation (1945–70) and today to *Jihad* vs. *McWorld*. Since the 1960s, demography has upset the sociological conditions of political expression, dissemination of learning, and manipulation of social *imaginaires*. One can speculate that in these circumstances an unforeseen subterranean evolution will operate towards the worst or the best. The visibility of the nearest horizon, the year 2010 for example, remains blurred, so much so that the social sciences confine themselves to the almost journalistic description of superficial events by depending upon the discourse of the most active actors, most directly engaged in the conquest of political and religious power.

I shall end with these brief observations. I know they demand more clarification, critical examination, and debate; but this is not possible so long as the great tasks involved in the general history of thought, of all the traditions of thought which seek to take their place and appointment with the generalized quest for one reliable, lasting, and universalizable meaning, mobilize only a limited number of exceptional researcher-thinkers.

CHAPTER 3

The Way (*Al-Sharia*) of Islam

Tariq Ramadan

Tariq Ramadan was born in Geneva in 1962, his father having fled there from Egypt after being prosecuted for his membership of the Muslim Brotherhood organization. Hassan al-Banna (1906–49), who founded the organization in 1928, is Ramadan's maternal grandfather, a fact about which Ramadan often writes with great pride. In addition to having studied Islam at the Al-Azhar, Ramadan holds two PhD degrees, one in philosophy and the other in Islamic sciences. A highly prolific author of books and articles, Ramadan was Lecturer in Philosophy and Religion at the University of Fribourg and the Collège de Saussure in Geneva until 2004, when he accepted a tenured, endowed professorship at the University of Notre Dame in the United States. He was forced to resign soon afterwards, however, after the US State Department abruptly revoked his visa. Despite the controversy that ensued, the State Department refused to provide an official explanation for its actions beyond vague references to Ramadan's support for terrorism, though at the time speculation revolved around his vocal denunciation of US foreign policy and his criticism of Western, especially French, intellectuals for their alleged silence over Israel's occupation and treatment of Palestinians in the Occupied Territories. In 2005, Ramadan accepted a Visiting Fellowship at Oxford University's St Antony's College.

Ramadan's writings have so far revolved around two main themes, one concerning the renewal and reform of Islam, the other dealing with the place of Islam as a world religion in Western societies. His primary goal has to been to present Muslims with a set of analytical and reasoning tools, which he claims are inherent in their religious values and traditions, in order to deal successfully with the challenges of modernity, whether they find themselves in Muslim-majority societies or in Europe. This line of reasoning is informed both implicitly and explicitly by the assumption that there is no inherent clash between the values of Islam and those that underlie Western civilization. The discrepancies and differences that historically have emerged between the two are due to their interpretations rather than their innate dispositions.

The two themes of constructing an Islamic hermeneutics and Islam's place in and its relationship with the West are both amply represented in the follow-

ing essay, drawn from Tariq Ramadan, Western Muslims and the Future of Islam *(Oxford: Oxford University Press, 2004), pp 31–61.*

In the West, the idea of *Sharia* calls up all the darkest images of Islam: repression of women, physical punishments, stoning, and all other such things. It has reached the extent that many Muslim intellectuals do not dare even to refer to the concept for fear of frightening people or arousing suspicion of all their work by the mere mention of the word.

It is true that scholars of law and jurisprudence have almost naturally restricted the meaning to their own field of study, that dictators have used it for repressive and cruel purposes, and that the ideal of the *Sharia* has been most betrayed by Muslims themselves, but this should not prevent us from studying this central notion in the Islamic universe of reference and trying to understand in what ways it has remained fundamental and active in the Muslim consciousness through the ages.[1]

If the idea of "establishing rules" is indeed contained in the notion of *Sharia* (from the root *sha-ra-a*), this translation does not convey the fullness of the way it is understood, unless its more general and fundamental meaning is referred to: "the path that leads to the spring." We have pointed out the tone of Islamic terminology, which systematically reflects a corpus of reference that sets a certain way of speaking of God, of defining the human being, and of understanding the relationship between them by means of Revelation. We have seen that this corpus of reference is, for the Muslim consciousness, where the universal is formulated: God, human nature, which makes itself human by turning in on itself and recognizing the "need of Him," reason, active and fed by humility, and, finally, Revelation, which confirms, corrects, and exerts a guiding influence.

Just as the *shahada* is the expression, in the here and now, of individual faithfulness to the original covenant by means of a testimony that is a "return to oneself" (a return to the *fitra*, to the original breath breathed into us by God), so the *Sharia* is the expression of individual and collective faithfulness, in time, for those who are trying in awareness to draw near to the ideal of the source that is God. In other words, the *shahada* translates the idea of "being Muslim," and the *Sharia* shows us "how to be and remain Muslim." This means, to put it in yet another way and extend our reflection, that the *Sharia* is not only the expression of the universal principles of Islam but the framework and the thinking that makes for their actualization in human history. There can be no *Sharia* without a corpus of fundamental principles that set, beyond the contingencies of time, a point of reference for faithfulness to the divine will. This corpus of principles, as we have seen, is a fundamental given of the Islamic universe of reference, which asserts, in the midst of post-modernism, that all is not relative, that there does indeed exist a universal, for it is a God, an only God, who has revealed timeless principles, which, while not preventing reason from being active and creative, protect it from getting bogged down in the contradictions and incoherences of the absolute relativity of everything.

By inviting Muslims to accept pluralism by a purely rationalistic approach, to express their faithfulness in a purely private way, or to define themselves in terms of minorities, some commentators have thought to ward off the danger of Islamic universality, which they perceive as inevitably totalitarian. Is this not how the West understands the quasi-summons to have to affirm one's "faith" in the autonomy of reason in order to prove one's open-mindedness or one's firm support for the "universal values of the West;" [2] or the new fashion of apologetic for a Sufism so interior that it has become disincarnated, almost invisible, or a façade with only blurred links to Islam; or, again, stigmatization and the exercise of constant pressure on Muslims driven to adopt the monochrome reaction of minorities on the defensive, obsessed with their only right—to be—and with their differentness? This is all happening as if, in order to ward off the "necessarily expansionist" universality of Islam, either Islam must be refused its claim to universality or Muslims must be pressed to accept this exercise in wholesale relativization.

Some Muslim intellectuals have accepted the imposition of these game rules. Others have opposed it and continue to oppose it by rejecting the West per se, with all it has produced, because it has forgotten God or because all that takes place there is Promethean, if not "satanic." Between these two extremes, there is a way, I believe, to change the terms of the debate: if, for Muslims, it is a matter of rejecting the insidious process of relativization of their universal values, it is also incumbent on them to explain clearly in what sense, and how, those values respect diversity and relativity. If the way to faithfulness, the *Sharia*, is the corpus of reference in which Islamic universality is written down, it is urgent and imperative to say how it is structured and how it expresses the absolute, and rationality, and the relation to time, progress, the Other, and, more broadly, difference. At a deeper level, the intuition that must feed this refusal of relativization and this presentation of the fundamental principles of Islam in the heart of the Western world is the conviction that this is the only true way to produce an authentic dialogue of civilizations and that this is now more necessary than ever. With globalization at hand, the fear is that the West—helped by an intangible Westernization of the world—will engage in a "dialogical monologue" or an "interactive monologue" with civilizations different only in name but so denatured or so exotic that their members are reduced, taking the good years with the bad, to discussing their survival and not the richness of their otherness. Muslims have the means to enter into this debate on an equal footing, and they should do so, and find debating partners ready for this worthy, enriching, and essential confrontation of ideas and ideals.

Comprehensiveness, the absolute, and the evolution

Wherever they find themselves, Muslim women and men[3] try, in their practice and daily lives, to conform as much as possible to Islamic teachings. In this they follow the path of faithfulness, "the path towards the spring." In other words, in the West as in the East, they try to actualize the *Sharia* as we have defined it beyond its merely legalistic form. In Europe and in North America, as soon as one pronounces the *shahada*, as soon as one "is Muslim" and tries to remain so by practicing the daily prayers, giving alms, and fasting, for example, or even simply by trying to respect Muslim ethics, one is already in the process of applying the *Sharia*, not in any peripheral way but in its most essential aspects.

This practice and moral awareness are the source and heart of the *Sharia*, which is personal, faithful commitment. Beyond that, the Way itself exerts its own influence more comprehensively with regard to the guidance that marks the elements or the actions. It touches all the aspects of existence, even if not in the same way, and we must mention this essential factor here, with regard to the methodologies, norms, and details of application of various regulations. This characteristic of Islam is contained within the concept of *shumuliyyat al-islam*, the comprehensiveness of Islam, which we could translate in a more immediately expressive form as "the comprehensive character of Islamic teaching." We certainly find in the sources regulations that touch on the intimate personal dimension (with regard to spiritual practices whose culmination is mystical experience)[4] and religious practice, but there are also directions concerning individuals' behavior with regard to the self, the family, and others, and again general principles pertaining to the management of inter-personal relations and of the community. It seems difficult to draw a line of demarcation here between the private and the public spheres, between the realms of faith and reason, between the religious and the political, so interconnected and mingled do these areas appear under the sole transcendent authority of the Book and the Prophetic traditions. Many Muslims have continued down through the ages to say formulaically, as if they were presenting evidence: "There is no difference, for us, between private and public, religion and politics: Islam encompasses all areas." Many Orientalists have fallen into step with them and affirmed, and still affirm, that Islam does not think in distinct categories and that all areas are governed by the same authority. Moreover, because of this kind of approach, it is often assumed that Muslims are by definition "not capable of integration" into secularized societies because their religion prevents them from accepting modern demarcations between the categories we have mentioned.

But one has the right to ask whether these statements are based on sound evidence. Islamic teaching certainly has "a comprehensive quality" that one cannot fail to notice even upon one reading of the Qur'an, but can it be so easily asserted that no distinction exists between the various realms of human activity? In other words, does the fact that there is one source necessarily require a similarity of approaches? Nothing is less certain, and Muslim scholars such as Abu Hanifa and al-Shafi'i, who in the earliest times tried to set the norms for reading and deducing rules, were deeply intuitive. For it must be said and remembered that the formulation of universal principles and the elaboration of a basic frame of reference, which give "the way to faithfulness" its meaning, were produced by human intelligence. It is from the reading of the scriptural sources, with the internal limitations this imposed (e.g. the Arabic language, grammar, the practice of the Prophet), that they decided upon the normative parameters from which it was possible to extrapolate principles, formulate regulations, and elaborate rules of morality faithful to the guidance of the Qur'an and the *sunna*. It is human intelligence that formulates the universal and elaborate methodologies, which vary according to the object of study to which they are applied (e.g. religious practice, social affairs, sciences), by working on the Qur'an and the *sunna*. In other words, the *Sharia*, insofar as it is the expression of the "the way to faithfulness," deduced and constructed *a posteriori*, is the work of human intellect. The Source and undisputed reference is the Book and then the Prophetic traditions: we have already said that these texts touch upon every area of life in ways both general and diverse and summon human intelligence to discern the difference between the categories, as well as the logic that underpins religious regulations, and to try to bring the whole of the message into harmony and make its guidance more accessible. This harmonization is rational, and, insofar as it tries to be faithful to the wisdom of Revelation, it does its utmost also to be reasonable.

The work of categorization left by scholars through the ages is phenomenal. Specialists in the foundations of law and jurisprudence (*usul al-fiqh*), who labored at this exercise of extrapolating and categorizing rules on the basis of a reading that was both careful to be faithful to the norm and profoundly rational, have bequeathed to us an unparalleled heritage. A careful reading of these works reveals that very precise modes of grasping the sources were set down very early. Consideration of the language was supported by a double process of distinguishing on the one hand between the unequivocal and the equivocal and on the other between the presence (explicit or implicit) or absence of a causal link (*illa*) in the pronouncement of rules. The other essential side of this work was the elaboration of methodologies differentiated according to the area being studied. Thus, in the area of religious practice (*al-ibadat*), it was determined that it was the texts that were the only ultimate reference because the revealed rites are fixed and not subject to human reason: here one can do only what is based on a text, and the margin for interpretation is virtually nil. In the wider area of human and social affairs, the established methodology is the exact opposite: bearing in mind the positive and trusting attitude of the Qur'anic message, as we have seen, towards the universe and human beings, everything is permitted except that which is explicitly forbidden by a text (or recognized as such by the specialists). Thus the scope for the exercise of reason and creativity is huge, in contrast with the situation in matters to do with religious practice, and people have complete discretion to experiment, progress, and reform as long as they avoid what is forbidden.[5] So the fact that the fundamental principles and prohibitions of Islam are stated can never allow Muslims to dispense with a study of the context and the societies in which they live. This is the price they must pay for their faithfulness.

It is on the basis of these same logical categorizations that it has been possible to differentiate, through reading the scriptural sources, between the universal principles to which the Muslim consciousness must seek to be faithful through the ages and the practice of those principles, which is necessarily relative, at a given moment in human history. We are here confronting the fundamental distinction that should be established between timeless principles and contingent models, a distinction that is a direct consequence of a normative reading of the sources and, as such, is in itself fundamental. So, a distinction should be made, in the case of the society of Medina, for example, between the fundamental principles on which it was established (e.g. the rule of law, equality, freedom of conscience and worship) and the form in which that society historically appeared. Faithfulness to principles cannot involve faithfulness to historical models because times change, societies and political and economic systems become more complex, and in every age it is in fact necessary to think of a model appropriate to each social and cultural reality.[6]

For example, one could investigate further the areas of custom and culture, because these concern Western Muslims very directly. The meth-

an independent source, though supplementary, of *Sharia* (and thus part of the latter, and whose scope should be limited),[18] or, finally, whether it should simply be seen as part of another source, such as *qiyas* (analogy).[19] These various positions also rely on another qualification that distinguishes three types of *masali* (this time differentiated according to their classification, not according to their hierarchical importance), by which the ulama established a typology based on the degree of proximity of *al-maslaha* to the sources. If *al-maslaha* is based on textual evidence (i.e. a quotation from the Qur'an or the *sunna*), it is called *maslaha mutabara* (accredited), and it must necessarily be taken into account. If, on the other hand, the *maslaha* invoked is contradictory to an undisputed text (*nass qati*), it is called *mulgha* (discredited) and cannot be taken into account. The third type occurs when there is no text: the Qur'an and the *sunna* do not confirm but neither do they reject a *maslaha* that became apparent after the age of Revelation. A *maslaha* of this type is call *mursala* (undetermined),[20] for it allows the ulama to use their own analyses and personal reasonings in order to formulate a legal decision in the light of the historical and geographical context, using their best efforts to remain faithful to the commandments and to the "spirit" of the Islamic legal corpus where no text, no "letter" of the law, is declared.

It is this last type that has given rise to much debate and polemic (an analysis of which is beyond the scope of this study). Suffice it to say here that the main cause of disagreement was the fear, on the part of those opposed to the very concept of *al-maslaha al-mursala*, that such a notion, with such broad scope, might then allow the ulama to formulate regulations without reference to the Qur'an and the *sunna* on the basis of exclusively rational and completely free reasoning, all in the name of a remote hardship or "an anticipated difficulty." These were the main arguments of the Zahirite school, as well as numerous Shafii and even Maliki ulama who did not recognize *al-maslaha al-mursala*—not referring back to the sources—as a legal proof; they saw it as a specious (*whamiyya*) proof, not valid for legislation. It was the same instinctive fear of an approach that was purely rational and not connected with the Law that pushed al-Ghazali to restrict work on *al-maslaha* to the area of the application of *qiyas* (analogy), which requires a close link with the text for the deduction of the cause (*illa*) on which analogical reasoning rests.

Some ulama in the course of history have formulated judgments in the name of *al-maslaha* and sometimes completely changed and disturbed the manner and conditions of the use of legal instruments within the Islamic framework. The particularly interesting example of the famous fourteenth-century Hanibali jurist Najm al-Din al-Tufi seems to have given them just

reason to be fearful: al-Tufi ended up giving *al-maslaha* priority over texts
from the Qur'an and the *sunna*, which, according to him, should be applied,
according to Mahmasani, only "to the extent that the common good does
not require anything else."[21] Moreover, in our own times, we see very
strange "modern Islamic legal decisions" based on "modern maslaha" that
are clearly contradictory to the sources. The notion of *al-maslaha al-mursala*
thus sometimes seems to justify the strangest behavior, as well as the most
obscure commercial dealings, financial commitments, and banking invest-
ments, under the pretext that they protect, or could or should protect, "the
common good."

But this kind of excess was not typical among those who supported
taking *al-maslaha al-mursala* into account as an authentic and legitimate
source of legislation. They believed that the formulation of Islamic legal
decisions should take place in the light of the Qur'an and the *sunna* and in
agreement with them and, moreover, upon certain demanding conditions
(even if *al-maslaha al-mursala* was taken into account as an authentic and
legitimate source in the absence of any text). A careful study of the various
opinions (for and against *al-maslaha al-mursala*) shows that the ulama are
in agreement on numerous important points, among the first of whom was
the *alim* of Grenada, al-Shatibi (fourteenth century). We find in his works
a series of conditions and precise definitions regarding recognition of the
"common good" as a reliable juridical source, which restrict its application
and prevent the ulama from having recourse to *al-maslaha* without justification. Without going into too much detail, we may summarize the three
generally recognized main conditions for situations in which it is sure that
no text has been enunciated:

1. The analysis and identification must be made with serious attention so
   that we may be sure that we have before us an authentic (*haqiqiyya*) and
   not an apparent or spurious (*wahmiyya*) *maslaha*. The scholar must reach
   a high degree of certainty that the formulation of an injunction will
   avoid a difficulty and not do the opposite and increase problems in the
   context of the Islamic legal structure.
2. The *maslaha* must be general (*kulliyya*) and be beneficial to the population and to society as a whole, and not only to one group or class or
   individual.
3. The *maslaha* must not be in contradiction to or in conflict with an
   authentic text from the Qur'an or the *sunna*. If it were, it would no
   longer be a *maslaha mursala* but would be a *maslaha mulgha*.[22]

These three conditions[23] give us broad guidelines by which we can understand the concept of *maslaha*, the common good, in the Islamic frame of reference. What is clear above all is the supremacy of the Qur'an and the *sunna* over all the other references and legal instruments. Yusuf al-Qaradawi[24] rightly recalls, taking up the ideas of al-Ghazali, Ibn al-Qayyim, and al-Shatibi, that everything found in the Qur'an and the *sunna* is, in itself, in harmony with "the good of humankind" in general, for the Creator knows and wants what is best for human beings, and He shows them what they must do to achieve it. We find in the Qur'an, referring to the revealed message:

> [the Prophet] who will enjoin upon them the doing of what is right and forbid them the doing of what is wrong, and make lawful to them the good things of life and forbid them the bad things, and lift them from their burdens and the shackles that were upon them [aforetime].[25]

> O human beings! An exhortation has come to you from your Lord, a healing for what is in your hearts, a guidance and a mercy for the believers.[26]

We find the preference for the good of humanity in the first Revelation (of the three that led to their eventual prohibition) concerning intoxicating drinks:

> They ask you about intoxicating drinks and games of chance. Say: "These two things contain great harm for men as well as benefits: but the harm found in them is greater than the benefit."[27]

Ibn al-Qayyim al-Jawziyya summarized the position as follows:

> The principles and fundamentals of the *Sharia* concerning the injunctions and the good of humankind in this life and the next are all based on justice, mercy, the good of man, and wisdom. Every situation in which justice succumbs to tyranny, mercy to cruelty, goodness to corruption, wisdom to foolishness, has nothing in common with the *Sharia*, even if it is the result of an allegorical interpretation [*tawill*]. For the *Sharia* is the justice of God upon His earth, and His wisdom, which is both the proof of His own existence and the best witness to the authenticity of His Prophet.[28]

To seek for the good (*maslaha*) of man, in this life and the next, is the very essence of Islamic commandments and prohibitions. If the latter are clearly proclaimed (*qati al-thubut wa-qati al-dalala*)[29] in the Qur'an and/or the *sunna*, they must be respected and applied in the light of an understanding of the whole body of the objectives of Islamic teaching, *maqasid al-Sharia*;[30] they are, and represent, the revealed good (*maslaha*) granted by the Creator of His creature to guide him towards the good.

Nevertheless, the sources are sometimes silent. When facing new situations and problems, the ulama cannot find specific responses in the Qur'an and the *sunna*: so, guided by the light of Revelation and the example of the Prophet, they have to formulate judgments that will protect the best interests of people without betraying the frame of reference. These interests are called *masalih mursala* and require the total and constant commitment of the ulama if they are to make it possible for individuals to live as Muslims in all times and places in order to prevent them from carrying too heavy a burden, for God said: "God wants things to be easy for you. He does not want it to be difficult for you."[31]

So this is the framework within which we must consider the notion of *maslaha*, which has been a controversial concept, often because there has been a lack of clarity in the way it is defined and because of the strict and demanding conditions required for its application. It has sometimes suffered from excessive use by some ulama and scholars when they have tried to justify some "modern judgment" or "progress" in the name of *al-maslaha*. We have seen that it is a very specific concept—in its definition, its levels, its types, and its conditions—and requires that the ulama constantly refer back to the sources so that they are able to formulate judgments in conformity with the revealed Message, even when there is no specifically relevant text. They must try—by carrying out a deep, thorough, and detailed study—to provide the Muslim community with new rational judgments guided by Revelation. This is the meaning of *itjihad* which is both the source and the legal instrument that allows a dynamism to be set in motion at the heart of Islamic law and jurisprudence.

Al-ijtihad

When the Prophet sent Muadh to Yemen, he asked him about the sources on which he would base his judgments and approved of his intention of "putting all his energy into formulating his own judgment" in cases where he could find no guidance in the Qur'an and the *sunna*. This personal effort undertaken by the jurist in order to understand the source and deduce the rules or, in the absence of a clear textual guidance, formulate independent judgments is what is called *ijtihad* in the field of Islamic law and jurisprudence. Hashim Kamali proposes the following definition:

> *Ijtihad* is defined as the total expenditure of effort made by a jurist in order to infer, with a degree of probability, the rules of *Sharia* from their detailed evidence in the sources. Some ulama have defined *ijtihad* as the application by a jurist of all his faculties either in inferring the rules of *Sharia* from their sources or in implementing such rules and applying them to particular issues. *Ijtihad* essentially consists of an inference [*istinbat*] that amounts to a probability [*zann*], thereby excluding the extraction of a ruling from a clear text.[32]

Like *al-maslaha*, the legal instrument of *ijtihad* has been used to justify all kinds of new judgments. So Hashim Kamali quite rightly recalls the general principle (about which the ulama are unanimous), according to which there can be no *ijtihad* when an explicit text exists in the sources (*la ijtihada maa al-nass*). This means that if there is an explicit Qur'anic verse whose meaning is obvious and leaves no room for any hypothesis or interpretation (*qati al-dalala*), no *ijtihad* is possible. Similarly, if the jurist finds an authenticated *hadith* (*mutawatir, qati al-thubut*) whose content is also completely explicit and unambiguous (*qati al-dalala*), he must use that as his reference and there is no room for the exercise of *ijtihad*.

Indeed, clear texts that are both authenticated and explicit, even though they are not very numerous, constitute the unalterable foundation, the fixed principles, on which the *Sharia* is based—principles to which the jurist must refer, from which he must analyze, comment on, and explain texts that contain some conjecture (*zanni*), and on the basis of which he should also formulate new judgments through a dynamic process when his community faces new situations. The laws and judgments provided by these clear texts together constitute a specific corpus, which the ulama *al-usul* call *al-malum min al-din bil-darura*, which means that they bring out the fundamental essence of Islamic law; to reject them leads to the negation of Islam (*kufr*).

But the great majority of the verses in the Qur'an and the traditions of the Prophet are not of a strict and compelling nature. The Qur'an is authenticated in itself (*qati al-thubut*, of indisputable origin), but most of the verses containing legal judgments (*ayat al-ahkam*) are open to analysis, commentary, and interpretation (*zanni al-dalala*), and this is also the case with the *ahadith*, most of which leave some scope for speculation as much concerning their authenticity (*thubut*) as concerning their meaning (*dalala*). This means that the *fuqaha* (jurists) had, and still have, an important and essential function in the formulation of laws that may be called Islamic. They fulfill this function particularly through their *ijtihad*, applied at various levels: to understand a specific text (in the light of the whole Islamic legal corpus); to classify texts on the basis of their clarity or their nature (e.g. *qati* (indisputable) or *zanni* (conjectural); *zahir* (obvious) or *nass* (explicit); *khass* (specific) or *amm* (general)); or to formulate judgments where no text exists.

Ijtihad taken as a whole (as both source and legal instrument) has in fact been considered by numerous ulama as the third principal source of *Sharia*, encompassing *al-ijma* (*ijtihad jamai*), *al-istislah*, and *al-istihsan*, as well as other subdivisions recognized among what are called the supplementary sources of the *Sharia*. As Muhammad Hashim Kamali has emphasized:

The various sources of Islamic law that feature next to the Qur'an and *Sunnah* are all manifestations of *ijtihad*, albeit with differences that are largely procedural in character. In this way, consensus of opinion, analogy, juristic preference, considerations of public interest [*maslahah*], etc., are all interrelated not only under the main heading of *ijtihad*, but via the Qur'an and the *Sunnah*.[33]

Al-Ghazali, al-Shatibi, Ibn al-Qayyim al-Jawziyya, and, more recently, al-Khallaf and Abu Zahra have referred to this type of classification, underlining the importance of *ijtihad* as the third source of Islamic jurisprudence, for *ijtihad* includes all the instruments used to form judgments through human reasoning and personal effort. *Ijtihad* is, in fact, the rational elaboration of laws either on the basis of the sources or formulated in the light of them. Thus even *ijma* (consensus) is the product of collective human, rational discussion, and so one can conceive—even if it would be very unlikely and rare—that a legal decision made by *ijma* might eventually become unsuitable and be referred again for debate. As Professor Hamidullah has said in connection with the Hanafi school of law:

> The opinion of a jurist can, however, be rejected by another jurist who can offer his own opinion instead. This applies not only to individual opinion or an inference but also covers collective opinion. At least the Hanafi school of law accepts that a new consensus can cancel an old consensus. Suppose there is a consensus on a certain issue. We accept its authority, but it does not mean that no one can oppose it till eternity. If someone has the courage to oppose it with due respect and reason, and if he can persuade the jurist to accept his point of view, a new consensus comes into being. The new consensus abrogates the old one. This principle has been propounded by the famous Hanafi jurist Abu al-Yusr al-Bazdawi and belongs to the fourth and fifth century of the Hijrah. This work is a great contribution to Islamic jurisprudence. It is on account of his statement that we can say that consensus cannot become a source of difficulty for us. If a consensus is reached on some issue and it is found subsequently to be unsuitable the possibility remains that we may change it through reasoning and create a new one canceling the old consensus.[34]

This analysis recalls an important principle from the realm of *usul al-fiqh*, which is that the Qur'an and the *sunna* are the only two indisputable sources, sources at whose core the prescriptive verses and *ahadith* (*ayat waahadith al-ahkam*)[35] are divided into two main levels: the *qati* (indisputable), which is clear in itself, and the *zanni* (conjectural, open to hypotheses and interpretations), which requires on the part of the ulama an attentive study of the texts in question before they can deduce appropriate judgments on passages taken from the sources. The aim of this type of *ijtihad* (applied to *zanni* texts)—sometimes called *bayani* (explanatory *ijtihad*)—is to analyze the text (*nass*) in order to draw from it a ruling and its *illa* (the

effective cause of this specific ruling); this allows both an adequate understanding of the text and consequent analogical reasoning (*qiyas*) in the light
of the historical context. This type of *ijtihad* has given rise to numerous and
diverse subdivisions following the various opinions of the ulama.

There is another type of *ijtihad* that is applied when there is no scriptural
reference. Here, too, we find numerous subdivisions because of the diversity
of opinion among the ulama and the collections of writings and commentaries that have been made in the course of history. At least three types
stand out:

1. *Ijtihad qiyasi* works by analogical reasoning, taking into consideration
   the effective cause (*illa*) of a ruling drawn from the sources.
2. *Ijtihad zanni* comes in when it is impossible to refer to an effective cause;
   this type is often linked with *ijtihad istislahi*.
3. *Ijtihad istislahi* is based on *al-maslaha* and seeks to deduce rulings in the
   light of the general objective of the *Sharia*.

But the ulama are not unanimous about the specific classification of *ijtihad*,
because they do not even agree on its definition and methods of application.

Another distinction has to do with the degree of *ijtihad*, which may be
absolute (*mutlaq*) or limited (*muqayyad*). The first type, also called *ijtihad fi
al-shar*, is based on the ability of the *mujtahid* (a scholar qualified to practice *ijtihad*) to extrapolate and formulate his own judgments on the basis
of a direct study of the sources. The second, also called *ijtihad madhhabi*
(pertaining to a school), is, by contrast, limited to a particular school of law,
and the *mujtahid* must formulate his judgments according to the rules of a
given juridical school.

The conditions (*shurut*) of *ijtihad*

The framework we have just presented, with the definition and classification
of *ijtihad*, has been taken into account by the ulama when determining the
conditions for *ijtihad*.[36] In order to analyze and classify, they have focused
on the qualities a scholar must possess in order to practice an authentic and
reliable *ijtihad*, in order to become a *mujtahid*. As with other classifications,
the conditions formulated by the ulama have been numerous and divergent
because of their various opinions about legal instruments, the applicability
of laws, or, simply, the priority allotted to their implementation.

Before going further in setting out the requirements of being a *mujtahid*,
it may be useful to refer here to the concise opinion of al-Shatibi, who differ-

entiated between the very nature of *ijtihad* and its instruments. His overall view is simple and edifying, for he brings together all the conditions under two main rubrics. Thus, according to him, "the level of *ijtihad* is attained when two qualities are present:

1. A deep understanding of the objectives (*maqasid*) of the *Sharia*.
2. A real mastery of the various methods of deduction and extraction (*istinbat*) based on knowledge and understanding." [37]

The "five essential principles" (*al-daruriyyat al-khamsa*) that we have already mentioned (religion, life, intellect, lineage, and property), as well as the necessary distinctions between the indispensable (*daruri*), the necessary or complementary (*haji*), and the embellishments or improvements (*tahsini*), constitute the framework provided by the lawgiver to guide the research of the *mujtahid* and so represent the fundamental terms of reference. The *mujtahid* must also know which instruments [38] he may resort to among the general maxims of *fiqh*, *qiyas*, *istihsan*, and so on.

From Abu al-Husayn al-Basri and his work *Mutamad fi usul al-fiqh* (eleventh century) to Ibn al-Qayyim al-Jawziyya, with his *Ilam al-muwaqqiin an rabb al-alamin* (fourteenth century), numerous ulama have proposed various classifications of the qualities required and the conditions to be met in order for a scholar to be considered a *mujtahid*. Some believed that the first condition was knowledge of the Arabic language;[39] others thought that what mattered above all was knowledge of the verses and *ahadith* that had legal significance. In spite of these divergences, which are in fact essentially procedural, since their respective conditions overlap, we may summarize the efforts of the ulama in this area in the following seven points. The *mujtahid* must possess:

1. A knowledge of Arabic, which enables him to understand the Qur'an and *sunna* correctly and particularly the verses and *ahadith* that contain rulings (*ayat wa-ahadith al-ahkam*).
2. A knowledge of the sciences of the Qur'an and *hadith*, which enables him to understand and identify the evidence (*adilla*) contained in the texts and, what is more, to deduce and extract judgments from them.
3. A thorough knowledge of the objectives (*maqasid*) of the *Sharia*, their classification, and the priorities they imply.
4. Knowledge of questions on which there was *ijma*; this requires knowledge of the works on secondary issues (*furu*).
5. Knowledge of the principle of analogical reasoning (*qiyas*) and its meth-

odology (the causes (ilal) and circumstances (asbab) for a specific judgment, conditions, e.g. shurut).

6. Knowledge of his historical, social, and political context, that is to say, the situation of the people living around him (ahwal al-nas), the state of their affairs, traditions, and customs, and so on.

7. Recognition of his own competence, honesty, reliability, and uprightness.[40]

As we have already mentioned, numerous other conditions, in different orders, have been proposed, but these seven points more or less cover the most important qualities needed by a mujtahid.[41] Some ulama believe that these conditions and qualifications are so advanced that it has not been possible to reach this standard since the time of the great ulama in about the ninth century. This is how they justify the pronouncement that forever closed the "doors of ijtihad" after this very rich period. Other ulama, the great majority, are of the opinion that the practice of ijtihad has been partly abandoned for historical reasons that have pressed either the political leaders or the ulama to declare that it was no longer necessary to practice ijtihad.[42] Consequently, the doors of ijtihad have never been closed; no scholar would have had the right to make such a decision in the name of Islam because a declaration such as this is, by its very nature, against Islam. In fact, ijtihad, as the third source of Islamic law and jurisprudence, is fard kifaya, a collective responsibility. Everyone recognizes that these conditions are demanding and that they are required for a qualified ijtihad, but they also say that these qualifications have never been beyond the reach of the ulama in recent times and up to the present. The progress that has been made in authenticating ahadith, easier access to reference works, and computer-aided classification make the work of the mujtahid easier and more effective. Consequently, the Muslim community, through its ulama, should still be fulfilling this fundamental duty today, even though it will be necessary to find a way to apply it appropriately in our contemporary context because of the new complexity of many sciences, such as medicine, technology, economics, the social sciences, and so on. Ijtihad remains the most important instrument the ulama have at their disposal to fulfill the universal vocation of Islam, through a constant dynamic of adaptation in response to the time and the context.

What is a fatwa?

To understand what a fatwa is, we should keep in mind the whole substance of the preceding analysis, for a fatwa is a part, an element, and, more precisely, a legal instrument, which must be understood in the light of the corpus of

Islamic law and jurisprudence. *Fatwa* (plural *fatawa*) literally means "legal decision," verdict," or, following the definition of al-Shatibi, "a reply to a legal question given by an expert (*mufti*) in the form of words, action, or approval."[43] A *fatwa* has two essential aspects: it must, first and above all, be founded on the sources and on the juridical inferences and extractions arrived at by the *mujtahidin*[44] who practice *ijtihad* when the sources are not clear or explicit (that is, when they are *zanni*) or when there is no relevant text. It must also be formulated in the light of the context of life, the environment, and the specific situation that justifies it being made—and which is in fact its cause.

The place of the *mujtahid* and the *mufti* is of prime importance. As al-Shatibi said, the *mufti*[45] within the community plays the part of the Prophet. Numerous evidences support his assertion. First there is proof of *hadith*:

> Truly the scholars are the heirs of the prophets, and what one inherits from prophets is not money [*la dinaran wa-la dirham*], but knowledge [*ilm*]. Second, he [the *mufti*] is the source of transmitting rulings [*ahkam*] in conformity with the words of the Prophet: "Let the one among you who is witness transmit [that to which he is witness] to those who are absent" and "Transmit from me, even if it is not the only one verse." If this is the case, it means that he [the *mufti*] stands in for the Prophet.

> In fact, the *mufti* is a kind of legislator, for the *Sharia* that he conveys is either taken [insofar as it has already been stipulated] from the Lawgiver [by the way of Revelation and the *sunna*] or inferred or extracted from the sources. In the first case, he is simply a transmitter, while in the second he stands in for the Prophet in that he stipulates rulings. To formulate judgments is the function of the legislator. So, if the function of the *mujtahid* is to formulate judgments on the basis of his opinion and efforts, it is possible to say that he is therefore a legislator who should be respected and followed: we should act according to the rulings he formulates and this is vicegerency [*Khilafa*] in its genuine implementation.[46]

Al-Shatibi underlines the importance of the *mujtahid* who stands in for the Prophet in the Muslim community after the death of Muhammad. In this way the *mujtahid* or the *mufti* represents the continuity of knowledge (*ilm*) guided by the two sources, so that it may be rightly applied throughout history. Al-Shatibi made a distinction between explicit evidence (that stipulated in the sources) and that which requires the exercise of deduction and inference and puts the *mujtahid* in the position of legislator (even though he must seek the guidance of God, the supreme Legislator, and follow the example of the Prophet). The distinction drawn by al-Shatibi has the great advantage of setting out the two different levels of *fatwa*: when questioned on legal issues, the *mujtahid* will sometimes find a clear answer in the Qur'an and the *sunna* because there is an explicit text. Then the *fatwa* consists of a quotation and a restatement of authoritative proof. If there is a text that is open to interpretation, or if there is no relevant text, the *mufti* must give a specific response in the light of both the objectives of the *Sharia* and the situation of the questioner. Al-Shatibi underlines that the *mufti* really does play the role of vicegerent who must come up with a legal judgment for the one who calls on him. The more the issue is related to an individual or a particular case, the more precise, clear, and specific it must be. Consequently, a *fatwa* is rarely transferable, because it is a legal judgment pronounced (in the light of the sources, of the *maslaha*, and of the context) in response to a clear question arising from a precise context. In the field of law, this is in fact the exact meaning of "jurisprudence."

Many questions have been raised in the course of history about the diversity of *fatwas*. If Islam is one, how could there be differing legal judgments on the same legal question? The ulama have unanimously affirmed that if geographical or historical contexts differ, it is no longer the same question, for it must be considered in the light of a new environment. Thus properly considered responses should naturally differ, as is shown by the example of al-Shafii, who modified some of his legal judgments after traveling from Baghdad to Cairo. So, even though Islam is one, the *fatwas*, with all their diversity, and sometimes contradiction, still remain Islamic and authoritative.

This kind of diversity was understood, accepted, and respected, while the problem of disagreement between ulama faced with an identical legal question has given rise to endless debates. Is this possible in the area of religious affairs, and, if so, how can Islam be a unifying force for Muslims? Two essential points have been emphasized by the vast majority of ulama.

1. There is no divergence of opinion on the principles, the fundamentals (*usul*) of Islamic law. There is a consensus among the jurists on the fact that these principles constitute the essence, the frame of reference, and the benchmark of the juridical corpus of Islamic law and jurisprudence (*fiqh*). However, it is impossible to avoid differences of opinion on points related to secondary issues (*furu*), for a legal judgment on these points is dependent on and influenced by many factors, such as the knowledge and understanding of the ulama and their ability to deduce and extrapolate judgments. The natural diversity in their levels of competence inevitably gives rise to divergent interpretations and opinions. This even happened among the Companions at the time of the Prophet, and, according to the ulama, such divergences should be recognized and respected, within their limits, as based upon the fundamentals of Islam.

2. A question naturally arises from this consensus: even if there are various "acceptable" legal opinions on one and the same problem (even a secondary problem (*far*)), does this mean that all the *fatwas* have the same value; in other words, are they all correct? If that were the case, it would lead to the conclusion that two divergent opinions could both be true at the same time, in the same place, and in respect of the same person, which is rationally unacceptable. The majority of ulama, including the four principal imams of the Sunni schools of law, are of the view that only one of the divergent opinions pronounced on a precise question can be considered correct. This is indicated in the passage in the Qur'an that relates the story of David and Solomon, where it is clear that although they had made judgments on the same case and although both of them had received the gift of judgment and knowledge, only Solomon's opinion was correct: "We made it understood to Solomon." [47] This position is also confirmed by the *hadith* already cited about the *mujtahid*'s reward: he will receive two rewards if he is right but only one if he is wrong, because his effort and sincere research will be taken into account by God.

So, to accept that there may be a diversity of legal opinions on precise questions (formulated in the same context, at the same time, and for the same community or individual) does not in the least lead to the assumption that there are several "truths" and that all these opinions have the same value and correctness. There is only "one truth," which all the ulama should try to discover, and they will be rewarded for the effort they make towards this. As long as there is no indisputable proof applicable to the problem in question, each Muslim should, after consideration and analysis, follow the opinion whose evidence and worth seem to him the clearest and most convincing.

Guided by the Qur'an and the example of the Prophet, which are for Muslims the sources of truth, the ulama should do their best to discover the truth when the texts are not clear or simply do not exist. In fact, the meaning and content of the delegation granted by God to humankind reaches its peak and is fulfilled when the ulama struggle constantly and tirelessly to arrive at the most correct judgment, or that which is closest to what is correct and true. So these ulama, both *mujtahids* and *muftis*, must be determined, demanding, and confident in their own judgments, while remaining humble and calm to face and accept the fact that there will necessarily and inevitably be a plurality of opinion. The imam al-Shafii aptly said, concerning the state of mind that should characterize the attitude of the ulama: "[As we see it] our opinion is right though it may turn out to be wrong, while we consider the opinion of our opponents to be wrong though it may turn out to be right." [48]

The principle of integration

A study of the three notions of *al-maslaha*, *ijtihad*, and *fatwa*, though rather technical, is unavoidable if we are to think from the inside about the presence of Muslims in the West, with their legitimate hope of remaining faithful to their religion and its scriptural sources. What emerges first from this presentation is a clear confirmation of what we brought out earlier: we are dealing with codifications and legal instruments thought up and elaborated by human intelligence on the basis of work on the Qur'an and the *sunna*. There are numerous differences among scholars, who are sometimes not even in agreement on the existence of some of these tools or how to define and apply them. It nevertheless remains true that, beyond these disagreements, a true frame of reference has been drawn up that has become, over time, the universe through which Muslim ulama have been given the means to think in terms of evolution and faithfulness at the same time.

It is nevertheless appropriate, particularly when we speak of the new realities that face us in the West, to stay within the spirit of the whole landscape at whose core are set the legal principles and instruments referred to earlier. And it is imperative to remember the meaning of these principles, their interactivity, and their hierarchy. There is a great temptation to use these notions incoherently, chaotically, or only selectively, without fully grasping the whole philosophical legal corpus and consequently to become detached from global progress. As a result, we hear in the West of intellectuals and scholars calling for a new *ijtihad* or for the formulation of innovative *fatwas* without integrating or even connecting this demand with the more general fundamentals of Islam concerning *tawhid*, the concept of the human being and the *Sharia* (with the universal principles it contains). This approach, which almost naturally tries to resolve the problems of integration faced by Muslims through attempts at legal adaptation that are based on circumstance, could soon prove to have serious limitations. First of all, because it is built on a dualistic vision of two universes that do not mingle and that make compromises at their boundaries, or in the limited area where they intersect, it assumes that it is Muslims, being in the numerical minority, who must adapt by force of circumstance. This approach also implicitly carries the idea (even if the discourse says the complete opposite) that Muslims must think of themselves as a minority, on the margin in their societies, which will continue to be the societies of "the Other" and in which they will live somewhat as strangers, their belonging at best being confined to symbolic "acts:" expressions of solidarity, voting, for example. And finally, and perhaps most seriously, the vision that underlies this approach is clearly the concern only that Muslims should integrate into their new environment, and not that they should contribute.

It is certainly quite normal that during the first decades of their new presence in the West, Muslims should have sought principally to protect themselves; they had no choice, and it was as much about the survival of their religious identity as about the preservation of the richness of their culture. This is how all the initial steps towards adaptation undergone by all immigrant populations should be understood. For Muslims, the process went from the building of mosques to the establishment of Islamic associations via the elaboration of a way of thinking, a discourse, and, little by little, a legal reference framework in the various continents and countries. The various meetings of ulama in the West (from the 1980s in the United States to the beginning of the 1990s in Europe), which tried to address the new questions faced by Muslims in industrialized societies, were part of this trend. The institutionalization of this dynamic with the establishment of the Fiqh Council (Council of Islamic Law and Jurisprudence) in the United States and the European Council for Fatwas and Research in 1997 made possible the formulation of a series of legal opinions in step with Western societies and available to the public.[49] There was then talk of a *fiqh al-aqal-liyyat*[50] (law and jurisprudence of minorities), which was to allow Muslims in the West to live their faith and religion more peacefully.

These achievements were, without a shadow of doubt, fundamental and particularly necessary; they constituted a new and important stage in the establishment of Muslims in the West. We must nevertheless be aware that it was just a stage and that we should rethink our presence in the West more comprehensively. Indeed, our own sources come to our aid and press us to go beyond three staging posts, which are in the long term to be considered as traps: the dualist approach, minority thinking, and integration through adaptation. Doubtless the coming generations will be better equipped to understand and take up these challenges, but the need to reformulate them from the inside is already being felt. To think of our belonging to Islam in the West in terms of Otherness, adaptation to limitations, and authorized compromise (*rukhas*) cannot be enough, and gives the impression of structural adjustments that make it possible to survive in a sort of imagined borderland but do not provide the means really to flourish, participate in, and fully engage in our societies. In his book *On Law and the Jurisprudence of Muslim Minorities*, Yusuf al-Qardawi adds a telling subtitle: *The Life of Muslims in Other Societies*. In his mind, Western societies are "other societies" because the societies normal for Muslims are Muslim-majority societies.[51] But this is no longer the case, and what were once thought of as some kind of "diaspora" are so no longer. There is no longer a place of origin from which Muslims are "exiled" or "distanced," and "naturalized:" "converted" Muslims—"Western Muslims"—are at home, and should not only say so but feel so.

It will be necessary to change the way we look at our societies. As we have been saying, our sources help us in this if we can only try hard to reappropriate for ourselves the universality of the message of Islam, along with its vast horizon. This reappropriation should be of a depth that will enable it to produce a true "intellectual revolution" in the sense intended by Kant where he spoke of the "Copernician revolution." Well before the tools that allow us to interact with the world, the Only One established a threefold relation with human beings—exactingness, trust, and humility. If the use of reason is essential for the return to self and the confirmation of the original breath, it also holds the key to applying the revealed books. We must engage with the world armed with faith, the scriptural sources, and an active intellect; in the course of the intellectual development of our universe of reference, we have learned to distinguish methodologies, grasp the religious rites (within the strict limits of its codification based on the texts), and observe the universe (with the methodology appropriate to social affairs) with assurance and confidence. In this we know that everything a society or culture produces and accepts that is not in opposition to a clearly stipulated prohibition is in fact integrated and considered part of the Islamic universe of reference.

It is precisely in this that the intellectual revolution for which we long must live. "The way of faithfulness," "the path to the spring," the *Sharia*, teaches us to integrate everything that is not against an established principle and to consider it as our own. This is, after all, the true universality of Islam: it consists in this principle of integrating the good, from wherever it may come, which has made it possible for Muslims to settle in, and make their own, without contradiction, almost all the cultures of the countries in which they have established themselves, from South America to Asia, through West and North Africa. It should not be otherwise in the West. Here, too, it is a matter of integrating all the dimensions of life that are not in opposition to our terms of reference and to consider them completely our own (legally, socially, and culturally). We must clearly overcome the dualistic vision and reject our sense of being eternal foreigners, living in parallel, on the margins or as reclusive minorities, in order to make way for the global vision of universal Islam that integrates and allows the Other to flourish confidently.[52]

Does this mean that this attitude will by itself make it possible for us to overcome all the problems and that there will be then no contradictions in the Islamic consciousness between the need to remain Muslim and the realities of life in the West? Of course not—but this is nevertheless the way to set the terms of the equation, which must change entirely. To begin by distinguishing all the dimensions of Western life that are already "Islamically based" and thus completely appropriated is to be already equipped with the means to understand this universe from the inside and to consider it truly our own. The next stage is to engage in a systematic work of selection, at several levels, in order to delineate from within the West the limits of the public good (*maslaha*) and to identify the margins available for maneuver between the situations in which we are free to act in accordance with our conscience and the rarer situations where we must find possible legal adaptations (through *ijtihad* and *fatwa*). These legal instruments must not be used only in the perilous area at the limits but must also find their place in a global vision that integrates and makes the West into an acquired territory, a land for Muslims: it is only this vision that will allow us to avoid the kind of adaptation that resembles a hodgepodge of *fatwas*, though, like so many accommodations, largely in response to arguments from necessity (*darura*) in order to justify a number of legal exemptions (*rukhas*) to make life less difficult. It all happens as if Muslims should ghettoize themselves and become spectators in a society where they were once marginalized. The universality of the message of Islam and the principle of integration that is at its heart invite us to integrate everything that is positive, to move forward selectively, and to act from within, as full members in our society, in order to promote what is good, to work against injustices and discrimination, and to develop alternatives that do not restrict *fiqh* in the West to thinking of itself as on the defensive, moving in a protective fashion, giving the name of "exemptions" (*rukhas*) to what in the long term could take on the color of surrender.[53] The intellectual revolution we are referring to here is extremely demanding: it compels us, from within, as free citizens in societies under the rule of law, to strengthen our faith and to use our intelligence to find solutions and alternatives to the problems of our societies—to move from integration to contribution, from adaptation to reform and transformation.

Faith, science, and ethics

The whole of the analysis we have proposed in the preceding sections will help us to deal with a question that is basic for the contemporary Muslim intellect.[54] We often recall the extraordinary contribution Muslims have made historically to scientific development and progress and emphasize the fact that they—more than any other civilization—have advanced the sciences to a higher level. If these facts prove that the current backwardness and difficulties in the area of science in Muslim countries are not intrinsic to Islam, it is nonetheless true that although they may comfort our hearts, they do not provide solutions to contemporary problems. In industrialized and technologically advanced countries. Muslims seem to suffer from a malaise, wedged between their particular ethics and science, which sometimes seems to contradict, or more often to jostle, their faith and convictions. What sort of relationship can be maintained among faith, the scriptural resources, ethics, and the human or hard sciences? Most Muslims ask themselves this question without always providing a clear answer. Are there aspects of the study of the sciences, or at least some of them, that have become "non-Islamic" under the pressure of modernity? How can we speak of the "comprehensive character" and the universality of Islam and at the same time feel ill at ease in the world of knowledge and progress? What is the source of the problem, and how can this apparent contradiction be resolved?

We have seen how necessary and crucial was the work of categorization undertaken by scholars in their reading of the sources. When they were carrying out this work, the sources themselves, as much as the demands of their studies and the vicissitudes of history, at the same time forced them to differentiate between the specific areas of religious study:[55] thus were born the sciences of the Qur'an (*ulum al-Qur'an*), the sciences of Prophetic tradition (*ulum al-hadith*), the science of creed (*ilm al-aqida*), the science of the fundamentals of law and jurisprudence (*ilm usul al-fiqh*), and others.

Between approximately the tenth and eleventh centuries, the corpus of these sciences was formed according to a design represented in Fig. 1. This was a stimulating typology appropriate for the clarification of the limits and objectives of each area. Moreover, it naturally lent itself to encouraging research in all the other sciences for at least three reasons: first, because the Qur'an and the traditions invited the human spirit to study and understand the world; second, because the religious sciences themselves very often referred to scientific discoveries (in medicine or astronomy, for example) to work out an aspect of practice; and third, because the framework of reference was so nourished by religion that the connection between ethics and science was immediate and natural and necessarily less at risk at that time because few situations were recognized as delimited.

When the Renaissance, humanism, and the Reformation—all deeply influenced and enriched by Islamic civilization—worked together in the West, although differently, to start the process of secularization and to set free the power of reason that has become more and more autonomous and scientific, Islamic civilization seemed to freeze. The natural and once coherent interaction between the "Islamic sciences" and other areas of

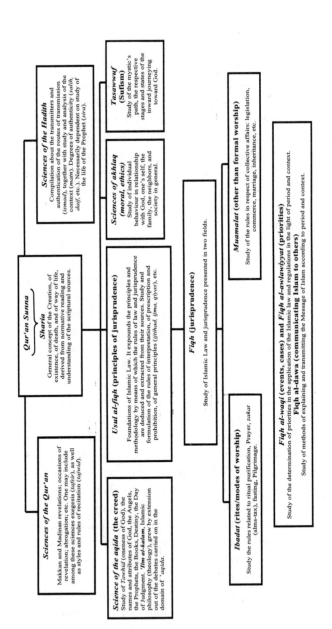

Fig. 1. Typology and Classification of the Islamic Sciences

knowledge—and some ulama had mastery of both—now seems defunct. The naturally ethical approach to the sciences that had characterized the Muslim stance till then seemed to suffer as, in the West, the successes of science took shape—a science that was becoming more and more distant from moral norms and also seemed to draw its power from a liberation from religious authority. Gripped by the ethical teaching of Islam, increasingly incapable of renewing the dynamic link between the moral frame of reference and the autonomy of reason, and feeling that they were in danger vis-à-vis the dynamism and expansion of Europe, the ulama were bound to the supreme authority of the religious sciences and preferred to sacrifice "the other knowledge," rather than norms of religion. For more than six centuries, no Muslim scholar has spoken out against science; rather, they all much prefer to recall the glorious past of Islam regarding the subject than the constant invitation of the religious sources to move science forward. Behind this sustained nostalgia and idealized dream, a deep malaise lies hidden, because we do not know, we no longer know, how to reestablish the connection between religion and science such that religion's ethical teachings give science a dignified finality without perverting its implementation or impeding its advances.

The overall sense is that the categorization of the Islamic sciences that was so useful in the context of the Middle Ages has become a stumbling block because it still retains a dualistic—and essentially very "Greek"—perception of the hierarchy of knowledge. For the Muslim spirit, the problem remains the same: the "all-comprehensive character of the message" comes face to face with a diametrically opposed reality whose terms of reference are apparently irreconcilable with its own. One of the solutions seems to be a wholehearted rush into activity, consisting of showing how the Qur'an contains scientific truths; but this collecting of scientific discovery in the text, this "harmonization," which too easily turns Revelation into a scientific text-book,[56] ill conceals an inability to engage with the scientific world while treating the texts with integrity. Another response, interesting in itself, has been suggested by the eminent Muslim intellectual Ismail al-Faruqi, who lived in the United States until his death and who was one of the founders of the International Institute of Islamic Thought (IIIT). He suggested the idea of an "Islamization of knowledge" and proposed discussion of the paradigms that underlay the various so-called profane sciences. This development has now revealed its limitations and has not met the hopes of its proponents. The question facing the Muslim mind remains: how can the connection be reestablished?

Once again it is a return to the scriptural sources that will make it possible for us to sketch the outlines of a solution. What they have taught us may be presented as two major theses:

1. The unity of the Source (God as revealed in the texts), which is where ethics finds its coherent foundation, never implies a similarity of approaches or a uniformity of methodologies.
2. Varieties of methodologies are constructed rationally, taking as the starting point the object of study,[57] not the relation to the Transcendent or to a system of knowledge that He has preordained.

Work on the scriptural texts, taken as an object of study in itself, demonstrated a diversity of methodologies and gave rise to a multitude of "Islamic sciences," each having its methodology, its field of investigation, and its limitations. Exactly the same logic should guide us in all areas of knowledge.

Faith connects the believer with the Creator in all areas of life, and life should stay committed as much as possible to the centrality of *tawhid* and the scriptural sources; this will produce a system of ethics built upon the meaning and the finality of life, which lie at the heart of the universal message of Islam. That same intellect will also, nevertheless, work out, completely autonomously and on the basis of its object of study, appropriate rules and methods that will set the boundaries for the science in question. In other words, and completely consistently, reason connected with the Source (God and the texts) formulates ethical teaching on the one hand and on the other sees itself as obliged by its object of study to set completely autonomous scientific rules and methods. There is no need to Islamize the sciences or to combine and confuse ethics and scientific methods: the universality of Islam offers a coherence that implies no confusion. So we must propose a new representation of the scientific universe if we want to avoid the dualistic impasse into which we were carried by the representation referred to earlier and produced by the medieval Muslim mind. We might present the picture as shown in Fig. 2.

In Fig. 2, from the centrality of *tawhid*, the arrows pointing from the center represent ethical teaching drawn from the scriptural sources. Along the concentric circles are the various sciences, each of which has its own methodology established by the autonomous efforts of reason on the basis of the object of study (e.g. the texts for the religious sciences, the human body for medicine, social dynamics for sociology). The various circles represent the various degrees of proximity (without any kind of hierarchy) that the different sciences may have with the scriptural sources. Thus the sciences

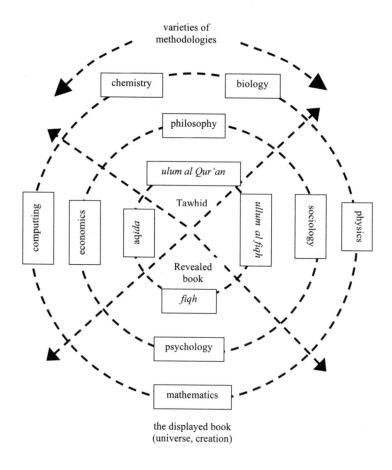

Fig. 2. *Tawhid*, Ethics, and the Sciences

traditionally called "Islamic" are naturally in the first circle; the humanities, where the scope for interpretation, subjectivity, and ideological orientation is considerable, are in the second circle (a particular view of the world may influence work in these sciences); the hard or pure sciences are in the last circle because their methodologies are virtually autonomous and are connected to the structure imposed by the object of study.[58] The universal and comprehensive message of Islamic ethics penetrates all the sciences without exception, calling for moral consistency, but it does not confuse the latter with the autonomy of scientific methods (in themselves morally neutral).

Thus human reason finds itself between two books, each of which, as an object of study, determines and imposes specific methodologies. From the revealed Book we must extrapolate and organize a grammar, a typology of rules, or the content of the credo. From the book of nature, we must discover the laws, functions, and logical patterns of organization, which give birth to medicine, chemistry, and physics. Ethics is the light that allows a "faithful' reading of the two books: it requires understanding of the laws, as well as respect for their balance.

This new representation makes it possible for us to change the old paradigms and rediscover ways that make a union possible. With reference to the elements that constitute the human being, we have shown that none of them is positive or negative "in itself" and that a moral quality can be acquired only through exactingness, discipline, self-control, and humility. It is exactly the same in the sciences, and it is the union of controlled scientific method and applied ethics that makes people faithful to the source at the heart of various fields of knowledge. So, like all the elements that make up the human being, all the scientific methods (imposed by creation itself, the open book) are "Islamic" *by nature*; mastered by mankind in the name of the ultimate values of life, they must, ethically, become so *by conscience*.

In order to achieve this, the consciousness of the believer will have to respond, in the very midst of scientific research and its application, to the three fundamental moral questions of the Islamic universe of reference:

1. What are my intentions (*al-niyya*) in engaging in the study of this science? There must be an active connection with *tawhid*.
2. What ethical boundaries must I respect? The concrete application of the ethical teaching must be rationally connected with the scriptural sources.
3. What are the ultimate objectives of my research? Scientific activity must be integrated into the "way of faithfulness," the "path to the Source."

At the end of this analysis we have come to understand that the principle of *shumuliyya*, the comprehensive character of the Islamic message, constitutes anything but a confusion of categories or, at the other extreme, a split between them such that one might legitimately be anxious about the emergence of a "science without conscience," to use Rabelais' phrase. The same logic we have already encountered, when considering relations with the texts, the human being, or the principle of integration, is at work here. Drawing on *tawhid*, faith demands of reason that it should unite, marry, pacify in full faithfulness: as a testimony to consciousness of the covenant.

It is also an expression of how demanding is this concept of "universality:" in practice, it means that Muslims must engage, within their own areas of competence, in groundbreaking specialization in all the areas of competence and contemporary knowledge and that, far from becoming intoxicated by that knowledge and changing it into a new idol of modern times, they must make their contribution to the ethical questions that it raises. The scientific challenges facing the new Muslim presence that seeks to act from within, not from the margins of society and science, are to master the rules and methods of the various humanities and pure sciences, to discuss hypotheses and applications, and to put forward new perspectives. The greatest challenge is to preserve the centrality of what is essential—the connection with the Source, a sense of responsibility, and retention of an awareness of "the need of Him," which gives birth to humility—even, and especially, in scientific activity.

CHAPTER 4

A Comparative Approach to Islam and Democracy

Fethullah Gülen

Born near Erzurum in 1938, Fethullah Gülen is today perhaps the most influential religious figure in Turkey and Central Asia, a prominence owed largely to his leadership of the Nurcu movement—which traces its genesis to the writings of the Turkish mystic Said Nursi (1876–1960)—and an expansive network of schools throughout Turkey and the Central Asian Republics. As a preacher in the 1960s, Gülen often gave sermons on the relevant social and scientific issues of the day, urging especially the young to synthesize between the ideal of Islam and the realities and promises of scientific progress. His broad appeal and his religious sentiments—coupled with his expanding popularity, particularly in the 1990s—earned him the suspicions of the authorities, having earlier resulted in a three-year jail sentence in 1971. A court case was initiated against him in 1995, and in 1997 he relocated to the United States, allegedly for "health reasons," where he currently lives and writes. Today, his "social movement" remains as vibrant as ever throughout Turkey and Central Asia, and is supported by a vast network of schools, media outlets, informal gathering circles, and wealthy sympathizers in Europe and elsewhere.

Recent years have seen a proliferation of Gülen's writing in English, most of the works having been translated from the Turkish by publishing houses affiliated with his movement. The published titles range from works dealing with tolerance and civilizational dialogue to expositions on Sufism and key concepts in the Qur'an. A number of the books start with the assertion that "Fethullah Gülen's long-standing dream has remained the same over the years: to raise a generation of young people combining intellectual 'enlightenment' with pure spirituality, wisdom, and activism." According to the author of the foreword to one of his books (Thomas Michel in Toward a Global Civilization of Love and Tolerance*), Gülen's works are "a call to Muslims to a greater awareness that Islam teaches the need for dialogue and that Muslims are called to be agents and witnesses to God's universal mercy."*

The brief essay that follows deals specifically with the relationship between Islam and democracy. It is taken from Fethullah Gülen, "A Comparative Approach to Islam and Democracy," SAIS Review, vol. 21, no. 2 (summer–fall 2001), pp 133–8.

Religion, particularly Islam, has become one of the most difficult subject areas to tackle in recent years. Contemporary culture, whether approached from the perspective of anthropology or theology, psychology or psycho-analysis, evaluates religion with empirical methods. On the one hand, reli-gion is an inwardly experienced and felt phenomenon, one mostly related to life's permanent aspects. On the other, believers can see their religion as a philosophy, a set of rational principles, or mere mysticism. The difficulty increases in the case of Islam, for some Muslims and policy makers consider and present it as a purely political, sociological, and economic ideology, rather than as a religion.

If we want to analyze religion, democracy, or any other system or philos-ophy accurately, we should focus on humanity and human life. From this perspective, religion in general and Islam in particular cannot be compared on the same basis with democracy or any other political, social, or economic system. Religion focuses primarily on the immutable aspects of life and exis-tence, whereas political, social, and economic systems or ideologies concern only certain variable, social aspects of our worldly life.

The aspects of life with which religion is primarily concerned are as valid today as they were at the dawn of humanity and will continue to be so in the future. Worldly systems change according to circumstances and so can be evaluated only according to their times. Belief in God, the hereafter, the prophets, the holy books, angels, and divine destiny have nothing to do with changing times. Likewise, worship and morality's universal and unchanging standards have little to do with time and worldly life.

Therefore, when comparing the religion of Islam with democracy, we must remember that democracy is a system that is being continually devel-oped and revised. It also varies according to the places and circumstances where it is practiced. On the other hand, religion has established immutable principles related to faith, worship, and morality. Thus only Islam's worldly aspects should be compared with democracy.

The main aim of Islam and its unchangeable dimensions affect its rules governing the changeable aspects of our lives. Islam does not propose a certain unchangeable form of government or attempt to shape it. Instead, Islam establishes fundamental principles that orient a government's general character, leaving it to the people to choose the type and form of govern-ment according to time and circumstances. If we approach the matter in this light and compare Islam with today's modern liberal democracy, we will better understand the position of Islam and democracy with respect to each other.

Democratic ideas stem from ancient times. Modern liberal democracy was born in the American (1776) and French Revolutions (1789–99). In democratic societies, people govern themselves as opposed to being ruled by someone above. The individual has priority over the community in this type of political system, being free to determine how to live his or her own life. Individualism is not absolute, though. People achieve a better existence by living within a society and this requires that they adjust and limit their freedom according to the criteria of social life.

The Prophet says that all people are as equal as the teeth of a comb.[1] Islam does not discriminate on grounds of race, color, age, nationality, or physical traits. The Prophet declared: "You are all from Adam, and Adam is from earth. O servants of God, be brothers (and sisters)."[2] Those who are born earlier, who have more wealth and power than others, or who belong to certain families or ethnic groups have no inherent right to rule others.

Islam also upholds the following fundamental principles:

1. Power lies in truth, a repudiation of the common idea that truth relies upon power.
2. Justice and the rule of law are essential.
3. Freedom of belief and rights to life, personal property, reproduction, and health (both mental and physical) cannot be violated.
4. The privacy and immunity of individual life must be maintained.
5. No one can be convicted of a crime without evidence, or accused and punished for someone else's crime.
6. An advisory system of administration is essential.

All rights are equally important, and an individual's right cannot be sacrificed for society's sake. Islam considers a society to be composed of conscious individuals equipped with free will and having responsibility towards both themselves and others. Islam goes a step further by adding a cosmic dimension. It sees humanity as the "motor" of history, contrary to the fatalistic approaches of some of the nineteenth-century Western philosophies of history such as dialectical materialism and historicism.[3] Just as every individual's will and behavior determine the outcome of his or her life in this world and in the hereafter, a society's progress or decline is determined by the will, worldview, and lifestyle of its inhabitants. The Qur'an (13:11) says: "God will not change the state of a people unless they change themselves (with respect to their beliefs, worldview, and lifestyle)." In other words, each society holds the reins of its fate in its own hands. The Prophetic tradition emphasizes this idea: "You will be ruled according to how you are."[4] This is the basic character and spirit of democracy, which does not conflict with any Islamic principle.

As Islam holds individuals and societies responsible for their own fate, people must be responsible for governing themselves. The Qur'an addresses society with such phrases as; "O people!" and "O believers!" The duties entrusted to modern democratic systems are those that Islam refers to society and classifies, in order of importance, as "absolutely necessary, relatively necessary, and commendable to carry out." The sacred text includes the following passages: "Establish, all of you, peace" (2:208); "spend in the way of God and to the needy of the pure and good of what you have earned and of what We bring forth for you from earth" (2:267); "if some among your women are accused of indecency, you must have four witnesses [to prove it]" (4:15); "God commands you to give over the public trusts to the charge of those having the required qualities and to judge with justice when you judge between people" (4:58); "observe justice as witnesses respectful for God even if it is against yourselves, your parents and relatives" (4:135); "if they [your enemies] incline to peace [when you are at war], you also incline to it" (8:61); "if a corrupt, sinful one brings you news [about others], investigate it so that you should not strike a people without knowing" (49:6); "if two parties among the believers fight between themselves, reconcile them" (49:9). To sum up, the Qur'an addresses the whole community and assigns it almost all the duties entrusted to modern democratic systems.

People cooperate with one another by sharing these duties and establishing the essential foundations necessary to perform them. The government is composed of all these foundations. Thus Islam recommends a government based on a social contract. People elect the administrators and establish a council to debate common issues. Also the society as a whole participates in auditing the administration.

Especially during the rule of the first four caliphs (632–61), the fundamental principles of government mentioned above—including free elections—were fully observed. The political system was transformed into a sultanate after the death of Ali, the fourth caliph, owing to internal conflicts and to the global conditions at that time. Unlike under the caliphate, power in the sultanate was passed on through the sultan's family. However, even though free elections were no longer held, societies maintained other principles that are at the core of today's liberal democracies.

Islam is an inclusive religion. It is based on the belief in one God as the Creator, Lord, Sustainer, and Administrator of the universe. Islam is the religion of the whole universe. That is, the entire universe obeys the laws laid down by God, so everything in the universe is "Muslim" and obeys God by submitting to His laws. Even a person who refuses to believe in God or follows another religion has perforce to be a Muslim as far as his or her bodily existence is concerned. His or her entire life, from the embryonic stage to the body's dissolution into dust after death, every tissue of his or her muscles, and every limb of his or her body follows the course prescribed for each by God's law. Thus in Islam, God, nature, and humanity are neither remote from each other nor are they alien to each other. It is God who makes himself known to humanity through nature and humanity itself, and nature and humanity are two books (of creation) through each word of which God is known. This leads humankind to look upon everything as belonging to the same Lord, to whom it itself belongs, so that it regards nothing in the universe as alien. His sympathy, love, and service do not remain confined to the people of any particular race, color, or ethnicity. The Prophet summed this up with the command, "O servants of God, be brothers (and sisters)!"

A separate but equally important point is that Islam recognizes all religions previous to it. It accepts all the prophets and books sent to different peoples in different epochs of history. Not only does it accept them, but also regards belief in them as an essential principle of being Muslim. By doing so, it acknowledges the basic unity of all religions. A Muslim is at the same time a true follower of Abraham, Moses, David, Jesus, and of all the other Hebrew prophets. This belief explains why both Christians and Jews enjoyed their religious rights under the rule of Islamic governments throughout history.

The Islamic social system seeks to form a virtuous society and thereby gain God's approval. It recognizes right, not force, as the foundation of social life. Hostility is unacceptable. Relationships must be based on belief, love, mutual respect, assistance, and understanding instead of conflict and realization of personal interest. Social education encourages people to pursue lofty ideals and to strive for perfection, not just to run after their own desires. Right calls for unity, virtue brings mutual support and solidarity, and belief secures brotherhood and sisterhood. Encouraging the soul to attain perfection brings happiness in both worlds.

Democracy has developed over time. Just as it has gone through many different stages in the past, it will continue to evolve and to improve in the future. Along the way, it will be shaped in a more humane and just system, one based on righteousness and reality. If human beings are considered as a whole, without disregarding the spiritual dimension of their existence and their spiritual needs, and without forgetting that human life is not limited to this moral life and that all people have a great craving for eternity, democracy could reach its peak of perfection and bring even more happiness to humanity. Islamic principles of equality, tolerance, and justice can help it do just that.

CHAPTER 5

Religious Liberty: A Muslim Perspective

Mohamed Talbi

Born in 1921 in Tunis, Mohamed Talbi is one of Tunisia's most respected historians and an influential figure in the current reformist Muslim discourse. An accomplished and well-respected Professor of History at the University of Tunis, he is also an acknowledged authority on Qur'anic exegesis and Islamic thought. As a historian, Talbi specializes in the history of medieval North Africa. As a scholar of Islam, his primary focus is to explore and elaborate on the essentially pluralist nature of Islam and its detailed attention to mutual respect (ihtiram mutabadal) and dialogue (hiwar). Not surprisingly, Talbi is an active advocate of interfaith dialogue between Islam and other world religions. Similarly, he has expounded on the synthesis between Qur'anic principles and modernity, particularly liberal democracy and equality between the sexes.

Talbi has published two highly significant works on Islamic thought, namely 'Iyal Allah (Families of God) and Ummat al-Wasat (Community of Moderation), both in Arabic. Families of God *comprises questions posed to Talbi on a variety of Islamic issues, and his answers.* Community of Moderation *contains a wide range of essays on topics related to Islam that Talbi considers important. The following essay, which in many ways encapsulates Talbi's thesis on the relationship between Islam and pluralism, is among one of his few publications in English. The essay originally appeared in Mohamed Talbi, "Religious Liberty: A Muslim Perspective," in Leonard Swindler (ed),* Muslims in Dialogue: The Evolution of a Dialogue *(Lewiston, NY: The Edwin Mellon Press, 1992), pp 465–82.*

From old relations to a new context

From the outset we have to remember that the problem of religious liberty as a common human concern and international preoccupation is relatively new. In former times the problem was totally irrelevant. During antiquity all felt that it was natural to worship the deities of their city. It was the task of these deities to protect the house, look after the family, and ensure the welfare of the state. Along with their worshippers, they took the rough with the smooth. The deities of Carthage, for example, were by nature the

enemies of the deities of Rome. In that context the refusal to worship the
deities of the city was felt essentially as an act of disloyalty towards the
state.

In the beginning the situation was almost the same in the biblical tradition. In the Bible, Yahweh acts as the Hebrews' God. God constantly warns
the people not to worship any other deity and to follow the Torah. This
people, with its one God, is also an association of an ethnic entity—the 12
tribes descended from Abraham via Isaac and Jacob—with a land, Israel.
The Hebrew community is an ideal prototype of unity: it obeys at one
and the same time the *ius sanguinis, loci, et religionis*, the law of blood,
place, and religion. It is the perfect prototype of an ethnically homoge-
neous community rooted in religion and a land shaped into a state. In a
way, to speak of religious liberty in such a case is literally absurd. There
was no choice other than adhering to the state community or leaving it.
Therefore Jews who converted to another religion *ipso facto* ceased to belong
to their state-community. Their conversions were felt as betrayals, and as
such they warranted the penalty of death. If we dwell on the case of the
Jewish community as a prototype, it is because that case is not without
some similarities to the classical Islamic *Ummah* as it has been shaped by
traditional theology.

For historical reasons, the situation changed completely with the appearance of Christian preaching and the destruction of the Jewish state in 70CE.
From the beginning Christian preaching was not linked with a state: Jesus
ordered his disciples "to render unto Caesar the things which are Caesar's, and
unto God the things which are God's" (Matthew 22:21). This revolutionary
attempt to dissociate the state and the religion and to ensure the freedom
of individual conscience failed. The time was not yet ripe. Consequently
the early Christians and the Jews after 70CE were often considered disloyal
subjects by the Roman Empire because of their refusal to pay homage to the
deities of their city and of their social group. Accordingly, they were often
treated as rebels, were even called atheists—because they were monotheists!
The right to self-determination and religious liberty was denied to them as
individuals.

To cut a long story short, let us say that political power and religion
preserved more or less, or resumed, their old relations. They needed each
other too much. The intolerance of the dominant social group asserted itself
everywhere in the world with internal and external wars and many forms of
more or less severe discrimination. Of course the Islamic world, though relatively tolerant, was no exception. As everywhere else in the world, human
rights have been violated in this area, and it still happens that they are, here

and there, more or less overridden. That does not mean, however, as we shall see, that Islam as such authorizes the violation of these fundamental rights.

Now, to avoid looking only on the dark side of things, we should note that our common past was not entirely so somber and so ugly. We can also cite some brilliant periods of tolerance, respect, comprehension, and dialogue. Nevertheless, we had to wait until the nineteenth century to see freedom of conscience clearly claimed. Political and philosophical liberalism were then in vogue, but in fact what was claimed was not so much the right of freedom of conscience as the right not to believe. Thus the concept of religious liberty unfortunately became synonymous with secularism, agnosticism, and atheism. As a result, a stubborn fight was launched against it. For us to deal with the subject honestly and with equanimity, we need to free ourselves of this false identification.

It must be granted that today religious liberty is, as a matter of fact, definitively rooted in our social life. Since the Declaration of Human Rights in 1948, this concept has become an essential part of international law. Moreover, we already live in a pluralistic world, and our world is going to be more and more pluralistic in the near future. I have written elsewhere that each person has the right to be different and that at the same time our planet is already too small for all our ambitions and dreams. In this new world, which is expanding rapidly before our eyes, there is no longer room for exclusiveness. We have to accept each other as we are. Diversity is the law of our time. Today, by virtue of an increasingly comprehensive and sophisticated mass media, every person is truly the neighbor of every other person.

In our Islamic countries we have since the beginning been in the habit of living side by side with communities of different faiths. It has not been always easy, as some recent events again make painfully clear. However, it is only recently that we have begun to be confronted with secularism. It is now our turn to experience from inside the growth of agnosticism and atheism. We have to be conscious of this overwhelming change in our societies and accordingly we have to exercise our theological thinking in this new and unprecedented context.

Before going further we must first ask more precisely what religious liberty is. Is it only the right to be an unbeliever? One may indeed say that religious liberty has very often been exclusively identified with atheism. However, this is only one aspect of the question, and from my point of view a negative one. In fact, religious liberty is basically the right to decide for oneself, without any kind of pressure, fear, or anxiety, whether to believe or not to believe, the right to assume with full consciousness one's destiny—the right, of course, to jettison every kind of faith as superstitions inherited from the Dark Ages, but also the right to espouse the faith of one's choice, to worship, and to bear witness freely. Is this definition in harmony with the Qur'an's basic teachings?

The Qur'an's basic principles

In my opinion, religious liberty is basically grounded, from a Qur'anic perspective, first and foremost on the divinely ordered nature of humanity. A human is not just another being among many others. Among the whole range of creatures only humans have duties and obligations. They are exceptional beings. They cannot be reduced to their bodies because, above everything else, humans are spirits, spirits which have been given the power to conceive the Absolute and to ascend to God. If humans have this exceptional power, this privileged position in creation, it is because God "breathed into him something of His spirit" (32:9). Of course humans, like all living animals, are material. They have bodies created "from sounding clay, from mud molded into shape" (15:28). But they received the Spirit. They have two sides: a lower side—their clay—and a higher side—the Spirit of God. This higher side, comments A. Yusuf Ali, "if rightly used, would give man superiority over other creatures." Humanity's privileged position in the order of creation is strikingly illustrated in the Qur'an in the scene where the angels are ordered to prostrate themselves before Adam (15:29, 38:72), the heavenly prototype of humanity. In a way, and provided we keep humanity in its proper place as creature, we may as Muslims, along with the other members of Abraham's spiritual descendants, Jews and Christians, say that humanity was created in God's image. A *hadith* (a saying of the Prophet), although questioned, authorizes this statement.

So we can say that on the level of the Spirit, all persons, whatever their physical or intellectual abilities and aptitudes may be, are truly equal. They have the same "Breath" of God in them, and by virtue of this "Breath" they have the ability to ascend to God and to respond freely to God's call. Consequently, they have the same dignity and sacredness, and because of this dignity and sacredness they are fully and equally entitled to enjoy the same right to self-determination on earth and for the hereafter. Thus from a Qur'anic perspective we may say that human rights are rooted in what every human is by nature, and this is by virtue of God's plan and creation. Now it goes without saying that the cornerstone of all human rights is religious liberty, for religion, which is the "explanation of the meaning of life and how to live accordingly," is the most fundamental and comprehensive of human institutions.

It is evident from a Muslim perspective that humanity is not the fruit of mere "chance and necessity." Its creation follows a plan and purpose. Through the "Breath" humanity has received the faculty to be at one with God, and its response, to have a meaning, must be free. The teachings of the Qur'an are clear: humans are privileged beings with "spiritual favors" (27:70); they have not been "created in jest" (23:115); they have a mission and they are God's "vicegerents on earth" (2:30). Proceeding from God, with a mission to fulfill, human destiny is ultimately to return to God. "Whoso does right, does it for his own soul; and whoso does wrong, does so to its detriment. Then to your Lord will you all be brought back" (45:15).

For that to happen it is absolutely necessary that each person be able to choose freely and without any kind of coercion. Every person ought in full consciousness to build his or her own destiny. The Qur'an states clearly that compulsion is incompatible with religion: "There should be no compulsion in religion. Truth stands out clear from Error. Whosoever rejects Evil and believes in God hath grasped the most trustworthy handhold, that never breaks. God is All-Hearing, All-Knowing" (2:256).

To the best of my knowledge, among all the revealed texts, only the Qur'an stresses religious liberty in such a precise and unambiguous way. Faith, to be true and reliable faith, absolutely needs to be a free and voluntary act. In this connection it is worth stressing that the quoted verse was aimed at reproving and condemning the attitude of some Jews and Christians who, being newly converted to Islam in Medina, were willing to convert their children with them to their new faith. Thus it is clearly emphasized that faith is an individual concern and commitment and that even parents must refrain from interfering with it. The very nature of faith, as is stressed in the basic text of Islam in clear and indisputable words, is to be a voluntary act born out of conviction and freedom.

In fact, even God refrains from overpowering humans to the point of subduing them against their will. This too is clearly expressed in the Qur'an. Faith is then a free gift, God's gift. Humanity can accept or refuse it. It has the capacity to open its heart and its reason to God's gift. A guidance (hudan) has been sent it. It is warmly invited to listen to God's call. God warns it in clear and unambiguous terms. As it is underlined in the cited verse stressing human freedom, "Truth stands out clear from Error." It is up to humanity to make its choice. The human condition—and that is the reason for humanity's dignity and sacredness—is not without something tragic about it. Humans can be misled. They are able to make the wrong choice and to stray from the right path. They have the capacity to resist God's call, and this capacity is the criterion of their true freedom.

Even the Messenger, whose mission properly is to convey God's call and message, is helpless in such a situation. He is clearly and firmly warned to respect human freedom and God's mystery. "If it had been thy Lord's will, all who are on the earth would have believed, all of them. Wilt thou then compel mankind, against their will, to believe?" (10:99). A. Yusuf Ali, in his translation of the Qur'an, comments on that verse in this way:

> men of faith must not be impatient or angry if they have to contend against Unfaith, and most important of all, they must guard against the temptation of forcing Faith, i.e., imposing it on others by physical compulsion, or any other forms of compulsion such as social pressure, or inducements held out by wealth or position, or other adventitious advantages. Forced Faith is no faith.[1]

The Apostle's mission—and all the more ours—is stringently restricted to advise, warn, convey a message, and admonish without compelling. He is ordered: "Admonish, for thou art but an admonisher. Thou hast no authority to compel them" (88:21–2). In other words, God has set humanity truly and tragically free. What God wants is, in full consciousness and freedom, a willing and obedient response to the divine call, and that is the very meaning of the Arabic word "Islam."

Now we must emphasize that this does not mean that we have to adopt an attitude of abandon and indifference. We must in fact avoid both Scylla and Charybdis. First, we must, of course, refrain from interfering in the inner life of others, and we have already stressed this aspect of the problem enough. It is time to add that, secondly, we must also avoid being indifferent to everything, being careless about others. We need to remember that the other is our neighbor. We must bear witness to and convey God's message. This too needs stressing.

We are too tempted today to shut ourselves up and to live comfortably wrapped in our own thoughts. But this is not God's purpose. Respectfulness is not indifference. God sets the example, for God is nearer to humanity "than the man's own jugular vein" (50:16), and God knows better than we do our innermost desires, and what these desires "whisper [*tuwaswisu*]" to us (50:16). Thus God stands by us and speaks unceasingly to each one of us, warning and promising with a divine pedagogy that fits all persons of different social and intellectual classes, at all times, using images, symbols, and words that only God may use with a total sovereignty.

And God urges us to follow the divine example and to turn our steps towards all our sisters and brothers in humanity, beyond all kinds of frontiers, religious ones included.

> O mankind! We created you from a male and a female; and we have made you into nations and tribes that you may know each other. Verily, the most honour-

able among you, in the sight of God, is he who is the most righteous of you. And God is all knowing, All-Aware (49:13).

This is addressed to all mankind, and not only to the Muslim brotherhood, though it is understood that in a perfect world the two would be synonymous. As it is, mankind is descended from one pair of parents. Their tribes, races, and nations are convenient labels by which we may know certain differing characteristics. Before God they are all one, and he gets most honor who is most righteous.[2]

In other words, humans are not created for solitariness and impervious individuality. They are created for community, relationship, and dialogue. Their fulfillment is in their reconciliation at once to God and to persons. We have to find the way, in each case, to realize this double reconciliation, without betraying God and without damaging the inner life of the other. To do so we have to listen to God's advice:

> Do not argue with the People of the Book unless it is in the most courteous manner, except for those of them who do wrong. And say: We believe in the Revelation which has come down to us and in that which came down to you. Our God and your God is one, and to Him we submit (29:46).

Let us note that the Arabic word used in the verse and rendered in the translation by the verb "to submit" is "*muslimun*" (= Muslims). So, to be a true Muslim is to live in a courteous dialogue with all peoples of other faiths and ideologies, and ultimately to submit to God. We must show concern to our neighbors. We have duties towards them; we are not isles of loneliness. The attitude of respectful courtesy recommended by the Qur'an must of course be enlarged to the whole of humankind, believers and unbelievers, except for those who "do wrong," that is to say, those who are unjust and violent and resort deliberately to the argument of the fist, physically or in words. In such a case it is much better to avoid a so-called dialogue in order to avoid worse.

In short, from the Muslim perspective that is mine, our duty is simply to bear witness in the most courteous way that is most respectful of the inner liberty of our neighbors and their sacredness. We must also be ready at the same time to listen to them in truthfulness. We have to remember, as Muslims, that a *hadith* of our Prophet states: "The believer is unceasingly in search of wisdom, wherever he finds it he grasps it." Another saying adds: "Look for knowledge everywhere, even as far as in China." And finally, it is up to God to judge, for we, as limited human beings, know only in part. Let me quote:

To each among you have We prescribed a Law and an Open Way. And if God had enforced His Will, He would have made of you all one people. But His plan is to test you in what He hath given you. So strive as in a race in all virtues. The goal of you all is to God. Then will He inform you of that wherein you differed (5:51).

Say: O God! Creator of the heavens and the earth! Knower of all that is hidden and open! It is thou that wilt judge between Thy Servants in those matters about which they have differed (39:46).

Beyond the limits imposed by traditional theology

Though all Muslims are bound by the Qur'an's basic teachings, Muslim traditional theology developed in a way that, for historical reasons, does not, in my opinion, always fit in with the spirit of the Qur'an. Let us briefly recall two important cases: on the one hand, the *dhimmis* case, that is to say, the situation of the religious minorities inside the Islamic empire during medieval times, and, on the other hand, the apostate case.

Let us start with the *dhimmis*. First, we must emphasize that, although the doors of many countries (not all of them, however) were opened (*fath*) by force or *Jihad*[3]—as it was the general custom then—to pave the way for Islam, in practice Islam itself has almost never been imposed by compulsion. On this point the Qur'anic teachings have been followed. They provided the *dhimmis* with a sound protection against the most unbearable forms of religious intolerance. In particular, with two or three historical exceptions, the *dhimmis* have never been prevented from following the religion of their choice, from worshipping, or from organizing their communities in accordance with their own law. We can even say that in the beginning their situation was often greatly improved by Islamic conquest. They enjoyed long periods of tolerance and real prosperity, very often holding high positions in the administrative, court, and economic activities.

But it is a fact that at certain times and places they suffered from discrimination. Roughly speaking, things began seriously to worsen for them from the reign of al-Mutawakkil (847–61CE). The discrimination, especially in matters of dress, took an openly humiliating shape. The oppression culminated in Egypt during the reign of al-Hakim (996–1021CE), who perhaps was insane.

In the medieval context of wars, hostilities, and treacheries, this policy of discrimination or open oppression was always prompted, or strongly backed, by the theologians. To understand that, we have to remember that it was not then a virtue—according to the medieval mentality everywhere in the world, and within all communities—to consider all human beings as equal. How could one consider as equal Truth and Error, true believers and heretics?

Thus in our appraisal of the past we must always take the circumstances into account, but above all we must strive to avoid the recurrence of the same situations and errors. In any case, the Qur'an's basic teachings, the inner meaning of which we tried to put into relief, lay down for us a clear line of conduct. They teach us to respect the dignity of the other and his/her total freedom. In a world where giant holocausts have been perpetrated, where human rights are still at stake, manipulated or totally ignored, our modern Muslim theologians must denounce loudly all kinds of discrimination as crimes strictly and explicitly condemned by the Qur'an's basic teachings.

However, we must consider the apostate case. In this field, too, traditional theology did not follow the spirit of the Qur'an. This theology abridged seriously the liberty of choice of one's religion. According to this theology, though the conversion to Islam must be, and is in fact, without coercion,[4] it is practically impossible, once inside Islam, to get out of it. The conversion from Islam to another religion is considered treason, and the apostate is liable to the penalty of death. The traditional theologians in their elaboration rely on the one hand on the precedent of the first caliph of Islam, Abu Bakr (632–34CE), who energetically fought the tribes that rejected his authority after the Prophet's death and refused to pay him the alms taxes, likening their rebellion to apostasy. On the other hand the theologians mainly put forward the authority of this *hadith*: "Anyone who changes his religion must be put to death."

I know of no implementation throughout the history of Islam of the law condemning the apostate to death—until the hanging of Mahmoud Taha in the Sudan in 1985.[5] This law has remained mostly theoretical, but it is not irrelevant to draw attention to the fact that during the 1970s, in Egypt, the Islamic conservatives narrowly missed enforcing this law against Copts who, without due consideration, converted to Islam, generally to marry Muslim women, and who, in case of the failure of the marriage, returned to their former religion. Recently, too, some Tunisian atheists expressed their concern. So, the case of the apostate in Islam, though mostly theoretical, needs to be cleared up.

Let us first point out that the *hadith* upon which the penalty of death essentially rests is always more or less mixed with rebellion and highway robbery in the Tradition books. The cited cases of "apostates" killed during the Prophet's life or shortly after his death are all without exception of persons who as consequence of their "apostasy" turned their weapons against the Muslims, whose community at that time was still small and vulnerable.

The penalty of death appears in these circumstances as an act of self-defense in a war situation. It is undoubtedly for that reason that the Hanafi school of *fiqh* does not condemn a woman apostate to death, "because women, contrary to men, are not fit for war."

Further, the *hadith* authorizing the death penalty is not, technically, *mutawatir*,[6] and consequently it is not, according to the traditional system of *hadith*, binding. Above all, from a modern point of view, this *hadith* can and must be questioned. In my opinion, there are many persuasive reasons to consider it undoubtedly forged. It may have been forged under the influence of Leviticus (24:16) and Deuteronomy (13:219)—where the stoning of the apostate to death is ordered—if not directly, then perhaps indirectly through the Jews and Christians converted to Islam.

In any case, the *hadith* in question is as a matter of fact at variance with the teachings of the Qur'an, where there is no mention of a required death penalty against the apostate. Even during the life of the Prophet, the case presented itself at various times, and several verses of the Qur'an deal with it. In all these verses, without a single exception, the punishment of the apostate who persists in rejection of Islam after having embraced it is left to God's judgment and to the afterlife. In all the cases mentioned in the Qur'an, and by the commentators, it is a question, on the one hand, of timeservers—individuals or tribes, who, according to the circumstances, became turncoats—and, on the other hand, of hesitating persons attracted to the faith of the "People of the Book" (2:109, 3:99–100), Jews and Christians. Always taking into account the special situation, the Qur'an argues, warns, or recommends the proper attitude to be adopted, without ever threatening death.

From a Muslim perspective, the Qur'an recognizes all the previous Revelations and authenticates and perfects them:

> Say: We believe in God, and in what has been revealed to us, and what was revealed to Abraham, Ishmael, Isaac, Jacob and the Tribes, and in that which was given to Moses, Jesus, and the Prophets, from their Lord. We make no distinction between anyone of them, and to God we submit (*muslimun*) (3:84).

It does not follow that all are permitted, at the convenience of the moment, to change their religion as they change their coats. Such behavior denotes in fact a lack of true faith. It is for this reason that the following verse insists on the universal significance of Islam, as a call directed to the whole of humankind: "If anyone desires a religion other than Islam, never will it be accepted of him; and in the Hereafter he will be among the losers" (3:85).

Accordingly, the apostates are warned: those who choose apostasy, after being convinced in their innermost thoughts that Islam is the truth, are unjust, and as such they are bereft of God's guidance, with all the consequences that follow for their salvation. "How shall God guide those who reject faith after they accepted it, and bore witness that the Apostle was true, and that clear signs had come to them? But God guides not a people unjust" (3:86; see also verses 87–91).

Nevertheless, the Qur'an denounces the attitude of "the People of the Book," who exerted pressure on the newly converted to Islam to induce them to retract. There is no doubt that the polemics between the dawning Islam and the old religions were sharp. In this atmosphere the Qur'an urges the persons who espoused Islam to adhere firmly to their new faith, till their death, to close their ranks, to refuse to listen to those who strive to lure them to apostasy, and to avoid their snares. They are also reminded of their former state of disunion when they were "on the brink of the Pit of Fire," and they are exhorted to be a people "inviting to all that is good" in order to ensure their final salvation. Let us quote:

> Say: O People of the Book: Why obstruct ye those who believe from the Path of God, seeking to make it crooked, while ye were yourselves witness thereof? But God is not unmindful of all that ye do.
>
> O ye who believe! If you obey a faction of those who have been given the Book, they will turn you back into disbelievers after you have believed.
>
> And how would you disbelieve, while to you are rehearsed the signs of God, and His Messenger is among you? And he who holds fast to God is indeed guided to the Right Path.
>
> O ye who believe! Fear God as He should be feared, and die not except in a state of Islam.
>
> And hold fast, all together, by the Rope of God, and be not divided, and remember God's favor on you: for ye were enemies and He joined your Hearts in love, so that by His Grace, ye became brethren; and ye were on the brink of the Pit of Fire, and He saved you from it. Thus doth God make His Signs clear to you, that ye may be guided.
>
> Let there arise out of you a Community inviting to all that is good, enjoining what is right, and forbidding what is wrong. They are the ones to attain felicity (3:99–104).

Thus, unceasingly and by all means, the Qur'an strives to raise the new Muslims' spirit, in order to prevent them from falling into apostasy. The argumentation is only moral, however. The Qur'an goes on: It is "from selfish envy" (2:109) that "quite a number of the People of the Book wish they could turn you back to infidelity" (2:109; see also 3:149); you have not to fear them, "God is your Protector, and He is the best of helpers, soon shall He cast terror into the hearts of the unbelievers" (3:150–1); "your real friends are God, His Messenger, and the believers ... it is the party of God that must certainly triumph ... therefore take not for friends those who take your religion for a mockery or sport" (5:58–60). And finally, those who, in spite of all that, allow themselves to be tempted by apostasy are forewarned: if they desert the cause, the cause nevertheless will not fail. Others will carry it forward:

> O ye who believe! If any from among you turn back from his faith, soon will God produce a people whom He will love as they will love Him, holy with the Believers, mighty against the Rejecters, striving in the way of God, and never afraid of the reproaches of a fault finder. That is the grace of God, which He will bestow on whom He pleases. And God is bountiful, All-Knowing (5:57; see also 47:38).

Finally the apostates are given this notice: they "will not injure God in the least, but He will make their deeds of no effect" (47:32).

The young Muslim community was thus given many reasons to adhere to its new religion. The members of this community are also warned that for their salvation they should not depart from their faith. They are urged to follow the true spirit of Islam, and this spirit is defined in two ways: first, they will love God and God will love them; second, they will be humble among their brothers and sisters, but they will not fear the wrongdoers, and they will not join with them. If by fear, weakness, or time-serving, they depart from this line of conduct and fall into apostasy, the loss will be their own, and the punishment will be hard in the hereafter. "And if any of them turn back from their faith, and die in unbelief, their works will bear no fruit in this life. And in the Hereafter they will be companions of the Fire, and will abide therein" (2:217). The apostates lay themselves open to "the curse of God, of His angels, and of all mankind" (3:87), "except for those who repent thereafter, and amend, for God is Oft-Forgiving, Most Merciful" (3:89). But there is no hope for those who persist in their apostasy (3:90–1). These obstinate apostates will "taste the penalty for rejecting faith" (3:106; see also 3:140). Such persons are entirely in the hands of evil (47:25). They secretly plot with the enemies (47:26–7), and "they obstruct the way to God" (47:2, 34). As a result "God will not forgive them" (47:34).

How should such obstinate and ill-disposed apostates be dealt with? How should those be treated who try to draw others into their camp or to manipulate others? Let us underline once more that there is no mention in the Qur'an of any kind of penalty, neither death nor any other one. To use the technical Arab word, we would say that there is no specified *hadd*[7] in this matter. On the contrary, the Muslims are advised to "forgive and overlook till God accomplishes His purpose, for God hath power over all things" (2:109). In other words, there is no punishment on earth. The case is not answerable to the Law. The debate is between God and the apostate's conscience, and it is not our role to interfere in it.

Muslims are authorized to take up arms only in one case, the case of self-defense, when they are attacked and their faith is seriously jeopardized. In such a case "fighting" (*al-qital*) is "prescribed" (*kutiba*) for them, even if they "dislike it" (*kurhun lakum*) (2:216), and it is so even during the sacred month of Pilgrimage (2:217, 2:194). To summarize, Muslims are urged not to yield when their conscience is at stake and to rise up in arms against "those who will not cease fighting you until they turn you back from your faith, if they can" (2:217).

It is thus evident that the problem of religious liberty, with all its ramifications, is not new within Islam. The Qur'an deals at length with it. At the heart of this problem we meet the ticklish subject of apostasy, and we have seen that with regard to this subject the Qur'an argues, warns, and advises, but it never resorts to the argument of the sword. This is because that argument is meaningless in the matter of faith. In our pluralistic world our modern theologians must take that into account.

We can never stress too much that religious liberty is not an act of charity or a tolerant concession towards misled persons. It is, rather, a fundamental right of everyone. To claim it for myself implies *ipso facto* that I am disposed to claim it for my neighbor too. But religious liberty is not reduced to the equivalent of atheism. My right and my duty also, are to bear witness, by fair means, to my own faith and to convey God's call. Ultimately, however, it is up to each person to respond to this call or not, freely and in full consciousness.

From a Muslim perspective, and on the basis of the Qur'an's basic teachings, whose letter and spirit we have tried to adduce, religious liberty is fundamentally and ultimately an act of respect for God's sovereignty and for the mystery of God's plan for humanity, which has been given the terrible privilege of shaping entirely on its own responsibility its destiny on earth and hereafter. Ultimately, to respect humanity's freedom is to respect God's plan. To be a true Muslim is to submit to this plan. It is to put one's self, voluntarily and freely, with confidence and love, into the hands of God.

CHAPTER 6

Freedom of Religion and Belief in Islam

Mohsen Kadivar

Mohsen Kadivar was born in Fasa in south central Iran in 1959. He received a religious education in Qom, specializing in fiqh, *philosophy, theology, mysticism, and* tafsir. *In 1997 he earned a degree in* ijtihad, *and two years later he was awarded a PhD degree in Islamic philosophy by Tehran's Tarbiat Modarres University, where he currently teaches. Kadivar's reformist interpretations of Qur'anic exegesis, articulated in numerous books and essays, ran foul of Iran's conservative religious establishment and eventually led to his arrest in 1998. Released after 18 months, he has since emerged as one of the most ardent advocates of religious reform in Iran.*

Kadivar is the author of three influential books and a score of essays and journal articles on religious reformism. His books, all in Persian, include Hokumat-e Velayati *(Government of the Jurisconsult),* Nazariye-haye Dowlat dar Feqh-e Shi'a *(Perspectives on Government in Shi'a Theology), and* Daqdaqe-haye Hokumat-e Dini *(Crises of Religious Government). Despite his highly influential role in the evolution of the modernist religious discourse in Iran, Kadivar and his writings remain largely unknown to the outside world, although that is beginning to change slowly thanks largely to the Internet, where many of his writings, some with English translations, can be accessed on* www.kadivar. com.

Published here with the author's kind permission, the following is the editor's English translation of a paper Professor Kadivar presented at the International Congress of Human Rights and the Dialogue of Civilizations in Tehran, held on May 6, 2001. All verses of the Qur'an quoted here are drawn from A.J. Arberry's The Koran Interpreted *(New York: Macmillan, 1955).*

Freedom of religion and belief means an individual's right to freely choose any and all ideologies and religions he likes. It also means the freedom and the right to think, to have beliefs and values, to express one's religion and opinions, to partake in religious rites and practices, and to freely teach religious values to one's children and to coreligionists. Similarly, freedom of religion entails the right to invite others to one's religion, to preach and propagate one's religion to other members of society, to build places of worship, to leave and renounce one's religion, and to be able to freely critique one's religion and religious teachings. Freedom of religion means doing all these freely so long as others' rights and liberties are not infringed upon, and public order and morality are not disturbed. Freedom of religion and belief will become possible when, regardless of the beliefs that an individual may have, he is not persecuted for them and his civic and individual rights are not taken away because of them.

Common interpretations of Islam divide people into the three groups: Muslims, the People of the Book, and *kuffar* (heathens). Each of these three groups faces obstacles in some of the liberties laid out above, resulting in the negation of some basic religious and doctrinal freedoms in Islam. These commonplace restrictions on religious liberty are frequently based on interpretations derived from Qur'anic verses and the traditions that are attributed to the Prophet Muhammad. As will be shown, these interpretations often fall significantly short of capturing the essence of the Holy Book or a particular Prophetic tradition and, in fact, often contradict them.

In my opinion, freedom of religion and belief is inherently and rationally good and is accepted by those with superior wisdom and knowledge. Also, the Holy Qur'an, in seven clusters of its verses, while introducing the correct and just religion, endorses the plurality of religions and beliefs. It recognizes people's rights to freely choose their own religions while forcefully renouncing the compulsion to impose a specific religion on others. Islam has not determined any type of earthly punishment for false religious and doctrinal beliefs, although it has warned those who turn their back on the Just Religion of divine punishment at the end of time.

The persecution of a heathen is unjustified in Islam. Through renewed *ijtihad* (independent reasoning), and based on the correct principles of the Qur'an and the *hadith*, freedom of religion and belief can be achieved through Islam.

One of the basic assumptions in the dialogue of the civilizations is accepting the plurality of beliefs and religions. Civilizations are based on different cultures, and different cultures have their foundations in various schools of thought and religions. Dialogue between civilizations and cultures is not possible without freedom of religion and thought.

Today there is a culture dominant in Iran that proposes the idea of dialogue between civilizations. This culture is, of course, based on Islam. However, popular interpretations of Islam, both official and traditional, do not seem to reflect such a desire for dialogue. Indeed, it appears as if the call for dialogue stems from a somewhat uncommon interpretation of Islam. The purpose of this paper is to highlight and outline that interpretation of Islam which supports and guarantees the freedom of religion and thought.

Doing so requires answering the following questions: What does freedom of thought and religion mean? What is the treatment accorded to freedom of religion in the Universal Declaration of Human Rights? How do popular Islamic interpretations treat the issue of freedom of belief and religion, and on what religious documents are such interpretations based? Are freedoms of belief and religion beneficial or are they destructive? What are some of the main characteristics of that interpretation of Islam that recognizes freedom of religion, and on what religious grounds is it based?

The thesis of this chapter is that freedom of belief and religion are desirable. To reach such freedoms through Islam requires studying some of the fundamental rules of the religion and a renewed *ijtihad* in certain aspects of Islamic *fiqh*.

The first section of this chapter examines some of Islam's fundamental concepts. In the second section, notions of freedom of religion and belief as understood in popular interpretations of Islam are analyzed, along with those references that support such notions. The paper then looks at why freedom of thought and religion are beneficial for society at large and ought to be sought after. The paper concludes with a critique of popular interpretations of Islam and asserts that a correct understanding of Islamic sources and its foundational principles would make the religion inherently supportive of the freedom of thought and belief.

Explaining concepts

Some of the concepts that are used in this discussion include notions such as freedom, belief, religion, freedom of thought, freedom of religion, Islam, popular interpretation (of religion), and the documents of the Universal Declaration of Human Rights.

Freedom: The right of choice in beliefs and in actions in all areas so long as these beliefs and actions do not deprive others of their rights or do not disturb public peace and order.

Belief: The collection of viewpoints, opinions, values, and impressions that each individual has concerning existence, society, history, humanity, religion, culture, etc. Every belief is considered correct, honest, useful, and superior by the person who believes in it, while, at the same time, it may be considered void, deceptive, and destructive by others.

Religion or creed: A kind of idea, a collection of viewpoints about human-ity, the physical world and beyond; ethical guidelines and practical rules for the believer to obey and follow in order to achieve eternal bliss through faith and the deeds that have been brought to humanity by the Prophet.

Freedom of belief: The right to choose and adhere to any idea; the right to think, believe, express, teach, promote, and act on one's beliefs so long as the rights of others are not obstructed and public peace and order is not disrupted; freedom of belief is realized when the beliefs of a person do not lead to the deprivation of his individual and social rights no matter what they may be.

Freedom of religion: The right to choose any religion; the right to practice one's faith and to worship freely, to express religious beliefs and to engage in its rituals freely; freedom of religion entails the right to invite others to one's religion, to preach and propagate one's religion to other members of society, to build temples, to leave and renounce one's religion, and to critique one's religion and religious teachings; religious freedom is realized when one's religious beliefs do not result in one's persecution and one's individual and civil rights are not taken away because of them.

Islam: Belief in Allah, resurrection, and the prophecy of Muhammad ibn Abdullah, the last Prophet of God. The Holy Qur'an—the collection of holy Revelations to His Prophet—and the Prophet's *sunna*, are the two main sources of Islam. Sunnism and Shi'ism are the main branches of Islam. Shi'ism means that after the Qur'an and the Prophetic tradition, exegesis (*tafsir*) by the Household of the Prophet (*Ahl-e Beyt*) of the Holy Book and the *sunna* are taken as the third source of main religious doctrine. Sunnism does not formally endorse the purity of anyone other that the person of the Prophet, although it does hold some members of the Prophet's household in high esteem.

The popular interpretation of religion: The dominant understanding of the Qur'an and the *sunna* that is often found in the judgments and enunciations of religious scholars and the ulama, and has generally become accepted and practiced throughout the Muslim world, thereby shaping Muslim history and deed. This popular interpretation of Islam is often dominant in coun-tries ruled over by Islamic governments. Over the last century, a number of reformist thinkers have questioned the legitimacy of this particular interpre-tation of Islam through reliance on the Qur'an and the *sunna* (and for the

Shi'as the examples set by those in the Prophet's immediate household).

The Universal Declaration of Human Rights: The international declarations, pacts, and protocols that have been legislated, with different dimensions, by a majority of sovereign states in the latter half of the twentieth century and are taken as universal standards to observe; signatory states may accept these documents either wholly or conditionally.

The most important documents concerning the freedom of thought and religion are the Universal Declaration of Human Rights, the International Covenant on Civil and Political Rights, and the Islamic Declaration of Human Rights, issued in Cairo in 1991.

Freedom of religion and belief in popular interpretations of Islam

From the perspective of religious beliefs, people can be divided into three groups: Muslims; Jews, Christians, and Zoroastrians, known collectively as the "People of the Book;" and others. The popular interpretation of Islam has rendered different judgments for each of these groups. We will first refer to the most original sources concerning these judgments, and then we will consider the references through which they are substantiated.

Muslims

Muslims are free to openly practice their religion, express their religious beliefs, practice their rituals alone or in groups, teach religion to their children and to all other believers, engage in the rituals of Hajj, propagate and promote their religious beliefs to others, and to build mosques. They have the right to critique other religions, reveal the shortcomings of other value systems, and to demonstrate the supremacy of Islam. Nobody has the right to force a Muslim to renounce his religion under duress or to prevent him from partaking in religious rituals.

On these points there is consensus and unanimity. But in a number of other areas, popular interpretations of Islam restrict one's freedom in many ways. They include:

1. The Muslim is not free to change his religion by becoming a Christian or a Buddhist, for example, or to become an atheist. A Muslim who for any reason leaves his religion, or, in other words, becomes an apostate, is to be severely punished. The child of a Muslim who has chosen to become a Muslim after maturity and then becomes an apostate will receive the following punishment: his repentance and embrace of Islam are not accepted;

he will be executed; his wife will be separated from him without divorce and will get the period of abstention in the case of the husband's death (three consecutive menstrual cycles); his property will be divided among his heirs.

A person born to non-Muslims who then embraces Islam before renouncing it has three days to repent. If the repentance takes place before the end of the third day after the renunciation, it is accepted. Otherwise, the person is considered an apostate and is subject to capital punishment. Additionally, as soon as he becomes an apostate, his spouse will be separated from him without divorce. If a Muslim woman becomes an apostate, her spouse will be separated from her without divorce and the period of abstention in the case of divorce (three consecutive menstrual cycles) will be necessary. If she repents, her repentance will be accepted and she will be spared. Otherwise, she will be imprisoned for life, with hard labor, until she either repents or dies. Therefore, a male Muslim who becomes an apostate and does not return to Islam will be executed, and a female Muslim doing so will be sentenced to life imprisonment with forced labor.

2. A Muslim is not free to deny the righteousness of, or to have opinions other than, the body of religious knowledge that has evolved through custom and tradition. An apostate is any Muslim whose beliefs and opinions cast doubt on the prophecy of God's Messenger or the *Sharia*, and he will be punished accordingly. During the course of Islamic history, a number of Muslim scholars have been accused of apostasy for these very reasons, Avicenna being a notable example.

3. A young person born to at least one Muslim parent must remain a Muslim after reaching puberty. If, for whatever reason, he chooses not to become a Muslim, he will be considered an apostate and will be sentenced accordingly. First he will be asked to repent, and if he does not accept, depending on his gender, he will be sentenced to death or to life imprisonment with hard labor, the sentence to be terminated by either death or repentance.

4. A Muslim may not knowingly and intentionally violate the tenets of Islam. If he does so, his punishment will be determined by a *Sharia* judge (an example of such a punishment would be flogging).

The People of the Book

The People of the Book include Christians and Jews. Zoroastrians and Sabians are also among the People of the Book. All others are infidels and may in no way be considered as belonging to the People of the Book. It is incumbent upon Muslims to wage war on the People of the Book in order to confront them with one of two choices: to either accept Islam, or, if choosing to remain loyal to another religion, to pay the *jizyah* (tax levied on non-Muslims) and to accept their separate treatment under Islam.

If they accept these terms, their lives, their property, and their women will be safe. The leader of the Muslim community will determine the amount of the *jizyah* and the conditions under which the protected subjects will live. If it is determined that they may eventually become Muslims, they are free to openly practice their own religion and express their beliefs. They may even be granted the permission to keep their places of worship and to freely partake in their religious ceremonies both individually and in groups. They are also free to critique their own religion, to leave it for another protected religion, or to become Muslim.

The People of the Book living under the protection of the Muslim ruler do not have the right to engage in certain types of religious activities. Most notably:

1. They may not raise their offspring such that they would adopt the religion of their fathers and be forbidden from attending Islamic gatherings and propaganda centers. Instead, the youth must be left alone to choose their own religion, and Islam is no doubt the natural choice.
2. They are not free to build churches, synagogues, monasteries, or fire temples.
3. They are not free to propagate and promote their religion and to weaken the beliefs of Muslims.
4. They cannot criticize the Islamic teachings.
5. They cannot openly practice what is permissible in their own religion but is prohibited in Islam.
6. They are not free to convert from their original religion to any religion other than Islam, Christianity, Judaism, or Zoroastrianism. Doing so is punishable by death.
7. They do not have permission to remain in the Islamic community if they do not abide by their obligations. There are varying opinions on whether they can seek refuge elsewhere or whether the leader of the Muslim community has the right to put them to death.

Infidels

All non-Muslims who have not accepted the conditions under which they are mandated to live in the Islamic community, whether or not they are People of the Book, are considered to be infidels and must face *Jihad*. The struggle against them shall continue until and unless they accept Islam or are all killed. All their wives and children will be taken as slaves and their land and property will be confiscated. Although most well-known Shi'a scholars do not see *Jihad* as permissible during the occultation (of the Hidden Imam), today the permissibility of *Jihad* before the Imam's arrival is widely accepted.

To sum up, then, the non-Muslim who refuses to accept Islam or to abide by its preconditions for the Book of People has forfeited the right to live, not to mention other civil rights, including the right of religion and belief.

A look at popular Islamic interpretations concerning the three groups—namely the Muslims, the People of the Book, and the infidels—reveals that these interpretations are inimical to freedom of religion and creed. Consequently, the more political power that the proponents of such interpretations get, the more scarce religious freedoms become. The evidence presented here is incontrovertible: most available interpretations of Islam do not welcome the freedom of religion and belief. There are innumerable *sunnas*, many of them authentic and verifiable, that support these interpretations of Islam and the judgments derived from them. Some of these *sunnas* and *hadiths* include the following:

> Kill anyone who changes his religion (The Prophet Muhammad).

> It is permissible to spill the blood of any Muslim who leaves Islam and denies Muhammad's prophetic mission and accuses him of falsehood. That apostate must also have his wife separated from him as he would be considered dead, his property divided among his heirs, and his repentance would not be accepted (Imam Ja'far Sadiq).

> A Muslim who converts to Christianity must be killed and his repentance will not be accepted. But if a Christian converts to Islam and then become an apostate, his repentance would be acceptable (Imam Musa ibn Ja'far).

> A Muslim woman who becomes an apostate shall not be killed but given life imprisonment with hard labor and must be deprived of all food and water except what is necessary to be kept alive. She must be given rough clothes to wear, and must be beaten in times of prayer (Imam Ja'far Sadiq).

Additionally, there are a number of Qur'anic verses that support the above traditions and the judgments based on them:

> Fight those who believe not in God and the Last Day and do not forbid what God and His Messenger have forbidden—such men as practice not the religion of truth, being of those who have been given the Book—until they pay the tribute out of hand and have been humbled (9:29).

> That is the right religion. So wrong not each other during them. And fight the unbelievers totally even as they fight you totally; and know what God is with the godfearing (9:36).

> Then, when the sacred months are drawn away, slay the idolaters wherever you find them, and take them at every place of ambush. But if they repent, and perform the prayer, and pay the alms, then let them go their way (9:5).

> Say to the unbelievers, if they give over He will forgive them what is past; but if they return, the wont of the ancients is already gone! (8:39).

Whether based on the Holy Book or the *sunna*, the evidence in support of Islam's denial of the freedom of religion and belief is substantial. These references will be analyzed critically below.

The desirability of freedom of religion and belief

This section will analyze the freedom of belief and religion from a rational perspective, without reference to narrative sources. First, the section will recreate the rationality of those who deny the validity of freedom of belief and religion. Then this rationality will be critiqued in order to demonstrate the superior rationality behind and the desirability of freedom of religion and belief.

Despite the seeming preponderance of evidence against freedom of religion and belief in Islam, the issue is not closed to discussion and can, in fact, be rationally discussed and critiqued. Undoubtedly, those who have expressed opinions in this regard have done so after rationally weighing its pluses and minuses. Religious scholars, commentators, and decision makers are no exception. Clearly, those issuing *fatwa*s in favor of restricting freedoms are more concerned about the disruptive and corrupting consequences that such freedoms might have, while those ruling in favor of them emphasize their advantages and benefits. Since the issue of freedom of religion and creed is a rational one, let us first examine it from a rational perspective.

Besides being a rational issue and not one of faith, the freedom to choose one's beliefs and creed predates religion. It is through this freedom that religion is chosen and belief is established. How could a religion, one that asks of its followers to explore for themselves and to choose their beliefs based on critical reason and thought, deny the necessity of freedom of religion and belief?

The results of a research project cannot be determined before the research itself takes place. It does not make sense to say that people are free to explore all religions and belief systems but must necessarily embrace Islam. If they are free then their choices cannot be predetermined, and if they have no options in their choices then they are not free. The key is the freedom of choice that is open to all thinking individuals. One cannot be expected to consciously choose a religion that will then take away one's free choice.

Unfortunately, religious scholars have not paid sufficient attention to the issue of freedom of religion and belief, therefore failing to construct an analytical framework for its understanding and exploration. This neglect has resulted in some key issues in Islam—such as the punishment of an apostate or the proper treatment of the People of the Book—not receiving the detailed attention that they deserve.

Let us critique some of the presuppositions on which denials of freedom of belief and religion are based. In addition to being influenced by prevailing popular sentiments, religious presuppositions against the freedom to choose one's religion are based on a number of assumptions. To begin with, it is often assumed that denying free choice in religion prevents unwanted views and values from polluting the popular mind, and guards people against the potential of becoming corrupted by deviant ideas and influences.

A second assumption revolves around the supposedly positive effects of heavy punishment in ensuring a morally upright society. Human nature is thought to require force and coercion to prevent its perversion. Excessive freedom is assumed to enable Satan to dominate one's life. With death as the prescribed punishment for apostasy, no one will dare leave Islam. If the People of the Book feel the humiliation of the *jizyah*, then they will surely convert to Islam, and if infidels have to choose between Islam and death, they will no doubt choose the former. Generally speaking, Islam is viewed as the only Just Religion that can dominate the world.

A third assumption deals with the forbidding of propaganda. The supposed inherent weakness of human nature makes it highly susceptible to propaganda. People are assumed to be gullible, easily to allow Satan into their lives, and just as easily lose their ways and values. The only plausible way to ensure that people do not lose their religion is to prohibit the propagation of other religions and beliefs. Otherwise, there is no guarantee that one's own religion will survive.

Fourth, the imposition of capital punishment for apostasy is seen as a common practice in many religions. Religions often clashed violently in the previous millennium. Therefore, stern dictates concerning remaining in one's religion were commonplace in the past and should not be shied away from or treated as an embarrassment.

The fifth assumption concerns the superficial propagation of Islam. It is obvious that the imperative to avoid a death sentence or the *jizyah* can prompt at best a superficial embracing of Islam. However, this will in no way lead to an in-depth, genuine acceptance of the faith. Indeed, it is worth asking if religious scholars do not have an obligation to ensure society's inner, true acceptance of religion rather that its superficial observance.

Despite the prevalence of each of these assumptions, their accuracy and depth is questionable. A summary critique of each is as follows:

First, astonishing innovations in means of communication have made closed societies impossible in today's world, and, whether we like it or not, there are numerous ways for different religious views to be expressed and propagated by their adherents.

Second, although fear and harsh punishments may compel people to engage in superficial observance of religion, they do little in bringing about true faith, and are in fact likely to have the opposite effect. We need to change our entire approach to the human race and to have trust in it. We must allow it to make free choices. The key is to make man realize that he can indeed make his own free choices.

Third, in today's world, hostile and violent encounters with other religious beliefs are uncalled for and cause repulsion and distaste rather than serving as a source of appeal and attraction.

Finally, how can one indeed endorse a set of religious dictates that repel others from that religion instead of causing them to endorse and internalize it?

The rational basis of religious and intellectual freedom

Given the above introduction to and critique of some of those religious justifications that seek to limit freedom of religion and opinion, we can now explore the dictates of reason concerning such liberties.

1. Religions and opinions are voluntary matters which people choose to endorse or abandon based on their own free will. Choosing a specific religion or set of beliefs requires the crystallization of certain conditions, and the disappearance of those conditions leads to the abandonment of that religion. So long as the conditions for the voluntary acceptance of religion are present, force and compulsion are not needed to draw people to it. And, inversely, if force and threats are used to keep people in a religion, then that religion is at best superficially observed rather than deeply internalized.

2. Obviously, not all religions and belief systems have the same degree of validity and, clearly, some are completely null and void. The most prudent way to reform and correct people's beliefs is through reason not compulsion. If they choose not to alter those beliefs that we consider void, there is not much more we can do. Force and compulsion lead to dissemination of false beliefs not their eradication. People will not accept a religion so long as they do not see it as a way of attaining inner peace and spiritual fulfillment. Historically, these have been the sustaining foundations of religions rather than the brute force with which some of their believers have sought to preserve and spread them. People change their beliefs and especially their religions very seldom. If they do change their religious beliefs, it is out of conviction rather than compulsion.

3. Going through life means being confronted with endless choices and tests. People are free to choose from among the endless array of religions and beliefs to which they are exposed, whether just or unjust, valid or invalid. In our opinion, they are answerable for their choices at the end of time. If God wanted to, he would have actually forced people to choose justice, or He would have brought about conditions in which people had no choice but to choose the just path. He would have created man from the same mold as angels and freed their world of struggles between the just and the unjust. If that were the case, however, the eternal rewards of those choosing justice and the punishment of those choosing injustice would have been meaningless.

4. History shows that a plurality of ideas and beliefs among people is inevitable. Amid the plethora of choices confronting people, limiting the choice of religion and belief leads to discord, deceit, and hypocrisy. Those who would be persecuted or killed for spreading false beliefs have no choice but to feign obedience to whatever religion happens to be dominant at the time. Hypocrisy undermines and destroys faith. Robbing people of their right to choose their religious beliefs only results in the spread of discord and hypocrisy.

5. Many religions and beliefs consider themselves to be the most exalted, most perfect, and the most definitive, and their believers no doubt accept them as such. The Almighty will decide whether or not they indeed are as exalted as they claim to be. Nevertheless, after centuries of such claims by competing religions, none has yet managed to convince everyone of its exclusive monopoly over the truth. If the followers of every religion claimed

such exclusivity, religious societies would become stalled and closed, and, instead, non-religious and secular societies would be highly dynamic and vibrant. The real danger would then be the attraction of the masses to the vibrancy and dynamicism of secular societies and, consequently, the inevitable undermining of religious values.

6. Restricting religious freedom requires an official reading of religion and the suppression of any type of innovative thinking and *ijtihad* (independent reasoning). Under such conditions, society is robbed of any fruitful contributions by its intellectuals.

7. Prohibiting religious freedom and the right to change religions, even denying coreligionists the right to change their religion, is ultimately counterproductive. In such a case, very few individuals from outside one's religion are likely to become believers.

8. The disadvantages of prohibiting religious freedom are so weighty that they discourage any rational individual from embracing it. If those religious scholars who issue *fatwas* in opposition to religious freedom were more rational and less narrow-minded, they would change their minds as well. It is especially important to properly educate children and youth, a task whose burden falls primarily on the parents. Additionally, in a free society, all the activities and efforts of religious propagandists are subject to the rule of law, and no person of faith may trample on the legal rights of others or disrupt public order, morality, and security under the pretext of religious activity.

9. Those religions and beliefs that rest on solid foundations do not fear competing in the marketplace of ideas with other religions. It is only weak value systems and religions that fear such a competition and, therefore, seek to avoid it by prohibiting the freedom to change one's religion.

10. It does not make sense to maintain that there is a fundamental difference between freedom of thought and freedom of belief and that the former is acceptable but the latter is not. Thought does not require permission from any source, and it cannot be granted as a favor or a privilege by anyone. The point of contention is over the freedom of belief and the right to act on those beliefs. Differentiating between thought and belief is not the solution to the issue. Those who engage in this type of hairsplitting are the same ones who advocate limiting freedom of religion and belief.

Based on the discussion above, we can conclude that from a rational perspective, freedom of religion and belief is reasonable and logical, and therefore beneficial and positive.

An alternative interpretation

This section addresses two issues. First, it presents Islam's perspective on the notion of freedom of religion and belief. Second, it critiques Muslim perspectives that negate such a freedom. Before exploring these two subjects, however, it is important to address the question of whether or not freedom of religion is a given fact: do we need a reason to justify freedom of religion, or is it accepted *a priori*? Obviously, by freedom of religion and belief we mean worldly freedom. For the true followers of the Just Religion—Islam— does belief in other religions and creeds mean apostasy and is it punishable or not? Establishing an *a priori* base ('*asl*), therefore, is important.

It appears that this *a priori* base rests on the premise that apostates and those People of the Book who refuse to pay the *jizyah* are free of guilt. Those who transgress against Islam are not guilty simply because they are transgressors. Their specific sins must be proven. Besides, worldly punishment cannot be meted out against all sins, and some sins are punished in the other world. Therefore, if a valid justification for a person's guilt and for his worldly punishment cannot be found, he must be found not guilty.

Scriptural proof of freedom of religion and belief in Islam

There are a number of Qur'anic verses that support the notion of freedom of religion and belief. These verses can be divided into seven categories. The first category of verses prohibit compelling people to change their religion to Islam or to remain within it. Of these verses, some are of particular importance, especially the following:

> No compulsion is there in religion. Rectitude has become clear from error. So whosoever disbelieves in idols and believes in God, has laid hold of the most firm handle, unbreaking; God is All-hearing, All-knowing (2:256).

This verse contains prohibitions and negations—negating the assumption that the Almighty has based faith on force and compulsion, and prohibiting the imposition of faith on others. After all, neither forced faith nor forced sin has any validity. The rejection of force and compulsion in this verse amounts to an endorsement of freedom to choose religions.

This requires freedom in two endeavors: the freedom to enter into a religion, and also the freedom to leave it. The choice between a particular religion or death is tantamount to denying people their freedom. If people are free to enter into a religion but are then prohibited from leaving it, their continued endorsement of that religion is possible only through the threat of punishment and fear. The Holy Qur'an has mandated that belief in God is a right. The Qur'an is also very clear in distinguishing between what is just and unjust without seeking to compel people to choose one or the other. As Ayatollah Ha'eri Yazdi had argued previously,

> an analysis of the exalted verses of the Qur'an demonstrates that the Holy Book has not prohibited religious compulsion in Islam alone and that any kind of force and compulsion in other belief systems and faiths is also null and void. The freedom of choice in faith is inherently congruent with human nature; it can be neither granted nor taken away.[1]

According to tradition, the verse quoted above was revealed in response to the forced conversion to Islam of a servant by one of the members of the Ansar, which the Qur'an henceforth prohibited. According to others, the verse was revealed in response to a query made by one of the Prophet's apostles named Abulhussien, a member of the Ansar whose merchant sons had converted to Christianity. In response, the verse states "there is no compulsion in religion."

There can be no doubt, therefore, that the administration of capital punishment for an apostate, or forcing infidels to choose between Islam or death, has no sanction in Islam and, in fact, contradicts the above verse.

> And if thy Lord had willed, whoever is in the earth would have believed, all of them, all together. Wouldst thou then constrain the people, until they are believers (10:99)?

While belief in God and Judgment Day is just and correct, the Almighty has not sought to control people's religions and has, instead, given them free will. If free will did not exist, sin and atonement would be meaningless. Religion and faith are meaningful only when people can freely choose them. When the Prophet disparaged some of the people's refusal to accept Islam, and when he become insistent that others must accept his religion, the Almighty reminded him that if God does not endorse the imposition of faith on people, then His messenger cannot do so either. In the same vein, if people cannot be coerced into becoming Muslims, then they cannot be forced to stay in the religion either. Despite the fact that Islam is the right and just religion, God has not given anyone the right to force this just religion on others. How can people be confronted with a choice between Islam and execution? Of course, the right thing to do would be to stay faithful and not to exchange faith for sin. But how can we use such threats as death and other forms of capital punishment to ensure that people remain Muslims?

According to the Qur'an, when Noah addressed his flock,

> He said, "O my people, what think you? If I stand upon a clear sign from my Lord, and He has given me mercy from Him, and it has been obscured for you, shall we compel you to it while you are averse to it?" (11:28)

When Noah declared his prophecy, he was confronted with resistance and denunciation. In response, he invited those who refuted him to contemplate the possibility that he might indeed be a messenger of God, a possibility that they had not considered before. A prophet does not have the right to force people to accept him. And, accordingly, that prophet's disciples do not have such a right either and may not coerce people into accepting their religion.

The conclusion to be drawn from the verses quoted here is clear: we cannot and may not force anyone to accept a particular faith, or resort to repression or the threat of punishment to ensure that someone does not abandon his religion. Freedom of religion means prohibiting the use of force and compulsion in religious matters.

A second category of verses in the Qur'an stipulates the necessity of freedom in finding or losing one's way in the world.

> Say: "The truth is from your Lord; so let whosoever will believe, and let whosoever will disbelieve." Surely We have prepared for the evildoers a fire, whose pavilion encompasses them (18:29).

Even though there is no doubt in the righteousness of Islam, the Qur'an clearly states that everyone is free to remain in Islam and that anyone who wishes to depart from it is free to do so. The sinner's only punishment is in the afterlife. The Qur'an does not mandate worldly punishment for the infidel. In the above verse, the Almighty reminds individuals that they are free to choose their religion and warns them of the punishment they will receive on Judgment Day if they make the wrong choice. He also reminds believers that they may not contradict divine logic and employ violence and threats against those embracing other religions.

> Say: "O men, the truth has come to you from your Lord. Whosoever is guided is guided only to his own gain, and whosoever goes astray, it is only to his own loss. I am not a guardian over you." (10:108)

Obviously, the Qur'an differentiates between Islam and the wrong path, and between believers and infidels. What is important and is worthy of reward, however, is for man to choose the right path by himself. If there were only one path that everyone had to follow—the right path—then there would be no need for independent judgment, and for God's rewarding of good and His punishment of evil. The principle of resurrection on the Day of Judgment would be meaningless without free will.

> Surely We have sent down upon thee the Book for mankind with the truth. Whosoever is guided, is only guided to his own gain, and whosoever goes astray, it is only to his own loss; thou art not a guardian over them (39:41).

The Qur'an has shown people the just path. People are free to choose it or to ignore it; either way, they will get their reward or their punishment on Judgment Day. We have no right to force on people what God found unacceptable for His Prophet. The Almighty and His messenger allowed people the freedom to choose their religions, while, at the same time, telling them what the right path is. Those who have accepted the right path will reap the rewards on Judgment Day.

> I have only been commanded to serve the Lord of this territory which He has made sacred; to Him belongs everything. And I have been commanded to be of those that surrender, and to recite the Koran. So whosoever is guided, is only guided to his own gain; and whosoever goes astray, say: "I am naught but a warner." And say: "Praise belongs to God" (27:91–3).

The Prophet warned people against false beliefs and religions, gave them the Qur'an, and showed them the right religion and belief. Fortunate are those who followed him. As for those who did not, they have only hurt themselves and will be answerable for their mistake on Judgment Day. The Almighty is a careful observer and pays close attention to every choice that is made.

To sum up, this group of verses emphasize worldly freedom and the importance of free will in choosing one's religious beliefs.

In a third group of verses, the Prophet simply *advocates* Islam as the Just Religion rather than seeking to impose it on people. The Holy Qur'an is very precise on the exalted position of the Prophet in relation to religion and the people. The Prophet's responsibility is to spread the message of justice, to guide, and to enlighten. He may not force people to choose the Just Religion.

> Then remind them! Thou art only a reminder; thou art not charged to oversee them. But he who turns his back, and disbelieves, God shall chastise him with the greatest chastisement (88:21–2).

The Prophet does not rule over people and is not allowed to compel them to choose his religion. The message of the following verses is important to keep in mind:

We know very well what they say; thou art a tyrant over them. Therefore remind by the Koran him who fears My threat (50:45).

And they serve, apart from God, what neither profits them nor hurts them; and the unbeliever is ever a partisan against his Lord. We have sent thee not, except good tidings to bear, and warning (25:56–8).

Whether We show thee a part of that We promise them, or We call thee to Us, it is thine only to deliver the Message, and Ours the reckoning (13:40).

It is only for the Messenger to deliver the Message; and God knows what you reveal and what you hide (5:99).

If the Prophet, who is the personal embodiment of righteousness and the primary guardian of Islam, has no right in relation to the religion of others and is merely a guide, how could others give themselves the right to infringe on people's freedom of religion under the banner of Islam? It is up to the Almighty to weigh the validity and righteousness of people's beliefs and religions, and it is His messenger's duty to enlighten and to show people the path to salvation. Standing in judgment on the beliefs of others is to ascribe to one's self God-like qualities, something that the Almighty prohibited to man and to his Prophet.

A fourth group of verses prohibit the imposition of punishment on those who change their religion. There has been a long tradition in Islam of using force to prevent people from abandoning their religion and of imposing heavy punishments for apostasy. On three separate occasions, however, the Holy Qur'an condemns the punishment of an apostate.

Said the Council of those of his people who disbelieved, "Now, if you follow Shuaib, assuredly in that case you will be losers" (7:88).

Tribal notables told Shuaib that he and his followers had to either renounce their religion or leave the group. Shuaib responded that religious belief could not be abandoned through the threat of coercion or exile and that neither he nor his followers were willing to do so. This logic is consistent with that of the Qur'an.

By the same token, people cannot be forced to convert from an unjust to a just religion in the same manner that they cannot be forced to convert from a religion that is considered just. The Holy Qur'an is quite emphatic on this point.

Now you shall know! I shall assuredly cut off alternately your hands and feet, then I shall crucify you all together. They said, "Surely unto our Lord we are turning.

Thou takest vengeance upon us only because we have believed in the signs of our Lord when they came to us. Our Lord, pour out upon us patience, and gather us unto Thee surrendering."

Then said the Council of the people of Pharaoh, "Wilt thou leave Moses and his people to work corruption in the land, and leave thee and thy gods?"

Said he "We shall slaughter their sons and spare their women; surely we are triumphant over them!" (7:121–4).

Witnessing the miracles performed by the prophet Moses, the sorcerers abandoned their false religion and began to worship the Almighty. In other words, they became apostates. Distraught at the conversions without his permission, the pharaoh accused the apostates of plotting against the public good and decreed that they have their limbs cut off and then be executed. The punishment for apostasy in the Pharaoh's religion was execution.

He said, "O my Lord, help me, for that they cry me lies" (40:26).

The Qur'an rejects this logic. Instead, it endorses the logic of freedom of religion and creed, as is evident from these and from other similar verses.

The manner in which the leaders and guardians of different religions have confronted one another, and the Almighty's acceptance of different beliefs by man, are the subjects of a fifth group of Qur'anic verses.

Or if there had been, of the generations before you, men of a remainder forbidding corruption in the earth—except a few of those whom We delivered of them; but the evildoers followed the ease they were given to exult in and became sinners.

Yet thy Lord would never destroy the cities unjustly, while as yet their people were putting things right (11:118–19).

It is not the Divine Will for everyone to be of the same mind. The Almighty has given sanction to freedom of religion and belief, and has warned wrongdoers of what awaits them in hell. Forced uniformity of religious beliefs stands in sharp contradiction with Qur'anic and Islamic precepts.

So spoke those before them as these men say; their hearts are much alike. Yet We have made clear the signs unto a people who are sure. We have sent thee with the truth, good tidings to bear, and warning. Thou shalt not be questioned touching the inhabitants of Hell (2:113).

The Qur'an has condemned mutual acrimony among religions. People have the freedom to choose their own religion; final judgment is only that of the Almighty.

Say: "O unbelievers, I serve not what you serve and you are not serving what I serve, nor am I serving what you have served, neither are you serving what I serve. To you your religion, and to me my religion!" (109:1–5)

This verse, entitled "The Unbelievers," is one of the most central proofs in support of freedom of religion and belief in Islam. Can the approach of Muslims to other faiths and religions be anything other than what is mandated here?

A sixth group of verses prohibit the imposition of earthly punishment for apostasy. Although the Holy Qur'an rejects turning away from the just religion and becoming an apostate, its logic does not determine any earthly punishments for apostasy and only warns of divine wrath on the Day of Judgment. In this connection, two verses are of great significance:

> They will question thee concerning wine, and arrow-shuffling. Say: "In both is heinous sin, and uses of men, but the sin in them is more heinous than the usefulness."

> They will question thee concerning what they should expend. Say: "The Abundance." So God makes clear His signs to you; haply you will reflect; in this world, and the world to come (2:216–17).

While these verses refer to the punishment of sinners, they do not speak of their execution or murder. The reference here is to death by causes other than intentional punishment for apostasy. In fact, the only punishment mentioned is in the afterlife, and there is no mention of capital punishment or exile. Elsewhere in the verse, the repentance of an apostate is accepted as valid so long as it leads to the true embracing of Islam.

> Surely those who disbelieve, and die disbelieving, there shall not be accepted from any one of them the whole earth full of gold, if he would ransom himself thereby; for them awaits a painful chastisement, and they shall have no helpers.

> You will not attain a piety until you expend of what you love; and whatever thing you expend, God knows of it.

> All food was lawful to the Children of Israel save what Israel forbade for himself before the Torah was sent down. Say "Bring you the Torah now, and recite it, if you are truthful."

> Whoso forges falsehood against God after that, those are the evildoers. Say: "God has spoken the truth; therefore follow the creed of Abraham, a man of pure faith and no idolater."

> The first House established for the people was that at Bekka, a place holy, and a guidance to all beings (3:85–90).

Even though the Holy Qur'an has expressly stated that after Muhammad's prophecy no religion other than Islam is acceptable, and that anyone with a different religion detracts from the public good, it has not mandated any worldly punishments for non-Muslims. Additionally, divine punishment will only be inflicted on those who knowingly turn their back on Islam and not on people who are unaware of this most exalted religion. The divine punishment for those who know of Islam's exalted merits but refuse to accept it includes eternal torment and damnation by the Almighty, the angels, and the people. These punishments will be inflicted if the infidel does not repent. If he repents, so long as he does not sin excessively, the Forgiving God may forgive him his sins. But even if the Almighty will not accept an infidel's repentance, he may not be subject to punishment in this world.

An analysis of the above verses leads us to the following conclusions:

1. Turning away from faith is unacceptable and must be condemned. The abandonment of faith may occur under two circumstances: research, theorizing, and debates, which are, of course, conducted on the wrong bases and sow doubts in a person's mind as to the validity of Islam; or through opportunism, Satanic pursuits, political corruption, or the prospects of material gain.
2. For those who abandon their faith through reason and logic, the Holy Qur'an has not stipulated any punishments either in this world or on the Day of Judgment. It is obvious that such a person will not benefit from divine grace and blessing.
3. Those who abandon their faith in favor of worldly pleasures and pursuits are condemned to divine punishment on Judgment Day in the form of eternal damnation in hell. This is what the Holy Qur'an refers to every time it discusses the punishment for apostasy.
4. The Holy Qur'an has stipulated absolutely no earthly punishments for apostasy.

A final, seventh group of Qur'anic verses provide guidelines for inviting others to join the faithful. The following verse is a prime example:

> The Sabbath was only appointed for those who were at variance thereon; surely thy Lord will decide between them on the Day of Resurrection, touching their differences (16:125).

The Qur'anic logic for the invitation to join Islam is conciliatory and emphasizes logic and reasoning, suggestion and advice. There is no room in it for coercion, death, and murder, or any kind of force. Islam is a religion of compassion, and invitation to join it also occurs compassionately.

Through examining these seven groups of Qur'anic verses, several important conclusions can be reached regarding the logic of Islam's Holy Book in relation to the issue of freedom of religion and belief. They include:

1. Islam is the just and correct religion and has warned people of the fallacies of beliefs that are null and void.
2. Islam sees the true salvation of man possible through his endorsement of the just and correct religion, and severely condemns deviation from it.
3. According to Islam, people are completely free to choose their religion and their beliefs, and no one may force and compel them to adopt the correct and just religion.
4. Islam recognizes the plurality of religions and beliefs even after the Revelation of the just religion, with some accepting the invitation to join and others refusing to do so. The Unbelievers have numerous religions and creeds.
5. In Islam, those who have not accepted the divine invitation to join the just religion will be punished on Judgment Day.
6. Islam does not sanction any earthly punishments for those believing in false religions and creeds.
7. Islam's logic and its approach towards the invitation of others to join the faithful are peaceful, conciliatory, and compassionate, devoid of any violence and compulsion.
8. Force and threats cannot be employed to prevent apostasy, and there is no earthly punishment for it. If apostasy is combined with violence and warmongering, its divine punishment is proportionately severe.

Given these considerations, it is obvious that the freedom of faith and belief has been guaranteed in Islam. Nevertheless, such a conclusion cannot be complete without a critical analysis of some of the documentary evidence presented by those who deny Islam's sanction of the freedom of religion and belief. This issue, therefore, needs greater attention.

Critique of popular documents concerning religious restrictions in Islam

A critique of all the documents and sources that advocate restricting religious freedoms is beyond the scope of this article. For our purposes here, non-scriptural sources will be examined in relation to three key areas: the death sentence for a male apostate and life imprisonment for a female apostate; the imposition of the *jizyah* on the People of the Book; and capital punishment for infidels.

Sunni Muslims attribute the imposition of the death sentence for apostasy to the Prophet, and Shi'as attribute it to members of his household.

Most Muslim scholars accept this tradition as valid and feel obligated to obey it even though it might contradict the logic and spirit of the Qur'an. There are, nevertheless, a number of issues to consider here.

First, there is no doubt that during the lifetime of the Prophet and the 12 Shi'a imams, the death sentence for apostasy was commonplace. These individuals knew the *Sharia* law and the divine will better than anyone else, and it is impermissible to doubt the validity of their judgment. What is open to interpretation, however, is the validity of such a judgment at the time of their absence. In fact, it is not clear whether such a dictate is valid for all times or was limited only to the time of the Fourteen Infallibles.[2] Shi'a scholars are of two minds on this issue. The more commonplace view prohibits the killing of an apostate when the Fourteen Infallibles are not present, a point over which a number of the Shi'a ulama have come to a consensus. Since the punishment for apostasy is addressed in the *Sharia*, it cannot be administered when the Fourteen Infallibles are not present. The significance of this opinion becomes magnified in light of other objections to the punishment of an apostate that have already been mentioned.

Second, all the traditions concerning capital punishment for apostasy come from a single source. The validity of a tradition is based on its genesis from, and its acceptance by, several religious scholars. On many key issues, the ulama do not rely on the strength of a single source for the veracity of a tradition. When the taking of a human life is concerned, a plurality of sources is most definitely needed. A person's inherent right to life can be terminated only when there is a specific dictate to that effect, such as a Qur'anic verse or an explicit injunction. The killing of an apostate cannot occur if based on only a single source.

Similarly, the question of the imposition of the *jizyah*, which is expressly mentioned in the Qur'an and was practiced at the time of the Prophet's life and afterwards, is open to interpretation. Again, it is unclear whether this is one of the permanent dictates of Islam or is a time-specific injunction that is rendered irrelevant with the passage of time and the dawn of modern conditions. This injunction had perfect validity when the Almighty dictated it to the Prophet. Today, however, it is no longer useful or applicable. Interestingly, the penal code of the Islamic Republic of Iran, which is based on the *Sharia*, makes no mention of either the *jizyah* or the punishment of apostasy by death.

Finally, the question of the killing of an apostate needs to be placed in the proper context. As we know, *Jihad* is one of the central dictates of Islam. But *Jihad* does not mean waging war on infidels and forcing them to become Muslim. *Jihad* means that if infidels who do not permit the free practice of religion control a land, and if Muslims are in a position to end this religious oppression, it is incumbent upon them to liberate the people so that they can freely choose their religion for themselves. It is inevitable that many of those liberated will choose the Just Religion. In many ways, then, *Jihad* is a defensive endeavor and is designed to ensure the people's right to choose their religion freely; it is not meant to confront them with a stark choice between Islam or death.

Conclusion

Non-Muslims living inside or outside Muslim lands have peace and security so long as they do not wage war on Islam. Whether or not they believe in one of the sanctioned religions or in falsehood, no Muslim has the right to disrupt their peace simply because their beliefs are different. This assertion is substantiated by the eternally valid verses of the Qur'an even if it is contradicted by popular interpretations that have been commonplace throughout the history of Islam.

To sum up, even though most of the interpretations of Islam that are prevalent today augur poorly for freedom of religion and belief, a more correct interpretation, based on the sacred text and valid traditions, finds Islam highly supportive of freedom of thought and religion and easily in accord with the principles of human rights.

CHAPTER 7

The Divine Text and Pluralism in Muslim Societies

Muhammad Shahrour

Muhammad Shahrour was born in Damascus in 1938 and trained as a civil engineer, first in the former Soviet Union and then in Ireland, where he earned a PhD from the National University of Ireland in Dublin in 1972. He is currently an Emeritus Professor of Civil Engineering at the University of Damascus. Shahrour's 1990 book, The Book and the Qur'an: A Contemporary Reading, *earned him both popularity and controversy. Three subsequent books—* Contemporary Islamic Studies on State and Society, Islam and Belief, *and* New Islamic Values—*have firmly established Shahrour as one of Syria's, and indeed the Arab world's, most formidable reformist Muslim thinkers.*

An ardent advocate of original ijtihad, *Shahrour's Qur'anic exegesis is at times accused of being "indigestible for the traditional scholar" and "incomprehensible for the common Muslim reader."[1] His exegesis is often, to say the least, "unique" and unconventional, unswerving in its conviction that the Qur'an as text is dynamic, moving, and contemporary. Despite his unconventional interpretations, or perhaps precisely because his exegesis represents such a radical departure from established* ijtihad, *Shahrour has emerged as one of the leading intellectual figures in the contemporary Muslim reformist discourse. Similar to Kadivar, Shahrour's writings are not readily available in English, although, again, the Internet is beginning to slowly introduce him to wider audiences. The following essay, originally published on the web site 19.org, is published here by the author's kind permission.*

Plurality may refer to religion, nationality, political views, political jurisdiction, and individual opinion, all gathered within a single society. Hence, speaking about pluralism in Muslim societies is to speak about freedom and democracy.

In a Muslim context, freedom and democracy should be understood in relation to Arab and particularly Islamic traditions and heritage, and the ways in which they are related to the events surrounding the establishment of a state in the seventh century at Medina. This state was based on the emergence of a new divine message that completed and sealed all previous ones. At that point, the existing Arab society was cohesive, with its own conventions, morals, and civilization.

In particular, we should understand how people at that time responded to this new state based on their political interests. During the time of the Prophet Muhammad's rule, conflicts of interest were not conducted openly. With his death, conflict immediately emerged within tribes, families, and other groups, each claiming to be the rightful followers of the Prophet, while also claiming a monopoly over absolute truth. These conflicts continue to this very day in the Arab-Muslim world, and are manifested in the existence of different Muslim sects.

Since the end of the nineteenth century, the slogan "Islam is the solution" has become increasingly popular. This means that Islam is the only guide to salvation, and offers the only way out of different crises. Islam is seen as the only way to build a just and free society; in other words, an Islamic society is the answer. But I often wonder, which Islam is meant by this? Is it the Islam of the Qur'an and the Prophet Muhammad, or is it the Islam that has emerged through many different historical events and circumstances? What kind of solution does Islam offer? What problems is Islam assumed to solve?

Under such circumstances, the Arab-Muslim population has divided into two tendencies. The first group holds tightly to the literal meaning of the heritage, in order to preserve its national identity and its character intact, or at least in ways that it imagines its national identity and character to be. Considering that this legacy contains absolute truth, these literalists believe that what was fit for the first community of Muslims at the Prophet's time is fit for all believers in all times. This belief has been absolute and exhaustive.

In today's circumstances, such beliefs are often encouraged by political and economic conditions, and people's dissatisfaction with the status quo in many countries leads them to accept the slogan that "Islam is the solution." Most members of this group consider parliaments and elections to be Western heresies that have no place in an Islamic state. Instead, they believe that only Allah provides legitimacy for a state, which means that professional clergy and the ulama should control the state, as is the case in Iran, for example.

For this group, the state is based on a legitimacy derived from the original human heritage, remaining untouched by changes in political thought over time. The group's political theory is based on the caliphate and the

Imamate—i.e. preeminent Islamic authority—and features absolute obedi-ence to decision makers, containing no provisions for an original theory of freedom and human rights.

The second group has tended to call for secularism and modernity, refus-ing the Islamic legacy altogether, including the Qur'an. It sees religion as part of an inherited tradition that only acts as an opiate of the masses and a narcotic on public opinion. For this group, ritual is an image of obscu-rantism. Leading this group have been Marxists, communists, and some Arab nationalists. But they have all failed to fulfill their promise of bring-ing modernity to their societies. They have attempted to construct a secular state that monopolizes truth, blocking any public expression of pluralism. This, however, is a perversion of secularism, which does not entail any state monopoly over the truth.

A return to text

Between these two groups, a third tendency has emerged. A few voices, including my own, have called for a return to *al-tanzil*, the original text of God's Revelation to the Prophet. There are actually two distinct aspects to what is commonly known as the Qur'an. The first is prophecy, which describes the difference between reality and illusion. The second concerns laws and moral behavior. In this sense, the first aspect is objective and thus independent of human acceptance. The second aspect is subjective, depend-ing on human knowledge, as, for example, in the human capacity to know right from wrong.

In my belief, *al-tanzil* is a divine whole, encompassing both the objective prophecy and the subjective message. It is a divine text, whereas everything else is part of the inherited legacy. All interpretations—including *tafsir* (exegesis) and *ijtihad* (independent reasoning)—are part of this inherited legacy, and are no more than human attempts towards understanding and acting on this divine text.

The sense of fatalism that afflicts many Arab Muslims comes from the confusion between God's prophecy and His message about how to live a moral life. Prophecy is limited to a certain number of things, above all that all men will die and be resurrected. But humans have the free will to deter-mine their own conduct in relation to God's message, and its relation to their lives. In the afterlife, they will be judged by God for the way they exercised their free will. Unfortunately, however, many Muslim Arabs have equated the inevitability of prophecy with an absence of free will. God may know all of the choices that I will face in mankind decisions tomorrow, but it will be me who chooses one of these options. This is my free will.

In 1970, when I was a student at the National University of Ireland in Dublin, a flood of questions started to form in my mind. I decided that the school of modernity, in the Arab-Muslim world, had made several mistakes. Most notably,

1. They understood religion by over relying on the views of the clergy and the religious establishment; they rejected the Islamic inherited legacy as a whole, which cut them off from their historical roots and their national affiliation.
2. They denied all divine messages, thereby disregarding morality itself as a principle for society; and they believed only in materialism as the basis of existence, resulting in a view of human beings as mere statistical units.

Moreover, I found that classicists, the traditionalist fundamentalists, and the extreme fundamentalists had also made several mistakes. These included:

1. They had transformed the universal message of Islam into a narrow, local one, intended only for the Muslims in their immediate vicinity.
2. They gave the traditional, inherited legacy a sacred aspect, even though such a legacy is only a product of human interpretation. Thus it became a dogma that people had to accept and apply literally. Over time, this approach reinforced itself, so that the original message of Islam was overwhelmed by human heritage. As a result, Islamic culture became petrified.
3. They treated different aspects of the divine Revelation as if they were the same thing.
4. They did not differentiate between the distinctive parts of *al-tanzil*. They concentrated on the beauty of the language, but ignored the brilliance of the divine logic.

In brief, I found Islam, Muslims, and Islamic thinkers sinking under the burden of ancestral traditions that pulled them backwards.

Under these circumstances, the formal religious establishment attempts to preserve the status quo in order to defend its accumulated privileges. In addition, extremist fundamentalists try to reclaim for themselves the authority of religion and to pry it away from the state. Average Muslims also face the burden of misunderstanding by non-Muslims, who often identify Islam in terms set by the religious establishment or by extreme fundamentalists.

Another ten years had to pass before I was able to free my thinking from this burden of man-made heritage. I have tried to clarify the definitions of a number of terms and ideas that were confused or obscured by traditionalist approaches and writings:

1. *Al-tanzil* is the revealed, divine text that had been given to Muhammad. And, like all Muslims, I am personally obliged to understand this prophecy and to carry out its injunctions, as if Muhammad had passed away yesterday. This is made clear in the text by hundreds of references, such as "O mankind," "O descendants of Adam," "O my worshippers," "O believers."

2. *Al-tanzil* is assigned for all mankind, and not for the Arabs only, and it has the ability to fit in with every human culture, at all levels of development.

3. With the exception of *al-tanzil*, all Islamic texts and religious literature are but a man-made legacy, and they represent human understanding of the divine Revelation within the conditions of the time and place of production. These conditions of time and place depend also on the state and means of scientific knowledge.

4. *Al-tanzil* need not be understood through the strict rules of interpretation established ten centuries ago. Obviously, there are rules of common sense that apply, such as an understanding of the Arabic language in order to read the Arabic text.

5. Rejecting the traditional legacy—which I do not believe gives a proper understanding of the divine messages, at least nowadays—does not mean that Muslims need be ashamed of their history and their identity. Our legacy is our roots, our history is our identity, and our ancestors are our forefathers. I argue only that we need not borrow others' glasses to see our own reality, or to solve our current problems.

In my opinion, Muslims do not need a new interpretation, or a new *tafsir*; we do not need a new Islam as some have imagined, or, God forbid, a heresy. In my own work, I believe I am making a serious, rational attempt to re-read *al-tanzil*, free from all the historic additions that were added arbitrarily by authoritarian governors and sultans. I try to look at this message through the eyes of the present, again, as if the Prophet Muhammad had passed away yesterday.

Remember that *al-tanzil* has characteristics that have been covered over by the literal adherence to human interpretations rather than adherence to the divine message. I see distinct differences between a number of terms that have been used as synonyms. For example, there is the difference between the term "Muslim"—which originally referred to all believers in God, the afterlife and the performance of good deeds—and the term *mu'minin*, which refers specifically to the followers of the Prophet Muhammad. For me, everything connected with God is "Islam."

Thus, in my view, all believers in God and the afterlife are Muslims. Those who follow the teachings of the Prophet Muhammad are Muslim *mu'minin*. Those who follow the teachings of Jesus are Muslim-Christians, while those who follow the teachings of Moses are Muslim-Jews.

What distinguishes the Prophet Muhammad from previous prophets is that God's Revelation to him by itself constitutes a miracle, whereas in Christianity and Judaism there are historical miracles outside the text. In the Prophet Muhammad's message, the text itself is the miracle, which teaches us that mankind must depend on reason alone and that no further Revelations or miracles are needed. We have to make our own miracles, like traveling in outer space.

Nature of the prophetic message

There are three noteworthy aspects of the message of the Prophet Muhammad: morality, legislation, and ritual. Morality, in my view, is the common heritage of all religions, and has been built over time from Noah to Muhammad, passing through Moses and Jesus. These prophetic messages constitute the moral pillars of Islam.

The legislative aspect refers to the limits that God sets for dealing with human behavior in different areas of interaction, as in marriage, business, inheritance, polygamy, and criminality. When Arab Muslims insist on the death penalty for murderers, they are confusing the maximum penalty with the required penalty. While murderers must be punished, they could be given a life sentence, rather than the death penalty. Both fall within the limits of punishment set by God in the Qur'an, but the torture of murderers is beyond these limits.

The idea that murderers must be put to death under all circumstances can be traced back to human interpretation that says there is only one punishment for murder, even though the Qur'an speaks only of the "limits" of punishment (*hudud*). Thus our heritage confines our ability to make proper legislation.

Yet at the same time, the theory of God's limits in legislation allows for different solutions to problems, hence different points of view, and, in time, pluralism within societies and parliaments. This means that, in a debate, if all parties respect God's limits, the accusation of heresy is out of place. Accusations of heresy become the way in which religious establishments try to control or limit pluralism. In this context, parliaments should replace clergymen and religious institutions in making legislation.

The development of pluralism also depends on our understanding of the distinction between God's doctrines as handed down to the Prophet Muhammad, and the Prophet's actual conduct as a man living at a certain time and in a certain society. Fundamentalists tell us that we must live as the Prophet lived, and that we have to follow his sayings and the examples he set. In my view, the Prophet lived an exemplary life within the limits set by God. But his behavior was only one of many choices he could have made, all within God's limits.

Thus the Prophet is a model to us in the sense that he observed God's limits, not in the sense that we must make the same choices that he made. The life of the Prophet is the first historical variant of how the rules of Islam can be applied to a tribal society of the time. But it is the first variant; it is neither the only one nor the last one.

Fundamentalists today confuse the choices that the Prophet made with Muslim rituals, and that distorts their view and understanding of Islam. By doing so, they prevent people from making legitimate choices and undermine pluralism in the name of the choices made by the Prophet. Everything is compared to what the Prophet did, or to the way the Prophet made choices. My interpretation puts the *sunna*, or the traditions and sayings of the Prophet, in a new light. As to ritual, these are specific to Muhammad's teaching of how to worship God, and Muslims know them as the five pillars: bearing witness to Muhammad as God's messenger, praying five times a day, giving to charity, making a pilgrimage to Mecca, and fasting during Ramadan. But this is only the ritualistic side of the universal message of God. Rituals may differ from one branch of Islam to another, that is, among *mu'minin*, Christians, and Jews.

Principles of pluralism

Through my reading of the text, I have come to conclusions that are relevant to the application of the Qur'an to contemporary society, particularly with regard to democracy and pluralism. First, one of the core principles of Muslim belief is the *shura*, or consultation. This was how the Prophet consulted with his Companions about making decisions for his society. In the Qur'an, the *shura* is mentioned twice, as a fundamental belief, just like prayer, and as a practice, according to the time in which one lives. In our times, genuine *shura* means genuine pluralism of points of view, and democracy.

Second, this view of the *shura* changes the concept of *Jihad*, about which we hear so much from the fundamentalists. To my mind, *Jihad* is justified in only two cases: to defend the homeland, or to fight for freedom and justice.

But if societies are governed within the limits set by God, then there is no need to confront them with *Jihad*. Fundamentalists again confuse limits with requirements, and so speak of *Jihad* against societies that do not share their view of God's requirements even if they may respect God's limits.

Attacks on others in order to spread Islam is a deformed historical concept of *Jihad*, because, as I have explained, Islam exists among all men, insofar as they believe in God, the afterlife, and good deeds. The Qur'an states clearly that it is not allowed to wage war against others in order to force them to believe in Muhammad or to become Muslim. The Qur'an recognizes that most people in the world will not be followers of the Prophet Muhammad; today, the *mu'minin* constitute approximately 20 percent of the global population.

A personal quest

Since 1990, I have become the target of different accusations. My first book, *The Book and the Qur'an: A Contemporary Reading (Al-Kitab wa'l-Qur'an: Qira'a Mu'asira)*, in which I explained my thesis, has been censored in more than one Arab or Islamic country. So I had to choose to invest my personal time either in defending myself or in writing further and developing my ideas. I chose the second option. I published my second book, *Contemporary Islamic Studies on State and Society (Dirasat al-Islamiyya al-Mu'as Ira fi 'l-Dawla wa 'l-Mujtama'a)*, and third book, *Islam and Belief (Al-Islam wa'l-Iman)*, which contained practical suggestions for the state and for individuals, based on my conceptual views.

I was fortunate to be living in Damascus, Syria. If not, I could have faced what thinkers in other Muslim countries have faced, like Nasr Abu Zaid, who lives exiled from Egypt (see Chapter 8). Perhaps my fate would have been even worse. The way I have chosen is very difficult. By training I am a civil engineer, and I know it is easier to build a skyscraper or a tunnel under the sea than to teach people how to read the book of the Lord with their own eyes. They have been used to reading this book with borrowed eyes for hundreds of years.

Nevertheless, the interest shown in my work by different groups was more than I expected. What attracted them was my total reliance on the Qur'an itself, not on the *sunna* or on other books that are written by men and are based on their personal interpretations. My critics also focus on my devotion to the Qur'an, as if I did not respect the Prophet. But, as I have said, I respect the Prophet in his human behavior, as the first Muslim who chose his options from within God's limits. What I do not respect is the way that heritage has become dogma in our thinking.

As far as I know, 13 books have been published attacking my first book, based on dogma. Since my starting point was not sectarian, people of all sects and religions have been interested in my work. Officially my first book has been circulated throughout the Middle East and North Africa. In many countries, the authorities have banned my second and third books. But I know that thousands of copies have been published, sold, and circulated—both in print form and on CD-ROM—under the table in these very same places.

I believe that the phenomena of traditionalism and fundamentalism in Islam will not disappear. Judaism and Christianity have not eliminated them either. But I hope that fundamentalism can have less influence, while still taking its place within a peaceful, pluralist society. I do not believe in violence against fundamentalists because their beliefs are at least partly rooted in the consciousness of many people. Cultural problems cannot be solved by force; attempts to do so have failed. A state that tries to enforce a single culture turns that culture into an ideology. I have seen that in the former Soviet Union myself. Modernity is not a new dogma that is replacing an older one. It is, instead, a rejection of fanaticism and offers pluralism to all members of society.

CHAPTER 8

The Nexus of Theory and Practice

Nasr Abu Zaid

Nasr Abu Zaid (b. 1943) is one of Egypt's most recognizable Muslim reformist thinkers, specializing in humanistic hermeneutics. He holds a doctorate degree in Arabic and Islamic Studies from Cairo University and was Professor of Arabic Literature there until 1995. In the process of his applying for promotion from the rank of associate to full professor, Abu Zaid's scholarship—especially his book The Concept of the Text, *published in 1990—was deemed insulting to Islam and he was subsequently declared to be an apostate, first by an Islamist colleague and eventually by the Egyptian legal system, to which the case against him was referred. Found guilty of apostasy, a forcible divorce decree was issued separating Abu Zaid from his wife, a fellow professor at Cairo University. Ayman al-Zawaheri, the Egyptian-born top commander of Al-Qaeda, also issued a death sentence and offered monetary reward for Abu Zaid's murder. Forced to leave Egypt, Abu Zaid and his wife moved to the Netherlands, where he currently holds the Ibn Rushd Chair in Humanism and Islam at the University for Humanistics in Utrecht.*

Abu Zaid perceives his main task as the deconstruction of traditional, ossified ijtihad *and the construction of a dynamic, contemporary one in its place. "My research and writing," he has been quoted as saying, "focus on the following problems: how to achieve a scientific understanding of the Qur'an, and how to brush aside layers of ideological imprepretations, in order to unearth the historical reality of the text."[1] His Qur'anic exegesis features three main themes: it traces the historical evolution of the various lines of interpretation of the text; it highlights the "interpretational diversity" that characterizes Qur'anic studies and the Islamic tradition in general; and it argues that these diverse interpretations have been increasingly neglected by Muslim scholars.[2]*

Abu Zaid's forced and hasty departure from Egypt has brought greater attention to his ideas and his writings in the West. The following excerpt, which represents a broad overview of some of his main ideas on Islamic exegesis, is from Nasr Abu Zaid with Esther R. Nelson, Voices of an Exile: Reflections on Islam *(Westport, CT: Praeger, 2004), pp 165–80 and 199–208.*

When I do research as an Islamic Studies scholar, I painstakingly look for those things initiated by the Qur'an—ways of being and doing that did not exist before Muhammad received the Revelation. When I find such phenomena, I take note. I delve into the text at this point, using this juncture to develop and steer Islamic thought. In so doing, I would say that I am moving in the same direction as the Word of God. I am convinced that people who think that everything mentioned in the Qur'an is binding, should be obeyed, and should be followed, literally are going against God's Word.

It is important for me to have a handle on the direction my research takes. So, for example, with regard to punishment for crime, the destination we are after is justice. In order to establish justice, a society needs to punish people who commit crimes against that society. But the form of punishment mentioned in the Qur'an is a historical expression of punishment carried out by a specific society in a specific time and place—it is not a divine directive. Punishment for crime is a principle that, when carried out, establishes justice. Justice is a principle reflected in the divine, universal Word of God. Punishment is part of constructing a just society, but the form punishment takes is historically determined—it is not fixed.

Reading classical Islamic thought should be a critical exercise. What did our ancestors accomplish? What can we add or develop as a result of their accomplishments? Through my research and study, I have concluded that the Qur'anic objectives that jurists long ago agreed upon were deduced from the penal code alive and well during the seventh century on the Arabian Peninsula. The objectives were not deduced from looking at the paradigm of the entire Qur'an.

The first objective—protection of life—emerged from the penal code's prohibition of illegal killing. Retaliation, according to the Qur'an, is sanctioned only to maintain life itself. Protection of sanity was deduced from the Qur'an's directive to abstain from alcohol. Protection of property was lifted from the penal code's condemnation of theft and then incorporated into the Qur'an. Protection of progeny can be traced to sanctions already in place against committing adultery. Regarding the protection of religion, the Qur'an doles out no earthly punishment for people who turn their backs on Islam. Those who reject the faith after once accepting it, and remain defiant, will suffer in the life hereafter. Later on, the death penalty for turning one's back on Islam became established as a way to maintain political authority in a region.

The Qur'an contains the penal code. We call it the *hudud*—all the verses that indicate specific punishment for certain crimes. I came to the conclusion that we need another reading of the Qur'an in order to make this particular manifestation of the Word of God meaningful in our present-day circumstances. If we look at the *hudud* in a historical context, we find that these particular passages reflect a historical reality. They do not reflect divine imperatives. For example, the killing for killing, the eye for an eye, stoning for adultery, the amputation of the hand for stealing, and death for changing religion—all this was in effect either before the Qur'an came along or instituted after Qur'anic Revelation. The Qur'an did not establish this kind of punishment. If the Qur'an did not initially establish a punishment, we cannot consider it to be Qur'anic. The Qur'an adopted particular forms of punishment from pre-Islamic cultures in order to have credibility with the contemporary civilization.

Punishment for crime is a Qur'anic principle, but should a form of punishment integrated into the body of the text from another source be considered Qur'anic and therefore binding on the community of believers? We can say that the Qur'an leads us to understand that those who commit crimes should be punished. True enough, but the Qur'an contextualizes itself within accepted practices during a particular time. Contemporary society has every right—even an obligation—to institute more humane punishment for crimes. To do so in no way violates God's Word.

The Qur'an took a particular shape so that people in seventh-century Arabia would "get it." If we elevate historical aspects of the Qur'an to divine status, we violate the Word of God. God's Word becomes twisted when we freeze it in a specific time and space. The absolute Word of God goes beyond its historical context—this is what we want to get hold of. If anything spoken about in the Qur'an has a precedent in pre-Islamic tradition—whether Jewish, Roman, or anything else—we need to understand that its being mentioned in the Qur'an does not automatically make it Qur'anic and therefore binding on Muslims.

What about slavery? Slavery as a socio-economic system is mentioned in the Qur'an—it is a historical reality. Human beings have developed their thinking since the seventh century. Slavery is no longer an acceptable socio-economic system in most parts of the world. How can we use the Word of God to legitimate a heinous system that human beings no longer generally practice? If we do legitimate such a thing, we freeze God's Word in history—but the Word of God reaches way beyond historical reality. Slavery is something that is not Qur'anic. Jurists, those folks in the Islamic world responsible for developing law, need to apply a healthy dose of critical thinking to their job as they go about the business of forming a just society—one that moves in the direction of the Word of God.

Another thing I have in mind when I do my research deals with discovering just what the ultimate objectives of the Qur'an really are. We learn, of course, from our ancestors. How did they go about deducing the meaning of the Qur'an? How did they read a text? To their accomplishments we add our modern disciplines of textual analysis, historical analysis, and hermeneutics.

Let us dig deeper into the subject of justice. This concept infiltrates all the passages of the Qur'an. "Just" is one of God's beautiful names. The Qur'an, when it admonishes people to avoid fraudulent practices, uses the image of a scale as a metaphor for justice.

> Woe betide the unjust who, when others measure for them, exact in full, but when they measure or weigh for others, defraud them! Do they not think they will be raised to life upon a fateful day, the day when all mankind will stand before the Lord of the Universe? (83:1–6).

Even the paradigms of the life hereafter are based on the concept of justice. The entire universe, the whole cosmos, is built on justice:

> We shall set up just scales on the Day of Resurrection, so that no man shall in the least be wronged. Actions as small as a grain of mustard seed shall be weighed out. Our reckoning shall suffice (21:47).

Keeping things balanced—establishing justice—is spoken about over and over again throughout the Qur'an. Every story and each commandment is there with the intention of establishing justice in a society. Justice easily emerges as one of the major objectives of the Qur'an.

The Qur'an took shape within Meccan society—an unjust society in many ways—where wealthy people oppressed poor people by charging them *riba* (usury). Why did the language condemning usurious practice have to be so strong? Mecca was smack dab in the middle of trade routes between the southern tip of the Arabian Peninsula and northern destinations such as Egypt, Jordan, Syria, and Turkey. Meccan citizens who enjoyed privilege and status became extremely wealthy as a result of trade. If poor citizens could not pay their debts, they were forced to borrow money from the wealthy (through usury) in order to save their own skins. There are many stories showing how the wealthy took advantage of the vulnerable in cities that dotted the trade routes in the Middle East. The Qur'an as a text emerged from the midst of this concrete and harsh reality. Usury, within the context of this particular reality, was used as an instrument that perpetuated injustice.

Why is the Qur'an so concerned about the orphans, the weak, and the poor? Muhammad himself was an orphan and poor. His father died before he was born. His uncle took him in after his grandfather died. He lost his mother when he was six years old. Because his uncle was so poor, Muhammad went to work early in his life. He belonged to the class of "have nots" in a society where the "haves" flaunted their wealth, not caring an iota about the lives of people living on the brink or, as we say in more modern times, falling through the cracks.

The opposition to and harsh criticism in the Qur'an of the practice of *riba* stand in sharp contrast to the giving of alms—something the Qur'an commands as a path towards achieving socio-economic justice. The two issues, alms and usury, are connected. The Qur'an gives us a nice image of those who give charitably, providing for needy folks without exposing them to embarrassment. This image stands in juxtaposition to the image of those who practice *riba*.

> God has laid his curse on usury and blessed almsgiving with increase. God bears no love for the impious and the sinful. Those that have faith and do good works, attend to their prayers and render the alms levy, will be rewarded by their Lord and will have nothing to fear or to regret. Believers, have fear of God and waive what is still due to you from usury, if your faith be true; or war shall be declared against you by God and His apostle. If you repent, you may retain your principal, suffering no loss and causing loss to none. If your debtor be in straits, grant him a delay until he can discharge his debt; but if you waive the sum as alms it will be better for you, if you but knew it (2:276–80).

During the past three decades, Islamic banks have been established all over the world, claiming to run on an economic system that practices no *riba*. But when it comes right down to it, these banks do not operate any differently than the existing banking system based on charging interest.

Many jurists (those responsible for enacting Islamic law) have ignored the circumstances surrounding the prohibition of usury. By ignoring the context of the Qur'anic position, the debate about *riba* has taken on a wooden character. The question has become focused on whether or not financial transaction in the modern banking system, based on a fixed interest rate on both savings and loans, is actually *riba*. This misses the point. The Qur'an forbade *riba* because it was used to oppress the poor. *Riba* has entered aspects of Islamic law as an acceptable practice under some circumstances. Modern Muslim scholars do not consider interest, used today by the modern banking system, to be *riba*. Jurists who tightly grasp those solutions more appropriate to another age (seventh-century Meccan society) believe that interest of any sort is *riba*, and therefore inherently wrong.

No matter what subject the Qur'an talks about—the universe, the cosmos, nature, God and His activities, social life, or the life hereafter—justice is at its core. Justice gives shape to all of them. In light of the Qur'an's emphasis on justice, it is surprising to me that the principle of justice is absent from the list of agreed-upon objectives in classical Islam. Justice should be right there on top. If there were to be a conflict between justice and freedom, justice ought to prevail. I think that is why we find the principle of freedom in the Qur'an somewhat limited. Even with our more modern understanding of freedom, freedom as a Qur'anic objective must be couched within the primary objective of justice.

Jahiliyyah is commonly known as the Age of Ignorance in the West. The phrase "the Age of Ignorance" does not convey an accurate meaning of the term. *Jahiliyyah* specifically refers to the pre-Islamic period, a time before Muhammad received divine Revelation. It refers to behavior based on the tribal code. The Qur'an condemns this code, a code insisting that members of the tribe comply with the group no matter what. (It is similar to the American expression, "My country, right or wrong.") According to the tribal code of conduct, the individual has no voice. The individual is expected to follow the leader and obey blindly. The Qur'an condemns this, admonishing us to follow our own conscience, built not on the tribal code but on right and wrong, just and unjust, good and bad. Here we see the Qur'an coming up with something different, something in contradiction to the tribal code.

The Qur'an's language in reference to the Bedouin (tribal people who inhabited the Arabian Peninsula) is harsh. The word "Arab" is not even used in the Qur'an—just the word *a'rab*—a word synonymous with "Bedouin" and always used negatively. We can conclude from this that the Qur'an espouses a set of values and rules that is in direct contradiction to the Bedouin tribal code; therefore, the Qur'an considers the Bedouin tribal code *jahiliyyah*.

Qur'anic values are built on the concepts of freedom and justice—freedom of thought in order to bring about a just society. So your tribe going to war is no reason to think that you, the individual, must automatically go with them. In this way, Islam established a community, not a tribe—a community that went beyond the strictures of the tribal system. This was part of Islam: to establish a sense of community based on another set of values, another code. In order to establish this community, freedom is understood as a way to get out from under the stultifying practice of blindly following tradition, copying the past.

If you look at Arab and Muslim societies, you will see that most of the time no government has come to power by the choice of the people. You will often find a military system in place, an archaic royal family at the nation's helm, or somebody who inherits power from his predecessor. Sometimes the new governing body takes a new name and puts on a modern appearance, but all you have to do is scratch the surface and you will see that it is the same old thing underneath. The tribal mentality is alive and well. The code is obedience. All our institutions—political, social, economic, and academic—have an authoritarian structure. Intellectuals have their own form of tribal behavior. You either belong to the right or belong to the left, but you had better not disobey the code of whatever intellectual tribe you belong to. It is a terrible situation.

For example, when the peace talks that led to the Oslo Accords began in 1992–93, many intellectuals were in favor of establishing communication and cooperation between the Palestinian territories and Israel. People from the intellectual tribe—both the left and the right—said they were in favor of peace. But when two groups say they are in favor of peace, does that mean that both groups have identical views about a situation? Not necessarily. In spite of that, some members of the intellectual tribe believed that here was an opportunity to speak from a united front. No way did this happen. The group in favor of the Oslo talks called those who expressed some reticence about the talks stupid, retarded, and belonging to the old world. The reticent group shot back by calling their accusers traitors, using peace as a way to conspire with the "enemy" in order to wield influence and power. I was appalled. What kind of discourse is this? If we all claim that we are looking for peace and we, those of us within the intellectual tribe, are not able to tolerate different opinions among ourselves—well, it is very easy to despair.

I was about to write against this kind of tribal code of discourse—it was just before the Supreme Court decided on a verdict in the case where I was accused of apostasy. I refuse to play the tribal game. Consequently I am one of those marginalized Arab intellectuals. Frankly I take some comfort in being marginalized. I do not try to vote with the center because it is only from the margins that I feel I am able to threaten the center. If I were to be integrated into the center, I would not have much impact on the development of Islamic thought, and, God knows, the Arab and Muslim world desperately needs to see the relevance of modern scholarship to individual lives and to societies.

When I applied my critical scholarship to the subject of women, I saw how well this subject nestled into the concepts of justice and freedom, two essential objectives of the Qur'an. The fourth chapter of the Qur'an is simply titled "Women." The opening verse tells us that God created a human being from one single soul, and from this one single soul God created its mate, and from there God created all humanity.

> You people! Have fear of your Lord, who created you from a single soul. From
> that soul, He created its spouse, and through them He bestrewed [scattered] the
> earth with countless men and women (4:1).

From this verse, we see the unity of human beings, of the human race. Male
and female are created from one single soul. The Christian understanding
of Eve, created from Adam's rib, has been integrated into Islamic thought—
into the exegesis of the Qur'an—and so it became part of Islam. I am aware
that Genesis gives two accounts of the creation of humanity, one of them
being more in line with Qur'anic understanding (not the account where
Eve emerges as a product of Adam's rib). But in the Qur'an, the chapter
on women begins by establishing the unity and equality of human beings.
There was one soul, and this one soul God divided into two, and from them
the whole human race came forth.

Let us consider polygamy, a subject not well understood even by most
Muslims. Polygamy, historically speaking, was a popular practice in human
societies long before the advent of Islam. It is a mistake to think of polygamy as part of the Islamic Revelation. Yes, the Qur'an does address the issue
of polygamy, but the verse so often used to legitimize polygamy is really
addressing the issue of orphans who needed protection and custody after
losing their parents in the battle of Uhud (625). Muslims lost ten percent
of the army—70 warriors—leaving many children orphaned. The historical context, as well as textual analysis, shows that permission was granted
to marry a widow or a female orphan so that she would be protected and
provided for in this particular society, a society that preyed upon widows
and female orphans—often stealing their inheritance from them. Therefore,
the Qur'an admonishes:

> Give orphans the property which belongs to them. Do not exchange their valu-
> ables for worthless things or cheat them of their possessions; for this would
> surely be a grievous sin. If you fear that you cannot treat orphans with fairness
> [giving them their inheritance], then you may marry other women who seem
> good to you: two, three, or four of them. But if you fear that you cannot main-
> tain equality among them [within a marital relationship], marry one only or
> any slave-girls you may own. This will make it easier for you to avoid injustice
> (4:3).

The syntax of the third sentence is conditional—if you are not sure that you
will be able to treat orphans with fairness, then you are allowed to marry
two, three, even up to four other women. What is the text talking about?
Justice is the goal, and the means to reach that goal in these particular
circumstances comes through the practice of polygamy. Polygamy is used

as a solution to establish justice. The plural "orphans" here is feminine. The focus is on doing justice for orphans. If that is not possible, there is a solution. Where does the solution come from? From pre-Islamic practice.

The Arabs living in the Arabian Peninsula of the seventh century mistreated orphans, denying them their rights. They took the orphans' inheritances and made them virtual slaves in their households. This was common practice. So the Qur'an asks, "OK, if you Arabs are so greedy, why do you not marry them?" Marriage brings about a whole new relationship. Marriage would be a means to bring about a more just society. The solution established by the Qur'an is not the same thing as establishing polygamy. It is using polygamy as a solution to a real problem in the seventh century, the problem of orphans. Polygamy was widely practiced already. So we cannot say that polygamy is Qur'anic law. It is not a law. It is a practical solution to a pressing, historical problem. Justice is the broader issue.

Through my research I have concluded that the Qur'an does not favor polygamy. The Qur'an, in its attempt to establish justice, realizes that even if the Arabs chose the path of marrying orphans, the goal of justice remained out of reach. I do not believe I can conclude that the Qur'an is against polygamy—that would be jumping over history. The Qur'an recommends polygamy as a solution to a social problem. Since the Qur'an is not in favor of the practice, jurists in the business of establishing modern law would be wise to put tight restrictions around its use. This way, Islam will be developing societies in the same direction the Word of God takes: the establishment of justice.

Given our present-day social circumstances, polygamy is insulting to women as well as to the children born into the family. I am appalled that there is no discussion in modern Islamic thought about what effects polygamy might have on children. The questions have remained the same over centuries: Is polygamy allowed in the Qur'an? Is it legal? It is time we asked, "What about the children? What impact does the practice have on them?" We have to consider this first and foremost: the Qur'an is all about establishing justice in society.

When we look at other verses in the Qur'an about women, we should envelop them in the same context—justice. If certain practices in the Qur'an appear to be contrary to this concept, the context can usually explain it. For example, the beating of wives. It is mentioned in the Qur'an—it cannot be ignored. So the thinking goes like this: if beating is mentioned in the Qur'an, I have the right to beat my wife. I remember hearing a professor from the Islamic University in Rotterdam say in an interview that the Qur'an allowed a husband to discipline his wife by beating her. It is not only the fundamentalist or radical people who think like this. Somehow, if something is mentioned in the Qur'an, people think it is permissible.

It is possible to state from a supposedly academic position that the Qur'an allows a husband to beat his wife in order to discipline her. If everything mentioned in the Qur'an is to be literally followed as a divine law, Muslims should be consistent and reinstate slavery as a socio-economic system. It is mentioned in the Qur'an, is it not?

When we speak of something being Qur'anic, we are talking about that which was initiated by the Qur'an and therefore is binding on Muslims. There is a distinction between the historicity of the Qur'an and the Word of God in its absolute form. We are back at the double nature of the Qur'an, human and divine. (According to Christian doctrine, not everything that Jesus said was said as the Son of God. Sometimes Jesus behaved just as a man.) The Qur'an is a mode of communication between God and humanity. When we take the historical aspect of that communication as divine, we lock God's Word in time and space. We limit the meaning of the Qur'an to a specific time in history. Far better—and more faithful to the Word of God—to ferret out that dynamic within the Qur'an which has been able to shape the lives of Muslims over centuries as they have wrestled with the question "How can I be a good Muslim in a changing world?"

Why is it, then, that when we read passages in the Qur'an dealing with women, the reading has concentrated on the historical aspect, not on the objective of establishing justice? Going back to the subject of polygamy, the Qur'an tells us, "Try as you may, you cannot treat all your wives impartially" (4:129). If you think that you will not be able to be fair with your wives, this verse confirms that fear. The problem comes as pre-Islamic social traditions have mixed with Islamic jurisprudence. This mixture has found itself woven into the fabric of Muslim societies, and then enforced there.

The name of the chapter—"Women"—is itself misleading. Muslims titled it according to its subject matter rather than the larger principle it encompasses—justice. The subject matter is women. The subject could just as easily have been war or the poor. Justice is the larger issue under which pressing social issues can easily be subsumed. A problematic verse reads:

> Men have authority over women because God has made the one superior to the other, and because they spend their wealth to maintain them. Good women are obedient. They guard their unseen parts because God has guarded them. As for those from whom you fear disobedience, admonish them, forsake them in beds apart, and beat them. Then if they obey you, take no further action against them. Surely God is high, supreme (4:34).

The English translation of this verse needs to be addressed. The Arabic word *qawwamun* is translated in some English texts as "protectors." Muslims generally understand this word to mean "superiors," meaning that men are financially responsible to maintain their families. The question comes down to this: is the Qur'an here descriptive, merely describing what is going on, or prescriptive, admonishing believers to carry on the practice? Many argue that it is prescriptive. Going to the context, though, gives us amazing insight. A woman came to Prophet Muhammad, complaining that her husband had slashed her face. Muhammad simply said, "Slash him back." What we note here is that Muhammad is going beyond the historical restraints placed upon women. (This anecdote always creates a lot of negative reaction from Muslim men.)

The Word of God continuously emphasizes equality between women and men. There is no distinction made regarding the rewards or punishments both women and men reap in the life hereafter. If there is equality in the spiritual realm, does it make sense that God would smile upon inequality in societies in the here and now? There is equality in creation itself and equality when Muslims perform religious duties and rites. We have seen how the Qur'an does not favor polygamy and how the entire thrust of the Qur'an is towards justice. How do we understand the Qur'an's directives regarding financial support, wife-beating, and inheritance?

Men have a superiority over women because of their contribution to the expenses of life. It has nothing to do with human worth. Human societies, though, have equated financial wealth with human worth, and this has shifted the balance of power between women and men unfairly. Men, as a rule in patriarchal societies, have more earning power than women. I understand this superiority that the Qur'an refers to as responsibility. This same term—responsibility—is a word used about God in relation to God's work in holding the universe together. Power is certainly involved, but the emphasis is on responsible action. We talk about God as being *qayyun* in regard to the heavens and earth. He keeps watch. He keeps things in order. He keeps the world from destruction. The Qur'an uses the same word with regard to men—they are *qawwamun*. They are responsible for the family, they keep the family in order. It has more to do with responsibility than authority. Of course, responsibility could imply some authority.

In modem times, because of the changes that have affected all our social institutions, and therefore our social structure, women can be considered *qawwamun*. If the woman is the major source of family income, then she is superior. Textual analysis shows that God considers some people to be superior (responsible), depending on their financial contribution. The pronoun used could refer to either women or men. It keeps open the possibility of interpretation, but certainly if the woman is the only source of income, and therefore responsible for protecting the family, then she is definitely *qawwam*.

The context of wife-beating revolves around instances where a wife's behavior threatens the stability of the family, and therefore the survival of the community. The expression *nushuz*, means "going way out of bounds." The Qur'an says that if a woman goes way beyond the boundaries, she should first be admonished about her behavior. If this is not successful, she opens herself up to punishment. Her husband may refuse to share their bed or may beat her. (The Qur'an also mentions a case where a husband goes beyond the boundaries—in the mode of *nushuz*.) Again, are these particular punishments mentioned through the Word of God or do they only reflect history? I believe these punishments were a historical solution to current social problems.

Of course it is entirely possible that some women would not have considered desertion from the marital bed to be punishment. We are dealing with the Qur'an, a historical text, coming into existence at a time when patriarchy was well established in cultures throughout the world. Patriarchy, literally meaning "rule by the fathers," is a social system with "domination over" somebody or something (men over women, masters over slaves, kings or queens over subjects, elite over commoners, human beings over nature) at its core. A patriarchal perspective sees things through a male-centered lens, and even though women can (and do) replicate the patriarchal order as their lives unfold, the gender roles that a society enforces on both women and men ensure that a male perspective remains dominant. Products of any given culture (and the Qur'an is a product of a specific culture) reflect the way things are in a society. The language of the text situates itself within a specific material reality—one that expresses itself through a patriarchal bent. Nevertheless, the absolute Word of God transcends the text. Part of my research has to do with distinguishing between the human and divine aspects of the Qur'an.

Before Islam made its appearance on the Arabian Peninsula in the seventh century, women inherited nothing. The eldest son received everything. Islam changed this.

> God has thus enjoined you concerning your children: A male shall inherit twice as much as a female. If there be more than two girls, they shall have two-thirds of the inheritance; but if there be one only, she shall inherit the half. Parents shall inherit a sixth each, if the deceased ha[s] a child; but if he leave[s] no child and his parents be his heirs, his mother shall have a third. If he ha[s] brothers,

his mother shall have a sixth after payment of any legacy he may be bequeathed or any debt he may have owed. You may wonder whether your parents or your children are more beneficial to you [nearer to you in benefit]. But this is the law of God; surely God is all-knowing and wise (4:11).

If you accept the reading that this verse establishes change—women have a right to be included in inheritance—and stop at that level, that is OK. The direction is towards justice. However, a deeper reading shows that this text is not about establishing the rights of women—it is about limiting the rights of men. The Qur'an here is moving in the direction of equality between women and men. It is a step in the right direction. Women should have a share in an inheritance just as men do.

"A male shall inherit twice as much as a female." The structure of the verse concentrates on the share of the male, not the share of the female. Suppose the structure were different? Suppose the text read, "A female shall inherit half of what a male inherits"? This gives us a different semantic reading. If the Qur'anic verse began, "A female shall inherit," we would know that the Qur'an is busy defining the share of the female. But it begins, "A male shall inherit." We see that the Qur'an busies itself defining just what the male's share is to be.

Remember that before Islam, the male received all of the inheritance. The Qur'an here is limiting the share of the male, not defining the share of the female. I believe the Qur'an's intention is limitation—it is the semantic focus of the text. Placing a limitation on what the male receives is not absolutely defining what he should get, but by saying "no more than this," it leaves open the good possibility that he could receive less.

Men should not go beyond what the Qur'an entitles them to. Grammatically speaking, the Qur'an limits the share that men inherit. The Qur'an does not give an absolute share to either women or men. The structure of the Qur'an clears the way for societies to enact inheritance laws that reflect equality between the sexes. Its structure does not box us into absolute numerical amounts.

How should we understand "You may wonder whether your parents or your children are more beneficial to you"? Just because the context reflects the *jahiliyyah* code of behavior, this does not necessarily imply that the Qur'an is trying to guide the believers to go beyond the blood bonds on which the inheritance passages rest. Nonetheless, reading the whole Qur'an in terms of its strong opposition to the tribal code would suggest such an implication. If we add the fact that the Prophet Muhammad clearly indicated that his inheritance was to be distributed for charity, we can suggest that the whole inheritance system is really historically determined.

Much work needs to be done in the field of Islamic studies. The nineteenth century saw a movement of revivalism in the Arab and Muslim world that for a variety of reasons lost its momentum. The process of reforming Islamic thought by looking at the Qur'an and trying to differentiate between what is history and what is the absolute Word of God has continued since then in spite of that loss of momentum. I do not consider my work exceptional. I do not come out of a vacuum. I count myself among those few who have been trying to keep the Qur'an relevant to life in the modern age. We experience heavy resistance.

There are reasons for this resistance. One of the reasons stems from the absence of what I call a "free market of ideas." The acceptance of the economic free market in Muslim societies does not include the acceptance of this free market of ideas. In the Arab and Muslim world, the media are totally controlled by the government. There is no space for free thinking to flourish. Yusuf Idris, one of our contemporary Egyptian writers (a playwright and novelist), said that all the freedom in the Muslim and Arab world is not enough for a single person. I agree with him. Political authority in Egypt is oppressive authority.

On my recent visit to Egypt, I spoke with a male lawyer—one with considerable standing and clout in Egyptian society—about the recent appointment of a woman judge, Tahani El-Gebali, to the Supreme Court. "You know I'm really liberal," he noted, "but I'm not happy at all about a woman being appointed as a judge."

I looked at him askance. "Why not?" "Because a judge must be somebody with experience—a judge needs to go from state to state and into the villages, examining evidence—it could be dangerous. You know the routine."

I had heard it all before. Under the guise of protecting women, we restrict their activities, a climate that perpetuates inequality between the sexes. Many Muslims are liberal and open-minded, but when it comes to the subject of women, they take refuge in an outdated ideology. With the advent of cloning, the possibility exists that one single woman can reproduce life on her own. Men—especially Arab men—feel threatened. Many Muslims point to the verse that shows life springing forth from a pair, and then refuse to discuss the issue further, claiming that the Qur'an settled that issue long ago.

Democracy, rationalism, and freedom are not instilled in our consciousness. All too often, as in the case of the lawyer who is unhappy with the recent appointment of Tahani El-Gebali to Egypt's Supreme Court, these concepts skim along the surface of our understanding. We have not incorporated these values into the way we go about living our lives. That is why it is easy to find refined, intellectual men talking about women and the rights of women, but treating their own wives with scorn and contempt.

An acquaintance of mine invited me to his home to have dinner with his wife and family. I had just met him and felt somewhat uncomfortable with the invitation. So I said, "You cannot just surprise your wife by bringing home a guest for dinner." "No, no, don't worry about it," he assured me. "My wife is gracious and hospitable."

I was still uncomfortable with the situation. I would not surprise Ebtehal in this way. I reluctantly accepted his invitation, thinking that perhaps he and his wife had some sort of understanding about bringing guests home for dinner. When we entered his home, his wife graciously received us. The husband took off his jacket, flung it across the room, not caring where it landed, and then clapped his hands three times as a signal to his wife that he wanted some service. "Cigarettes, get me my cigarettes." His cigarettes were in his jacket pocket—the same jacket that he had just thrown across the room.

What kind of freedom is this? Where is the respect, especially in front of a guest? Perhaps a man might behave like this when he is alone with his family, showing how spoiled he is—but to do this in front of a guest! But the man was not staging a scene. This was ordinary, everyday behavior. This showed me what a wide gap exists between people's talk about freedom and justice; all that talk has yet to make a dent on the way many people live. Clearly, we have not integrated our talk into our walk. Or, to put it in academic terms, theory has not made its way into practice.

The way forward

Islam, like any religion, speaks on several levels and from more than one perspective. Religious thinking in Islam, above all, is human expression of metaphysical reality. Islamic scholarship attempts to give a comprehensive and coherent understanding to the Qur'an, God's speech revealed to the Prophet Muhammad by the angel Gabriel. Islamic thinkers—scholars, jurists, and philosophers—have applied their own particular disciplines to the Qur'an in order to ferret out meaning from the text. Human effort, grounded in and informed by a particular historical and social setting, distilled (and continues to distill) the material of Revelation into a precise intellectual form.

The Arab-Islamic Reform Movement, begun in the nineteenth century, has been sidetracked. Under the wider heading of justice, we had begun to address issues concerning human rights, women's rights, and the rights of minority groups. We also started to deal with issues such as education, freedom, democracy, and progress. Today we must not let ourselves be defined by a phony identity that manifests itself in terms of backwardness and resistance to progress, under the guise of defending Islam and our identity. Our aborted renaissance looked to the future as it attempted to break free from outdated structures of thinking. It is high time for us to pick up the ball where it was dropped, and carry on. To carry on, we need an orderly way to talk about religion—a discourse.

Religious discourse is human discourse—it consists of people talking about religion. Therefore, religious discourse has the ability to stimulate progress or defend the status quo. Discourse that envisions progress will be inherently critical. This criticism will be aimed at the past along with the present, and will encompass other cultures as well. Critical examination of Islam digs deep. Pioneers of modern Islamic discourse, such as Muhammad 'Abduh (1848–1905), Taha Hussein (1889–1973), and 'Ali Abdel Raziq (1887–1966), contextualized social and political issues within religious discourse, attacking the thoughtless imitation of the past as a way to move Islamic culture forward. These men called for religious renewal, yes, but their discourse integrated the whole public realm into their understanding of that religious renewal. How can we think of ourselves as good Muslims when injustice runs rampant? Why is there such disparity (economic, social, political) between the so-called elite and ordinary citizens?

Conservative discourse, on the other hand, most often resists criticism and looks for pragmatic solutions to problems in the modern world that uphold the status quo. The Egyptian market became glutted with books on Arab nationalism and Islamic socialism during the 1950s and 1960s in an attempt to superimpose a practical, political ideology on the Egyptian people. These books lacked any kind of critical analysis. In the 1970s, books abounded that denounced market-oriented policies. These authors tried to make a case that agrarian reform, inheritance taxes, and interest rates were un-Islamic practices. As a result, many citizens supported Islamic investment companies as alternative institutions to Westernized banks. These Islamic investment companies were later exposed as fraudulent pyramid schemes—too late for many Egyptians, who by this time had been swindled out of their life savings. Conservative, pragmatic, religious discourse can generate alternative ways of interacting in the modern world, but does so without grappling effectively with changing circumstances. Conservative Islamic discourse merely spreads itself like a veneer over problems that emerge from the changes we experience in the ebb and flow of a world that is in constant flux.

Often the phrase "religious discourse" becomes synonymous with sacred propaganda and the rhetoric of Friday sermons. That is certainly not what I have in mind when it comes to a conversation about religion. Religious discourse is not preaching—something in dire need of reform and modernization in the Muslim world—but consists of a process that engages the intellect while grappling with the question "How can I hold on to Qur'anic values in a changing world?" Referring to words uttered by somebody, somewhere, at some time or another and expecting those words to magically effect a solution just does not work.

It is imperative for us to understand that in order to create a society based on freedom and justice, we must change the way we think. A new religious discourse is part of the broader call for freedom. For any endeavor—such as creating a just society—ultimately to be successful, citizens must be able to think critically and express themselves freely. Unfortunately, most of the Arab world today remains shackled with chains of fear, chains that squeeze free thinking and its expression.

For renewal of religious discourse to take root, we need to take a long hard look at our own religious legacy. There can be no safe doctrinal havens or sacred cows inaccessible to critique. Safe havens and sacred cows restrict the process of renewal and, bottom line, amount to censorship. Censorship and stagnation go hand in hand. Because religious discourse is tied to public discourse, all facets of society deteriorate as a result of censorship. Only confident and free societies have an ability to repel stagnation and decay. Challenging the status quo opens the pathway to progress. People must be free to hold what other folks deem to be erroneous opinions. People must be free to challenge opinions in the marketplace of ideas. Islam must protect this right. It is the only way to move forward with integrity. It is the only way to establish a just and free society.

Just what is it that fuels nothing less than panic nowadays when Muslims critique established Islamic thought? Why does Islamic culture today consider critique of our historical past and orthodox religious expression to be a crime? What do we make of the fact that the fifteenth-century encyclopedist Jalal al-Din al-Suyuti (d. 1505) forthrightly stated that Prophet Muhammad received Revelation (the Qur'an) only in content, and that the actual phrasing of the Qur'an came from the Prophet himself? Today, such an idea cannot be discussed or even mentioned publicly. People have lost their lives for speaking out in this manner.

What is it that offends so many people when historians speak of the failure of Prophet Muhammad's preaching to win over Meccan society, forcing him to flee with his small band of followers to Medina? Why is there such animosity towards the arts, particularly the performing arts? Are not Qur'anic recitals a form of vocal performing art? Is not the Qur'an a work of literature? Why do we prohibit the personification of historic, religious figures, thus impoverishing even further our culture's theatrical expression? Are we not able to distinguish between the represented figure and the actor playing a part? Can we not sort out reality from fiction? More to the point, are we not able to find spiritual meaning for our lives through artistic expression? Is it possible that we are so dull? It is as though Islamic culture has become incarcerated by literal and concrete thinking. No distinction is made between language (a symbolic system) that a culture uses to express and create itself, and divine reality.

This is an odd phenomenon, given our broad historic legacy, one based on the Qur'an, a book that opposes *jahiliyyah* (the pre-Islamic tribal code of behavior) while calling for the engagement of an individual's conscience in the quest for justice and freedom. Islam gave birth to intellectual and philosophical structures that challenged the ways of the past. Intellectual and philosophical structures, though, cannot by themselves transform a culture. People must integrate these structures into the way they live. This is difficult to do. A culture's familiar ways of going about living in a society carry a momentum, and those familiar ways of being and doing have staying power.

It is at this juncture (where thought and practice meet) that we can begin looking for those fault lines that have led to ignorance, injustice, and tyranny in much of the Muslim world. The faults lie within Islamic social history, not Islamic religious texts. Arab-Islamic culture, not Islam, showed no confidence or faith in democracy and critical thought. Islamic history is human history, a history based on social, political, and economic factors. Understanding the Qur'an and applying its message has developed through social, political, and economic forces. Religion does determine and shape social life, but religion gets its shape, to a great extent, from factors present in that society. There never has been any such thing as a pure, abstract Islam situated above the rough and tumble of geography and history. We cannot speak of any one manifestation as being the true Islam, whether that manifestation takes form in the shape of the al-Azhar of Egypt, the Taliban of Afghanistan, the Hawza in Iran, the Zaytuna of Tunisia, the Wahhabi of Saudi Arabia, or the Diyanat of Turkey.

We can, though, speak about two dimensions of Islam—the historical dimension that presents its particular teaching regarding belief and ethics in a seventh-century context, and the universal dimension that presents values transcending time and place. Some Muslim thinkers emphasize the historical dimension, considering this interpretation essential to Islam. The field of jurisprudence emphasizes the historical dimension. Jurists deal with practical actions of individuals within their society. A variety of political Islamist groups, known as fundamentalists, see the jurist view of the Qur'an as the only true and valid understanding of Islam. It follows then that *Sharia* law—human law deriving largely from the foundational texts of Islam (the Qur'an and Prophetic tradition) along with the consensus of earlier generations—must be implemented in an Islamic society. Throughout most of Islamic history the jurists' understanding of religion has taken hold and often has been held in place by force.

Reading the Qur'an from a different perspective suggests more universal and inclusive objectives. For example, creating a community of believers, rather than relying on behavior that a tribal system of kinship dictates to the individual, ushered in what I call human rational conduct. Rational thought and conduct freed the individual from the mindless duty of submitting to the tribal code of conduct. One was expected to replace *jahiliyyah* with human, rational understanding. Another example would be establishing the practice of almsgiving. Social justice became an important facet of religious expression. Freedom to act according to one's conscience and caring for the poor in a society go beyond specific geographical boundaries and take us into a more universal understanding of religion.

This broader, more universal understanding of Islam, representing basic human principles, remains politically and intellectually marginalized in the Muslim world. Modern Muslim intellectuals (and I consider myself in this category) who try to perpetuate this broader understanding of Islam through our writing and through public dialogue are in the minority. I am convinced we need a broader understanding of Islam if we are to be effective in the modern world. The Mu'tazilites produced a rational theology able to cope with the demands of modernity in the ninth century.

The Mu'tazilites established the principle that knowledge starts from this world. We can speak about the unseen world only on the basis of indications furnished by the evident reality of the seen world. God and His attributes can be known only by reflection and acquired knowledge, not necessarily by direct or revealed knowledge. Ibn Tufayl's twelfth-century allegory, *Hayy ibn Yaqzan*, illustrates this point well.

This is a story about two islands. No human being had ever lived on one of the islands until a child, known as Hayy ibn Yaqzan, comes ashore one day, having floated there in a box. His name means "The Alive, son of The Awake." A gazelle suckles him until her death, at which time he is left on his own to provide for his needs. His innate intelligence, feeble at first, develops. Through the tedious process of observation and reflection, he acquires knowledge of the physical universe. His thinking takes him into the realm of metaphysics, and the existence of an all-powerful Creator becomes obvious to him. Through ascetic discipline of his mind and body, he seeks union with this One Eternal Spirit—as he has come to understand the Creator. Ultimately, he arrives at a state of ecstasy where his intellect merges with the Active Intellect and he is able to apprehend those things which his eye has not seen or his ear heard. Without prophet or Revelation, he achieves full knowledge and everlasting happiness in metaphysical union with God.

One day, while walking on his island, he is astonished to discover a creature like himself. It is none other than a holy man named Asal, a recent arrival from the neighboring island, where the good king Salaman rules. Life on Asal's island revolves around a conventional religious system that uses rewards and punishments to keep people in line. Asal has reached a deep level of spirituality—deeper than his peers have been able to achieve— and has come to what he believes to be an uninhabited island in order to reach even more depth through asceticism and solitude.

Asal teaches Hayy language, and Hayy is amazed to discover that the pure Truth he struggled to attain in solitude is the same Truth symbolized by the religion Asal professes. When Hayy learns about the condition of people on the other island, he is moved with compassion, and vows to go and offer them the benefit of his knowledge. Asal and Hayy set out on this mission together. However, the mission is an abysmal failure. Most of their audiences cannot grasp Hayy's exposition of the Truth. They call it a dangerous innovation and become hostile towards him. Because they are fettered by their senses, they can respond only to concrete imagery. Their moral nature responds only to a crude system of rewards and punishments. Hayy soon realizes that the Prophet Muhammad's way with them, as expressed in the Qur'an, is the only effective method for them. He apologizes for his intrusion, exhorts them to be faithful to their religion, and returns with Asal to his home island.

The name of the hero of this allegory is suggestive. *Hayy* means "alive," *ibn* means "son of," *Yaqzan* means "awake." "The awakened" refers to the intellect. Human beings are alive only when their intellect becomes activated. With intellectual reflection, a human being can acquire knowledge of God. Divine knowledge need not depend on Revelation, although Revelation need not contradict knowledge obtained through human intellect. Enlightenment, however, is not purely an intellectual exercise. Our hero, Hayy, practicing asceticism in mind and body as well as developing his intellect, achieves union with God, something that happens only through this synthesis of rationalism and mysticism.

Ibn Rushd (1126–98), known as Averroës in the West, influenced both Jewish and Christian philosophers (Maimonides, Thomas Aquinas, and Albertus Magnus) with his rationalistic thought. Averroës argued that real knowledge took shape in the form of philosophical, rational knowledge. Only a small, elite minority of society should be privy to this knowledge—knowledge, he thought, would harmfully affect the belief system of most people. We saw this illustrated in our allegory. Hayy felt compelled to withdraw his message and insights from the people living on the other island. Because they strictly followed religious teachings and adhered to their literal meaning, they were unable to apprehend Hayy's "higher" discourse.

Before Averroës, Abu Hamid Muhammad al-Ghazali (d. 1111), a Sufi, wrote a book considered to be his masterpiece, *The Revival of the Religious Sciences (Ihya 'Ulum al-Din)*. This work became extremely popular—only the Qur'an and the *hadith* (text based on the life of the Prophet) surpassed it in popularity. Al-Ghazali emphasized that mystical knowledge is not meant for the public. Simply stated, he believed sound knowledge (and to his way of thinking, sound knowledge took the shape of mystical understanding) is revealed to a chosen elite.

Despite their different philosophical orientations, Averroës and al-Ghazali agreed about the necessity of keeping ordinary people distanced from true knowledge. This legacy has stayed with us in the Muslim world, especially since al-Ghazali's writings dominated Islamic discourse until the nineteenth century.

The nineteenth century ushered in a new age. The Muslim world felt threatened by European political aggression. Islam became identified not just as a nationality or an ethnicity, but as a repository of specific characteristics of the collective "self" (Muslim) opposed to the "other" (European). Intellectuals responded to this aggression by defending Islam and Islamic culture against those who simply pronounced Islam to be backward rather than looking at the social, economic, and political realities of the Arab world in order to understand why Arab societies took on a particular configuration. Islam was put on the defensive. It felt it had to explain and interpret itself as a religion that encourages progress, is rational as well as scientific, and accepts modern institutions.

I continuously struggle with where to place myself as I wrestle with creating a modern Islamic discourse. Does modern Islamic thought have to start with Averroës' philosophy and the rational understanding held by the Mu'tazilites? I used to think so. Today, I am not so sure. The huge chasm that exists in Averroës' philosophy between the elite and the public will never help to achieve enlightenment—a free and just society.

According to Averroës, knowledge is not for everybody, it is not open to all—it is an elite privilege. Enlightenment, therefore, can never be institutionalized in society. Enlightenment has never been a public movement in any Muslim country. Our history is riddled with examples of how those who hold political authority have been able to impose their thinking on the majority through the force of inquisition. Ignoring the individual's intellectual freedom only perpetuates this thinking, and hence repressive societies abound. This notion of dividing people into the elite (knowledgeable) and the public (ignorant), the cultured and the commoner, and the statesman and the ordinary citizen, dominates the Muslim world even though education is free and open to all.

The ideals of the Enlightenment—freedom of speech and freedom of thought—values that have become part of my academic research, are not fully embraced in the Muslim world. The fear, of course, is that Islamic values will be rendered null and void if freedoms, as envisioned by the Enlightenment, are unleashed. There is this sense that there should be security zones, places not accessible to intellectual discussion or academic investigation. Academic research, freedom of thought, and freedom of speech are guaranteed only as long as they do not impinge on what is known as absolute truth. Of course, truth is the interpretation given to the Qur'an by the orthodox, those who have the political power to enforce their views. Orthodox Islam, it should come as no surprise, emphasizes obedience as a religious, obligatory duty. Political rulers often combine political and religious authority and become known as God's authority on earth. (Christianity had this understanding for years, something known as the divine right of kings.)

Many Muslims are persuaded that freedom of thought and freedom of speech are products of Western culture and European civilization—a culture and civilization seen as antithetical to the essence of Islamic culture and civilization. In order to avoid being swallowed, controlled, and manipulated by powers that once sought to conquer them, many Muslims believe it cannot be in their best interest to adopt values associated with the West.

Is there hope? Is it possible to envision Muslims embracing freedom within a framework of democracy? Yes, of course. However, it is imperative that citizens in what are generally known as democratic nations understand how their countries' own economic and political interests often subvert the very thing (democracy) they purport to want established in Islamic states. It is also important to understand that it is not Islam that prevents Muslims from accepting democracy, but rather a religious and political dogmatic trend of thought, ever prevalent, which claims that Islam and modernity contradict one another.

Political regimes in the Muslim world to a large extent unfold in what I call modernity without rationality. Since democracy is not based solely on respect for the individual, but takes into account through free elections the individual's opinion, it seems that this lack of rationality found throughout the Muslim world blocks democracy at every turn. Turkey, the only Muslim country ever to claim to be a secular state, controls its so-called democracy through military censorship. Iran's ayatollahs, upon seizing power, interestingly enough did not restore the caliphate, but established a republic. All the democratic accoutrements—popular election, a constituent assembly, a parliament, a president, political factions, a constitution, and so forth—emerged. But can there be democracy when clerics wield authority? Can *Sharia* law as interpreted by the ayatollahs yield a democratic society? Would a secular party be welcomed in Iran? I doubt it. Both countries, under different guises, reflect this idea of modernity without rationality.

The West places an inordinate amount of pressure on the Muslim world in order to protect its economic and political interests. There have been a number of puppet political regimes in Muslim countries (Iran, Iraq, Afghanistan), held in place by Western powers against the will of the Muslim people. This is not democracy. In addition, how many times is Islam portrayed, especially by the Western media, as an inherently violent religion and antithetical to Western values? How is it that in many developing countries a wider and wider gap exists between the haves and the have nots? Modernity, human rights, and democracy seem to be the domain of the privileged, who, more often than not, turn a deaf ear to underprivileged people crying out for justice. This cry for justice, when it goes unheeded by those with privilege and power, easily turns violent. The seeds of violence are found at this juncture, not in Islam—or in any religion, for that matter.

How do we go forward? I trace the conflict between secular and religious forces that we experience within Muslim cultures to an absence of a public forum for debate and dialogue. Many ideas and opinions circulate among us. I believe that defending democracy unconditionally is the only way to crystallize these ideas and opinions. It is imperative that we defend a democracy that does not shunt aside any of those opinions coming from our perceived enemies.

The developed world navigated this ideological terrain by agreeing to organize its disagreements through the mechanism of democracy, relying heavily on freedom of speech—the ability to express one's opinion. It is high time that we in the Arab world began to organize our disagreements. The saying "I may disagree with you, but I am ready to give my life to defend your right to express your opinion" needs to seep into the marrow of our collective bones. Those who are afraid of disagreement should look again at our history. When did Arabs ever agree with each other about anything? Historically, there has always been a difference of opinion among us.

In modern history, Muslims have managed to present a united front in their struggle against Western imperialism and Zionism. These two threats have managed to suppress the establishment of civil, democratic society based on multiplicity, diversity, and the peaceful circulation of power.

At the same time, I believe that those democratic countries that have inherited the values of the Enlightenment—freedom of thought, freedom of expression—need to reclaim those freedoms and apply those eroding values in their own societies. The West badly needs to put its own house back in order.

Muslims need to focus on creating just and equitable societies based on creatively formulating and integrating thoughtful religious and political discourse into daily life. Seeing in a new way—an act that enables us to create a better society based on a fresh perspective—then becomes useful in the modern world. It is high time we shed this *jahiliyyah*, blind obedience to the echoes of our ancestor's voices.

CHAPTER 9

Women and the Rise of Islam

Leila Ahmed

Born in Cairo in 1940, Leila Ahmed received a doctorate degree from the University of Cambridge and was later appointed to professorships first at the University of Massachusetts, Amherst, and later at the Harvard Divinity School, where she currently holds an endowed chair. After publishing a book in 1978 on Edward Lane, a British Orientalist, Ahmed turned her attention to issues of gender in Islam and Western stereotypes of Muslim women, both products of her personal experiences as a Muslim woman living in the West. In 1992 she published her seminal work Women and Gender in Islam, *from which the following essay is drawn, in which she examined the treatment of women in Arab Muslim societies from the establishment of Islam up to the present. The two themes of critically analyzing women's position in the theory and practice of Islam, and simplistic Western stereotypes of Muslim women figure prominently in this work, as they also do in Ahmed's more autobiographical* A Border Passage: From Cairo to America—A Woman's Journey, *published in 1999.*

The following essay comes from Women and Gender in Islam: Historical Roots of a Modern Debate *(New Haven, CT: Yale University Press, 1992), pp 41–63. An earlier version of the essay appeared in* Signs, *vol. 11, no. 4 (summer 1986), pp 665–91.*

In the sixth century CE Arabia formed, as it were, an island in the Middle East, the last remaining region in which patrilineal, patriarchal marriage had not yet been instituted as the sole legitimate form of marriage; although even there it was probably becoming the dominant type of marriage, the evidence suggests that among the types of marriage practiced was matrilineal, uxorilocal marriage, found in Arabia, including Mecca, about the time of the birth of Muhammad (*c.*570)—the woman remaining with her tribe, where the man could visit or reside with her, and the children belonging to the mother's tribe—as well as polyandrous and polygamous marriages.

Neither the diversity of marriage practices in pre-Islamic Arabia nor the presence of matrilineal customs, including the association of children with the mother's tribe, necessarily connote women having greater power in society or greater access to economic resources. Nor do these practices correlate with an absence of misogyny; indeed, there is clear evidence to the contrary. The practice of infanticide, apparently confined to girls, suggests a belief that females were flawed, expendable. The Qur'anic verses condemning infanticide capture the shame and negativity that *jahiliyya* Arabs associated with the sex:

> When one of them is told of the birth of a female child, his face is overcast with gloom and he is deeply agitated. He seeks to hide himself from the people because of the ominous [bad] news he has had. Shall he preserve it despite the disgrace involved or bury it in the ground? (16:58–61).[1]

However, the argument made by some Islamists, that Islam's banning of infanticide established the fact that Islam improved the position of women in all respects, seems both inaccurate and simplistic. In the first place, the situation of women appears to have varied among the different communities of Arabia. Moreover, although *jahiliyya* marriage practices do not necessarily indicate the greater power of women or the absence of misogyny, they do correlate with women enjoying greater sexual autonomy than they were allowed under Islam. They also correlate with women being active participants, even leaders, in a wide range of community activities, including warfare and religion. Their autonomy and participation were curtailed with the establishment of Islam, its institution of patrilineal, patriarchal marriage as solely legitimate, and the social transformation that ensued.

The lives and the marriages of two of Muhammad's wives, Khadija and Aishah, encapsulate the kinds of changes that would overtake women in Islamic Arabia. Khadija, Muhammad's first wife, was a wealthy widow who, before her marriage to Muhammad, employed him to oversee her caravan, which traded between Mecca and Syria. She proposed to and married him when she was 40 and he 25, and she remained his only wife until her death at about 65. She occupies a place of importance in the story of Islam because of her importance to Muhammad: her wealth freed him from the need to earn a living and enabled him to lead the life of contemplation that was the prelude to his becoming a prophet, and her support and confidence were crucial to him in his venturing to preach Islam. She was already in her 50s, however, when Muhammad received his first Revelation and began to preach, and thus it was *jahiliyya* society and customs, rather than Islamic, that shaped her conduct and defined the possibilities of her life. Her economic independence; her marriage overture, apparently without a male guardian to act as intermediary; her marriage to a man many years younger than herself; and her monogamous marriage all reflect *jahiliyya* rather than Islamic practice.

In contrast, autonomy and monogamy were conspicuously absent in the lives of the women Muhammad married after he became the established Prophet and leader of Islam, and the control of women by male guardians and the male prerogative of polygyny were thereafter to become formal features of Islamic marriage. It was Aishah's lot, rather, which would prefigure the limitations that would thenceforth hem in Muslim women's lives: she was born to Muslim parents, married Muhammad when she was nine or ten, and soon thereafter, along with her co-wives, began to observe the new customs of veiling and seclusion. The difference between Khadija's and Aishah's lives—especially with regard to autonomy—foreshadows the changes that Islam would effect for Arabian women, Aishah, however, lived at a moment of transition, and in some respects her life reflects *jahiliyya* as well as Islamic practice. Her brief assumption of political leadership after Muhammad's death doubtless had its roots in the customs of her forebears, as did the esteem and authority the community granted her. The acceptance of women as participants in and authorities on the central affairs of the community steadily declined in the ensuing Islamic period.

The evidence regarding marriage practices in pre-Islamic Arabia is fairly scant and its implications uncertain. Evidence of matriliny and of sexual mores consonant with matriliny, including polyandry, is, however, distinct enough for the nineteenth-century scholar Robertson Smith to have suggested that the society was matriarchal and that Islam therefore displaced a matriarchal order with a patriarchal one. More recently, Montgomery Watt has put forward a modified version of this theory. Gathering evidence of the practices of uxorilocal marriage and polyandry in some parts of Arabia, he suggests not that pre-Islamic Arabia was matriarchal but that it was predominantly matrilineal, a society in which paternity was of little or no importance, and that the society was in the process of changing around the time of Muhammad's birth into a patrilineal one—a change that Islam was to consolidate. Watt speculates that the commercial growth of Mecca during the fifth and sixth centuries and the progressively sedentary ways of its preeminent tribe, the Quraysh, led to the breakdown of tribal values, particularly the notion of communal property, which disappeared as individual traders accumulated wealth. Men now wished to pass on property to their offspring, which gave new importance to paternity and led eventually to the displacement of matriliny by patriliny.[2]

Smith's and Watt's theories aside, the evidence does at least unambiguously indicate that there was no single, fixed institution of marriage and that a variety of marriage customs were practiced about the time of the rise of Islam, customs suggesting that both matrilineal and patrilineal systems were extant. Uxorilocal practices, for instance, can be found in Muhammad's background. His grandfather had been taken from his mother's clan and appropriated by his father's only with difficulty. Muhammad's mother, Amina, remained with her clan after her marriage to 'Abdullah, who visited her there, and after Muhammad's birth ('Abdullah died before his son was born). Muhammad passed to the care of his paternal kin only after her death.[3]

Other indications of a variety of types of union being practiced include al-Bukhari's account of Aishah's description of the types of pre-Islamic marriage. According to Aishah, there were four types of marriage in the *jahiliyya* period: one was the "marriage of people as it is today," and two of the other types were polyandrous.[4] Polyandrous marriages are known to have taken place in both Mecca and Medina. Also, although there is evidence of polygyny before Islam, it is speculated, on the basis of lack of reference to the practice, that the virilocal polygyny that Muhammad practiced was rare and that, rather, polygyny in a matrilineal context probably entailed a husband's visiting his different wives where they resided with their tribes.[5] Similarly, some wives might have been visited by different husbands.

Divorce and remarriage appear to have been common for both men and women, either of whom could initiate the dissolution. *Kitab al-aghani* reports:

> The women in the *jahiliyya*, or some of them, divorced men, and their [manner of] divorce was that if they lived in a tent they turned it round, so that if the door had faced east it now faced west … and when the man saw this he knew that she had divorced him and did not go to her.

Divorce was not generally followed by the *'idda*, or "waiting period" for women before remarriage—an observance Islam was to insist on—and although a wife used to go into retirement for a period following her husband's death, the custom, if such it was, seems to have been laxly observed.[6]

From early on, evidently, the institution of a type of marriage based on the recognition of paternity was part of the Islamic message. The pledge of allegiance to Islam, later formalized in the Qur'an (60:12, known as the Pledge of the Women; the men's pledge differed only in that it included the duty of defense), seems from the start to have included an undertaking to refrain from *zina*, a term usually translated as "adultery." What *zina* meant before the advent of Islam—in a society in which several types of union were legitimate—is not clear, nor, apparently, was it always clear to converts to Islam. After being conquered by Muhammad, the men of Taif complained on taking the oath that *zina* was necessary to them because they were merchants—in other words, they attached no stigma to the practice. One woman taking the oath said, "Does a free woman commit *zina*?"—a response construed to mean that she felt any union that a free woman entered into could not be termed *zina*.[7] When first used in Islam, therefore, the term may have referred to other types of marriage, including polyandrous ones, and to forms of "temporary" marriage also practiced in the *jahiliyya*, which Islam would outlaw. Aishah, in her remarks about the different types of marriage in the *jahiliyya*, concluded: "When Mohamad (God bless and preserve him) was sent with the Truth, he abolished all the types of marriage [*nikah*] of the pre-Islamic period ... except the type of marriage which people recognize today."[8] If, in prohibiting *zina*, Islam was to some degree outlawing previously accepted practices, this perhaps would account in part for the otherwise extraordinary Qur'anic ruling (4:19) that four witnesses are required to convict anyone of *zina*. The ruling suggests both that those engaging in such sexual misconduct were doing so with some openness—the openness appropriate to relatively accepted rather than immoral or prohibited practices—and that Muhammad realized that such practices could not be instantly eradicated.

Islamic reforms apparently consolidated a trend towards patriliny in sixth-century Arabia, and particularly in Mecca, where, as a result of commercial expansion, the entire fabric of the old nomadic order was undergoing change. In addition to internal economic change, external influences no doubt played some part in transforming the culture. The infiltration of Iranian influences among the tribes of northern Arabia, along with Meccan trade linking Syria and the Byzantine Empire to the north with Yemen and Ethiopia to the south, meant increasing contact with and exposure to the social organization of gender in these neighboring societies. A form of monotheism, characteristic of the predominant religions in these adjoining regions, as well as patrilineal marriage, in which men controlled women's sexuality, had also begun to gain ground in a hitherto polytheistic Arabia before Muhammad began to preach Islam. The mechanisms of control, seclusion, and exclusion of women from community affairs already elaborately developed in these societies must also have become familiar to Arabians, particularly traders.

The type of marriage that Islam legitimized was, like its monotheism, deeply consonant with the socio-cultural systems already in place throughout the Middle East. Within Arabia patriarchal, patrilineal, polygynous marriage was by no means starkly innovative. Rather, Islam selectively sanctioned customs already found among some Arabian tribal societies while prohibiting others. Of central importance to the institution it established were the preeminence given to paternity and the vesting in the male of proprietary rights to female sexuality and its issue. Accordant customs, such as polygamy, were incorporated while discordant or opposing customs were prohibited. Through these changes Islam fundamentally reformulated the nexus of sexuality and power between men and women. The reconceptualization of marriage implied by the Islamic regulations might justly be regarded as critical to the changes in the position of women and to the crushing limitations imposed on them following the establishment of Islam.

The laws regulating marriage and women's conduct that were developed by later Islamic societies represent their interpretations of a series of Qur'anic verses revealed to Muhammad chiefly in the Medinian period and their decisions about the legal significance of Muhammad's own practices. The sources I draw on in exploring key moments in the development of marriage and in exploring those practices of Muhammad in relation to women that were to prove decisive for Muslim women thereafter are largely the *hadith* and other early biographical literature on Muhammad and his Companions.

The *hadith* are short narratives about Muhammad and his Companions which contemporaries collected into written form in the three or four centuries after Muhammad died. They are based (as the biographical literature also is) on memorized accounts first related by Muhammad's contemporaries and transmitted by a carefully authenticated chain of individuals of recognized probity. Although orthodox Islam has regarded certain collections as authentic accounts of acts or utterances of Muhammad, Western and Western-trained scholars have revised their thinking on the matter; earlier this century most scholars regarded the material essentially as fabrications of a later age. More recently some Western-based scholars have come round to the view that some *hadith* probably did originate in very early Muslim times—that is, in the period immediately after Muhammad's death, when many of his Companions were alive.[9] The narratives cited below are drawn from texts generally considered among the most authentic, and the circumstances and behaviors described are typical of the lifestyles portrayed in the *hadith* corpus.

In its account of pre-Islamic customs this early material has already been ideologically edited from an Islamic standpoint. All the material we have on the *jahiliyya* dates from at least a century after Muhammad's death and thus was written down by Muslims. For example, when Ibn Sa'd asserts that none of Muhammad's foremothers through 500 generations was a "fornicator" in the manner "of the *jahiliyya*," he refers presumably to the forms of union, including polyandry, that were accepted practice (Ibn Sa'd, 1, pt. 1:32). Practices endorsed by Islam, such as polygyny, are mentioned without parallel censure. That is, the texts themselves discretely and continually reaffirmed the new Islamic practices and branded the old immoral.

Furthermore, although these early reports were written down by men, a significant proportion of the accounts of Muhammad and his times—the literature revered as the authentic annals of early Islam and looked to for a model of Muslim conduct and as a source of Muslim law—were recounted on the authority of women; that is, the accounts in question were traced back as having been first recounted by a woman of Muhammad's generation, a Companion, and often a wife or daughter, of Muhammad. Women therefore (and Aishah most particularly) were important contributors to the verbal texts of Islam, the texts that, transcribed eventually into written form by men, became part of the official history of Islam and of the literature that established the normative practices of Islamic society. This very fact indicates that at least the first generation of Muslims—the generation closest to *jahiliyya* days and *jahiliyya* attitudes towards women—and their immediate descendants had no difficulty in accepting women as authorities. It also means that the early literature incorporates at least some material expressing the views of women fairly directly, such as Aishah's indignant response to the notion that women might be religiously unclean. "You equate us [women] with dogs and donkeys!" she exclaims in one *hadith*. "The Prophet would pray while I lay before him on the bed [between him and the *qibla*, the direction of the Ka'aba in Mecca, which Muslims face when they pray]." [10] Obviously, this does not mean that opinions or actions unacceptable to the order represented by the men who transcribed women's words into written form were not suppressed and omitted.

In a cave in Hira, a hill near Mecca, to which he often retired for solitary contemplation, Muhammad, then 40 years old, received his first Revelation: a vision of the angel Gabriel, commanding him to read. Shivering from the experience, he hurried to Khadija, who comforted him physically and mentally, wrapping him in a blanket and assuring him that he was sane. Later she took Muhammad to her cousin Waraka (to whom she had been betrothed), a Christian versed in the Hebrew scriptures, who confirmed what had evidently occurred to her: he said that Allah had also sent the angel Gabriel to Moses. Thereafter, the Judeo-Christian framework was to be that which Muhammad declared as the framework of his prophethood. [11]

Khadija became his first convert. The faith of this mature, wealthy woman of high standing in the community must have influenced others, particularly members of her own important clan, the Quraysh, to accept Islam. [12] From the earliest years women were among the converts, including women whose clans were fiercely opposed to Muhammad, such as Umm

Habiba, daughter of Abu Sufyan, Muhammad's formidable enemy. They were also among the Muslims who, under the pressure of the growing Meccan opposition to and persecution of Muhammad and his followers, emigrated (c.615) to Abyssinia. None of the women, however, is mentioned as having emigrated independently of her husband.[13]

It was during the period of persecution in Mecca that Muhammad spoke verses sanctioning the worship, along with Allah, of the three Meccan goddesses, the "daughters of Allah," Allat, Manat, and al-'Uzza, a development that briefly appeased the Meccans. The verses, however, were shortly abrogated, having been "thrown" upon Muhammad's tongue by Satan, according to tradition, at a time when Meccan persecution was growing intense and the Meccans were offering Muhammad position and wealth to cease reviling their goddesses. As they stand in the Qur'an, the verses in their amended form (53:19–22) point out the absurdity of Allah's having daughters when mortals could have (the preferred) sons—therefore confirming what the practice of female infanticide indicated anyway, that the existence of goddesses in the late *jahiliyya* period did not mean a concomitant valuation of females above or equal to males.[14]

In 619 Khadija and Ali Ibn Abu Talib, Muhammad's uncle and protector and head of their clan, both died within days of each other. Muhammad himself "went down into the pit" to place Khadija in her tomb in the Hujun, a hill near Mecca that was the burial place of her people. Neither Muhammad nor Khadija's daughters seem to have inherited anything from her, and it is possible that she lost her wealth in the Meccan persecution.[15]

Ali Ibn Abu Talib had not converted to Islam, but he nevertheless granted Muhammad the full protection of a clan member and thereby made it possible for him to survive the Meccan persecution. His successor as head of the clan was Abu Lahab, another uncle of Muhammad, who was married to Umm Jamil, sister of Abu Sufyan, Muhammad's enemy. Soon after Abu Talib died, Abu Lahab sided with his wife's clan and refused to give Muhammad clan protection. When Abu Lahab and Umm Jamil were then cursed in a Qur'anic Revelation, the latter, carrying a stone pestle, went searching for Muhammad and came to where he sat with his Companion Abu Bakr, by the Ka'aba. God made Muhammad invisible to her, so she asked Abu Bakr where Muhammad was. "I have been told that he is satirizing me, and by God, if I had found him I would have smashed his mouth with this stone." She then declared herself a poet and recited:

> We reject the reprobate.
> His words we repudiate.
> His religion we loathe and hate.[16]

Bereft of the clan's protection, Muhammad began actively to seek converts and protectors beyond Mecca. He initiated a series of negotiations with people from Medina who, while on pilgrimage to Mecca in 620, had converted to Islam. The following year they returned with more converts, and in June 622 75 Medinians, including two women and their husbands, came to a secret meeting with Muhammad at 'Aqaba, where they pledged to protect and obey him. Their allegiance meant that he would be received in Medina not as the reviled leader of a sect seeking protection but as an honored prophet and designated arbiter of the internal tribal dissensions of Medina.[17]

Meanwhile, Muhammad had also set about his own remarriage—to Sawda and Aishah. The idea for the marriages reportedly came from Khawla, an aunt of Muhammad who was a convert to Islam. After Khadija's death she "served" Muhammad, presumably seeing to the housework, along with his daughters. Muhammad had in the past intervened on her behalf, rebuking her husband for his celibacy and his consequent neglect of his duties towards his wife. When Khawla broached the idea of Muhammad's remarriage, he asked whom she would suggest. Aishah if he wanted a virgin, she said, and Sawda if a non-virgin. "Go," he is said to have replied, "bespeak them both for me." Having two wives concurrently was not a new practice in that society, but it was new for Muhammad, leading some investigators to speculate that he may have had a marriage contract with Khadija specifying that during her lifetime she would be his only wife.[18]

Sawda, a Muslim widow and former emigrant to Abyssinia, described as "no longer young," sent back with Khawla the message "My affair is in your hands," indicating her consent (Ibn Sa'd, 8:36). This point confirms that as Khadija's case had suggested, widows in the *jahiliyya* were apparently free to dispose of their persons in marriage without consulting any guardians (Ibn Sa'd, 8:36).[19] The marriage of Muhammad and Sawda probably took place shortly after Khadija's death.

Aishah's case was different. She was the six-year-old daughter of Muhammad's closest and most important supporter, Abu Bakr. Khawla took the proposal to Umm Rumman, Aishah's mother, who deferred the matter to her husband. He said that because Aishah was already betrothed, he would first have to release her from that commitment. There is no suggestion that anyone thought the marriage inappropriate because of the discrepancy in their ages, though Aishah's prior betrothal was evidently to a boy. Abu Bakr went to seek her release from the boy's parents and found the mother, who was not a Muslim, particularly anxious to release her son from that betrothal because she was afraid it might lead to his converting to

Islam.

Aishah later recalled that she had realized she was married (that is, that the marriage agreement had been concluded) when her mother called her in from her games with her friends and told her she must stay indoors; and so "it fell into my heart," she said, "that I was married." She did not, she recalled, ask to whom (Ibn Sa'd, 8:40). Muhammad thereafter continued his regular daily visits to Abu Bakr's house, but the marriage was not consummated until after the Muslims had migrated to Medina.

The Muslims migrated to Medina in small groups in the three months after the agreement with the Medinians at 'Aqaba had been concluded. Among the men, Muhammad and Abu Bakr left last and in secret, to escape a Meccan plot to murder Muhammad, for the Meccans now feared that at Medina he would grow too strong for them. The two hid in the hills near Mecca, waiting for the search to be given up. Asma, Aishah's sister, took them provisions at night and helped load their camels when they were ready to depart. After they left, she returned home and found a group of hostile Meccans searching for the two men. When she denied knowledge of their whereabouts, she was slapped so hard, she related, that her earring flew off.[20]

Muhammad arrived in Medina with a large religious following and an important political standing. The year of the migration, or *Hijrah* (Hegira), 622, is reckoned by Muslims as the first year of the Islamic era, and the migration did indeed inaugurate a new type of community, one that lived by the new values and the new laws of Islam—many of which were elaborated over the next few years.

Work was immediately begun on the building that was to be Muhammad's dwelling, the courtyard of which was to be both a mosque and the place where he would conduct community affairs. He meanwhile lodged on the ground floor of a two-room house belonging to the couple who lived nearest the construction. Some sense of the material privation of their lives and Muhammad's is suggested by the couple's response to breaking a jar of water: fearing it would leak through on to Muhammad and having no cloth to mop it up with, they used their own garments.[21]

Muhammad had Sawda and his daughters brought from Mecca. Like the dwellings built later for Muhammad's other wives, Sawda's was built along the eastern wall of the mosque and consisted of one room about 12 by 14 feet, with possibly a veranda-like enclosure looking on to the mosque courtyard; the courtyard had pillars of palm trunks and a roof of palm branches. Muhammad had no separate room, sharing in turn those of his wives.[22]

Abu Bakr also had his family fetched, and they joined him in a house in the suburb of Sunh. When Aishah was no more than nine or ten, Abu Bakr, anxious no doubt to create the further bond of kinship between Muhammad and himself, asked Muhammad why he was delaying consummation of the marriage. When Muhammad replied that he was as yet unable to provide the marriage portion, Abu Bakr forthwith provided it himself (Ibn Sa'd, 8:43). Thereafter, the marriage was consummated in Aishah's father's house in Sunh. As Aishah recalled the occasion:

> My mother came to me and I was swinging on a swing. ... She brought me down from the swing, and I had some friends there and she sent them away, and she wiped my face with a little water, and led me till we stopped by the door, and I was breathless [from being on the swing] and we waited till I regained my breath. Then she took me in, and the Prophet was sitting on a bed in our house with men and women of the Ansar [Medinians] and she set me on his lap, and said, "These are your people. God bless you in them and they in you." And the men and women rose immediately and went out, And the Prophet consummated the marriage in our house.[23]

Aishah became and remained Muhammad's undisputed favorite, even when he had added beautiful, sought-after women to his harem. Her most recent scholarly biographer, Nabia Abbott, stresses Muhammad's tender care and patience with her; he joined even in her games with dolls. To modern sensibilities, however, details such as Aishah's recollections of her marriage and its consummation, do not make the relationship more comprehensible. If anything, they underscore its pathos and tragedy. Nevertheless, Abbott is right to assume that the relevant matter is not the sensibilities of other ages but rather the accurate representation of the relationship. Consequently, other aspects, such as their apparent emotional equality and their mutual dependence, should also be noted. These are suggested by, for instance, Muhammad's sullen, wounded withdrawal following the famous necklace incident: Aishah was left behind at a campsite because she had wandered off looking for the beads of her necklace. Returning the following morning, her camel escorted by a young man, she was suspected by the community, and finally by Muhammad, of infidelity. Muhammad's distress over the matter became so intense that his Revelations ceased for the duration of their estrangement; his first Revelations at the end of that period were the verses declaring her innocence.[24] Complementarily, Aishah must have felt reasonably equal to and unawed by this prophet of God, for his announcement of a Revelation permitting him to enter into marriages disallowed other men drew from her the retort, "It seems to me your Lord hastens to satisfy your desire!" (Ibn Sa'd, 8:112). In other words, in all its aspects their relationship was defined by the particular social context—not only in the sense of the mores of the society but also in the sense of the ways in which the mores of a society shape the inner psychic and emotional structures of its members.

The details of Aishah's betrothal and marriage indicate that parents before and around the time of the rise of Islam might arrange marriages between children, male or female, and their peers or elders. They indicate, too, that for girls betrothal entailed control and supervision of their sexuality, some form of seclusion (Aishah understood she was married when told she had to stay indoors). A patriarchal notion of marriage and sexuality apparently, then, already pertained in Aishah's childhood environment. Similarly, the arrangements for Muhammad's simultaneous betrothal to two women were represented in the literature not as innovatory but, again, as ordinary. It is, however, possible that the reports coming from the pens of Muslim authors do not accurately reflect late *jahiliyya* and early Islamic practices but rather conform to a later Islamic understanding of marriage.

Aishah's removal to Muhammad's dwelling, where Sawda already lived and where they would soon be joined by more wives, introduced into Islam the type of polygyny—virilocal polygyny—that some investigators believe was Muhammad's innovation.

Three months after Muhammad's marriage to Aishah he married Hafsa, daughter of Omar ibn al-Khattab, who along with Abu Bakr was among Muhammad's closest supporters. Hafsa had lost her husband in the battle of Badr. The majority of Muhammad's wives thereafter were also widows of Muslims slain in support of Islam. Soon after this marriage, and after the battle of Uhud (625), which widowed many Muslim women, the Qur'anic verses encouraging polygyny—"Marry other women as may be agreeable to you, two or three or four" (4:3)—were revealed. Many of these widows were Meccan immigrants and so could not return to the support of their clans. The Muslim community consequently found itself with the responsibility of providing for them. Encouraging men to marry more wives both settled the matter of support for the widows and consolidated the young society in its new direction: it absorbed the women into the new type of family life and forestalled reversion to *jahiliyya* marriage practices.

There was little intermarriage between Medinians and Meccans, perhaps chiefly because of their different attitudes towards marriage and especially towards polygyny. Medinian women apparently were noticeably more asser-tive than Meccan women. Omar ibn al-Khattab complained that before coming to Medina "we the people of Quraysh [Mecca] used to have the upper hand over our wives, but when we came among the Ansar [Helpers], we found that their women had the upper hand over their men, so our women also started learning the ways of the Ansari women." [25] One Medinian woman is said to have offered herself in marriage to Muhammad—who accepted—then to have withdrawn her offer when her family, which disapproved, pointed out that she could never put up with co-wives (Ibn Sa'd, 8:107–8).

Women's right to inherit property—generally speaking, a woman is entitled to about half a man's share—was another Islamic decree that Medinians found novel and apparently uncongenial. Medina being an agricultural community presumably made the new inheritance law, involving the division of land, more complex in its consequences than for commercial Mecca, where property was in herds and where even before Islam it was apparently the custom for women to inherit. [26]

Accounts of the battle of Uhud portray women, including Muhammad's wives, actively and freely participating in the ostensibly male domain of warfare. One man described seeing Aishah and another wife of Muhammad, their garments tucked up and their anklets showing, carrying water to men on the battlefield. Other women on the Muslim side are mentioned as caring for the injured and removing the dead and wounded from the field. On the opposing side Hind bint 'Utbah, wife of the Meccan leader Abu Sufyan, led some 14 or 15 women of the Meccan aristocracy on to the battlefield, playing out women's traditional *jahiliyya* role in war of singing war songs and playing tambourines. [27] The Meccans won, and Hind, who had lost a father and brothers to the Muslims in previous wars, cut out the liver of the man who had killed her father and cut off his nose and ears and those of other dead men on the field. Wearing necklaces and bracelets of the severed parts, she stood on a rock declaiming, in satirical verse, her triumphant revenge (Ibn Sa'd, 3:1, 5–6). The extreme ferocity attributed to her, reported in works compiled in the Abbasid age, perhaps owes its bloodiness to Abbasid hatred of the Umayyad dynasty, founded by Hind's son.

Such free participation in community affairs would soon be curtailed by the formal introduction of seclusion. The lives of Muhammad's wives were the first to be circumscribed, and during Muhammad's lifetime the verses enjoining seclusion applied to them alone. Early texts record the occasions on which the verses instituting veiling and seclusion for Muhammad's wives were revealed and offer vignettes of women's lives in the society Islam was displacing, as well as record the steps by which Islam closed women's arenas of action. These texts do not distinguish in their language between veiling and seclusion but use the term *hijab* interchangeably to mean "veil," as in *darabat al-hijab*, "she took the veil"—which in turn meant "she became a wife of Muhammad's," Muhammad's wives but not his concubines donning the veil—and to mean "curtain" (its literal meaning) in the sense of separation or partition. They also use the same term to refer generally to the seclusion or separation of Muhammad's wives and to the decrees relating to their veiling or covering themselves.[28]

The feast at Muhammad's wedding to Zeinab bint Jahsh, according to one account, was the occasion for the revelation of a number of these verses. Some of the wedding guests stayed on too long in Zeinab's room chatting, which annoyed Muhammad and thus occasioned the revelation of the verses instituting seclusion for his wives. At this or some other meal, according to another account, the hands of some of the male guests touched the hands of Muhammad's wives, and in particular Omar's hand touched Aishah's (Ibn Sa'd, 8:126). The Qur'anic verses instituting seclusion read as if they followed such events:

> O ye who believe, enter not the houses of the Prophet, unless you are invited to a meal, and then not in anticipation of its getting ready. But enter when you are called, and when you have eaten, disperse, linger not in eagerness for talk. This was a cause of embarrassment for the Prophet. ... When you ask any of the wives of the Prophet for something, ask from behind a curtain. That is purer for your hearts and for their hearts (33:54).

An account attributed to Aishah connects these and the further verses—which enjoined Muhammad's wives and Muslim women generally to draw their cloaks around them so that they could be recognized as believers and thus not be molested (33:60)—with another occasion. Omar ibn al-Khattab, according to Aishah, had been urging Muhammad to seclude his wives, though unsuccessfully. One night she and Sawda went outside (there was no indoor sanitation), and Sawda, being tall, was recognized by Omar from a distance. He called out to her, saying that he recognized her, and later again urged Muhammad to seclude his wives.

According to one account, Omar wanted Muhammad to seclude his wives to guard against the insults of the "hypocrites," a group of Medinians whose faith was lukewarm, who would abuse Muhammad's wives and then claim that they had taken them for slaves (Ibn Sa'd, 8:125–7).[29]

According to another account, Omar urged Muhammad to seclude his wives because Muhammad's success was now bringing many visitors to the mosque.[30] (That several different occasions and reasons are given for those verses does not mean that they are all untrue but rather that they were part of the background to the new edicts and represented the kinds of situations that were becoming unacceptable to new Muslim eyes.) The mosque was the place where Muhammad conducted all religious and community affairs and the center of lively activity. Muhammad once received there the leaders of a tribe not yet converted to Islam; during the negotiations three tents were put up for them in the courtyard. Envoys from other tribes came there looking for Muhammad. Medinian chiefs spent the night there after a battle. One warrior brought the head of an enemy to the mosque. People without means slept in the arbor of the north wall. People also simply sat or lay about or put up tents. One woman, an emancipated slave, "put up a tent or hut in the mosque" and visited and talked with Muhammad's wives, according to Aishah. Many who came hoping for some favor from Muhammad approached one or another of his wives first to enlist their assistance.[31]

By instituting seclusion Muhammad was creating a distance between his wives and this thronging community on their doorstep—the distance appropriate for the wives of the now powerful leader of a new, unambiguously patriarchal society. He was, in effect, summarily creating in non-architectural terms the forms of segregation—the gyneceum, the harem quarters— already firmly established in such neighboring patriarchal societies as Byzantium and Iran, and perhaps he was even borrowing from those architectural and social practices. As a successful leader, he presumably had the wealth to give his wives the servants necessary for their seclusion, releasing them from tasks that women of Muhammad's family and kin are described as doing: Asma, Abu Bakr's daughter, fetched water, carried garden produce, ground corn, and kneaded bread, and Fatima, Muhammad's daughter and Ali Ibn Abu Talib's wife, also ground corn and fetched water (Ibn Sa'd, 8:182–3).[32]

Veiling was apparently not introduced into Arabia by Muhammad but already existed among some classes, particularly in the towns, though it was probably more prevalent in the countries that the Arabs had contact with, such as Syria and Palestine. In those areas, as in Arabia, it was connected with social status, as was its use among Greeks, Romans, Jews, and Assyrians, all of whom practiced veiling to some degree.[33] It is nowhere explicitly prescribed in the Qur'an; the only verses dealing with women's clothing, aside from those already quoted, instruct women to guard their private parts and throw a scarf over their bosoms (24:31–2).

Throughout Muhammad's lifetime veiling, like seclusion, was observed only by his wives. Moreover, that the phrase "[she] took the veil" is used in the *hadith* to mean that a woman became a wife of Muhammad suggests that for some time after Muhammad's death, when the material incorporated into the *hadith* was circulated, veiling and seclusion were still considered peculiar to Muhammad's wives. It is not known how the customs spread to the rest of the community. The Muslim conquests of areas in which veiling was commonplace among the upper classes, the influx of wealth, the resultant raised status of Arabs, and Muhammad's wives being taken as models probably combined to bring about their general adoption.

There is no record of the reactions of Muhammad's wives to these institutions, a remarkable silence given their articulateness on various topics (particularly Aishah's, as the traditions well attest)—a silence that draws attention to the power of suppression that the chroniclers also had. One scholar has suggested that it was probably the wives' reaction to the imposition of seclusion that precipitated Muhammad's threat of mass divorce and the tense situation that culminated in the verses presenting Muhammad's wives with the choice of divorce.[34] Muhammad's wives were presented with the choice between divorce and continuing as his wives, which meant accepting the special conduct expected of them in this life and eventually receiving the special rewards awaiting them in heaven.

The threatened divorce was no mere domestic affair. During the month in which Muhammad remained withdrawn from his wives, the community became gravely concerned about the potential consequences, because Muhammad's marriages cemented crucial ties with important members of the Muslim community in Medina and with tribal leaders outside Medina as well. The rumor of a possible divorce reportedly caused greater public concern than an anticipated Ghassanid invasion: Abu Bakr and Omar, fathers of Aishah and Hafsa respectively (and the first and second caliphs after Muhammad's death), became so deeply perturbed that they reprimanded their daughters.

Given the seriousness of the situation, any of the purported causes of the breach were, as several scholars have noted, astonishingly trivial. The described activities and rivalries seem to have been part of ordinary life and therefore do not seem to be grounds enough for precipitating a serious political crisis. According to one account, Muhammad's wives were clamoring for more worldly goods than he had means to provide. Another account blames the bickering between Aishah and Zeinab over the equitable distribution of a slaughtered animal. Yet another claims that Hafsa had caught Muhammad with Miriam, his Egyptian concubine, in her own (Hafsa's) apartment, but on Aishah's day. In spite of promising Muhammad that she would not tell Aishah, Hafsa broke her vow. Soon after "Aisha confronted him, the entire harem was up in arms over the matter" (Ibn Sa'd, 8:131–9).[35]

The verses of the Qur'an that specifically enjoin and stress the importance of "obedience" indeed suggest that some kind of protest or disobedience had been under way among Muhammad's wives.

Say, O Prophet, to thy wives: If you desire the life of this world and its adorn-
ment, come then, I shall make provision for you and send you away in a hand-
some manner. But if ye desire Allah and His Messenger and the Home of the
Hereafter, then Allah has prepared for those of you who carry out their obligations fully a great reward. Wives of the Prophet, if any of you should act in a
manner incompatible with the highest standards of piety, her punishment will
be doubled. That is easy for Allah. But whoever of you is completely obedient
to Allah and His Messenger, and acts righteously, We shall double her reward;
and We have prepared an honorable provision for her. Wives of the Prophet, if
you safeguard your dignity, you are not like any other women. So speak in a
simple, straightforward manner, lest he whose mind is diseased should form an
ill design; and always say the good word. Stay at home and do not show off in
the manner of the women of the days of ignorance (33:29–35).

Muhammad first put the choice to Aishah, advising her to consult her parents
before making a decision. Replying that she had no need to consult her
parents—"You know they would never advise me to leave you"—she chose
to stay. The other wives followed suit. Verses conferring on Muhammad's
wives the title and dignity of Mothers of the Believers—perhaps in compen-
sation—and forbidding them to remarry after his death also probably
belong to the same period as the verses that put to his wives the choice of
divorce.[36]

In 630 the Muslims took Mecca with little bloodshed. Abu Sufyan, after
surrendering at the Muslim encampment, returned to Mecca and called on
his people to convert to Islam. His wife, Hind bint 'Utbah, enraged by his
surrender, denounced him publicly and then, realizing the cause was lost,
shattered the statues of her gods. Some sources say that Hind was among
the three or four women condemned to death and that she saved herself
only by hastily converting to Islam, but this may be an anti-Umayyad
embellishment of her story.[37] In any event she spiritedly led the Meccan
women in taking the oath of allegiance to Islam. Muhammad led and Hind
responded.

"You shall have but one God."
"We grant you that."
"You shall not steal."
"Abu Sufyan is a stingy man, I only stole provisions from him."
"That is not theft. You will not commit adultery."
"Does a free woman commit adultery?"
"You will not kill your children [by infanticide]."
"Have you left us any children that you did not kill at the battle of Badr?" (Ibn
Sa'd, 8:4)

With the conquest of Mecca the Muslims received the key of the
Ka'aba, which at the time was in the hands of Sulafa, a woman. According
to Muslim sources, Sulafa's son had merely entrusted her with it for safe-
keeping, just as Hulail, the last priest-king of Mecca, had previously—also
according to Muslim sources—entrusted his daughter Hubba with the key.
Although no other women are mentioned as keepers of the key, Sulafa's and
Hubba's minimal role in Islamic records probably reflects Muslim assumptions projected on to the earlier society. However, in a society such as that of
the *jahiliyya*, which had *kahinas* (female soothsayers) and priestesses, Hubba
may well have been at least in some sense a successor to her father or a trans-
mitter of his powers.[38]

Muhammad died two years after the conquest, following a brief illness.
Lying sick in his wife Maimuna's room, where his other wives visited him,
he began asking in whose room he was due to stay the next day and the
next, in an attempt, they realized, to figure out when he was due at Aishah's.
Finally, he asked to be allowed to retire there, and a few days later, on June
11, 632, he died. His unexpected death precipitated a crisis in the Muslim
community. Abu Bakr was able to settle the question of where he should
be buried by recalling that Muhammad had said that a prophet should be
buried where he expires (Ibn Sa'd, 2, pt. 2:71). Thus Muhammad was buried
in Aishah's room, which is now, after the Ka'aba, the most sacred spot in
Islam.[39] Abu Bakr and Omar were also buried there, as they requested,
although Aishah had hoped to keep the last space for herself. After Omar's
burial, she had a partition built between her section of the room and the
tombs: she had felt at home, she said, sharing the room with her husband
and father, but with Omar there she felt in the presence of a stranger (Ibn
Sa'd, 3, pt. 1, 245, 264).

Muhammad's death sparked off a series of rebellions in various parts of
Arabia, most of which had converted to Islam by then. At least one armed
rebellion was led by a woman, Salma bint Malik, and one of the "false
prophets" who appeared as leader of a revolt against the Islamic state was a
woman, too. Captured by the Muslims in a battle led by her mother in 628,
Salma bint Malik was given to Aishah by Muhammad. She served Aishah
for a time and later married a relative of Muhammad's. Upon Muhammad's
death she withdrew and returned to her people, who were among those
now rebelling against Islam. Her mother, when captured by the Muslims,
had been executed by having each foot tied to a different beast, which then
rent her in two. Salma, determined to avenge her or die, led her soldiers in
person, riding on her mother's camel. She was finally killed, but not before
"a hundred others" had fallen around her.[40]

The false prophet was Sajah bint 'Aws of the Tamim, whose mother was of the Banu Taghlib, a largely Christianized tribe. The Tamim were divided between supporting and opposing Islam. Those wanting to throw it off supported Sajah. When her faction lost in a civil war and she was forced to leave Tamimi territory with her army, she headed for Yamama, the capital of another false prophet, Musailamah, and apparently made a treaty with him—but nothing is known of her after that. Her deity was referred to as *Rabb al-sirab*, "The Lord of the Clouds," but her teachings have not been preserved.[41]

Salma and Sajah were, it seems, a rebel and a prophet who happened to be women. But in Hadramaut women may have rebelled as women, rejoicing at Muhammad's death because of the limitations Islam had brought to them. "When the Prophet of God died," reads a third-century (Islamic) account of this rebellion, "the news of it was carried to Hadramaut."

> There were in Hadramaut six women of Kindah and Hadramaut, who were desirous for the death of the Prophet of God; they therefore (on hearing the news) dyed their hands with henna and played on the tambourine. To them came the harlots of Hadramaut and did likewise, so that some twenty-odd women joined the six. ... [The text then lists the names of some women, including two it describes as grandmothers.] Oh horseman, if thou dost pass by, convey this message from me to Abu Bakr, the successor of Ahmad [Muhammad]: leave not in peace the harlots, black as chaff, who assert that Muhammad need not be mourned; satisfy that longing for them to be cut off, which burns in my breast like an unquenchable ember.[42]

Abu Bakr sent al-Muhagir with men and horses against the women, and although the men of Kindah and Hadramaut came to the women's defense, al-Muhagir cut off the women's hands. This account is intriguing, for why should the opposition of harlots have been threatening enough to Islam to merit sending a force against them? Three of the women listed here were of the nobility, and four belonged to the royal clan of Kindah. Their status and the support of their men suggest that they were priestesses, not prostitutes, and that their singing and dancing were not personal rejoicing but traditional performances intended to incite their tribespeople to throw off the yoke of the new religion. They were evidently successful enough in gathering support to constitute a threat worthy of armed suppression.[43]

Furthermore, some Arabian women at the time of the institution of Islam, and not only priestesses, doubtless understood and disliked the new religion's restrictions on women and its curtailment of their independence. For them Muhammad's death would have been a matter for celebration and the demise of his religion a much desired eventuality. That some women felt Islam to be a somewhat depressing religion is suggested by a remark of Muhammad's great-granddaughter Sukaina, who, when asked why she was so merry and her sister Fatima so solemn, replied that it was because she had been named after her pre-Islamic great-grandmother, whereas her sister had been named after her Islamic grandmother.[44]

Muhammad's wives continued to live in their mosque apartments, revered by the community as the Mothers of the Believers. Financially they seemed to depend on private means, on their families, or on money they earned through their skills. Sawda, for instance, derived an income from her fine leatherwork. They apparently inherited nothing from Muhammad, Abu Bakr maintaining that Muhammad had wished his modest property to go to charity. In 641, as a result of the immense revenues brought by the Arab conquests Omar, the next caliph, initiated state pensions and placed the Mothers of the Believers at the head of the list, awarding them generous sums. This recognition further confirmed their already prominent status. Aishah, as Muhammad's favorite wife, received the state's highest pension. Acknowledged as having special knowledge of Muhammad's ways, sayings, and character, she was consulted on his *sunna*, or practice, and gave decisions on sacred laws and customs.[45] Other wives were also consulted and were cited as the sources of traditions, though none was as prominent and prolific as Aishah.

Omar's reign (634–44) is regarded as the period in which many of the major institutions of Islam originated, for Omar promulgated a series of religious, civil, and penal ordinances, including stoning as punishment for adultery. He was harsh towards women in both private and public life: he was ill-tempered with his wives and physically assaulted them, and he sought to confine women to their homes and to prevent their attending prayers at the mosques. Unsuccessful in this last attempt, he instituted segregated prayers, appointing a separate imam for each sex. He chose a male imam for the women, another departure from precedent, for it is known that Muhammad appointed a woman, Umm Waraka, to act as imam for her entire household, which included, so far as can be ascertained, men as well as women (Ibn Sa'd, 8:335).[46] Moreover, after Muhammad's death Aishah and Umm Salama acted as imams for other women (Ibn Sa'd, 8:355–6). Contrary to Muhammad's practice, Omar also prohibited Muhammad's wives from going on pilgrimage (a restriction lifted in the last year of his reign). This prohibition must have provoked the discontent of the Mothers of the Believers, although "history" has not recorded any, just as it has not recorded any opposition on the part of Muhammad's widows to Omar's attempt to prevent women from attending prayers at the mosques (Ibn

Sa'd, 8:150).[47] The consistent silence on such issues now speaks eloquently. Given the harsh suppression at Hadramaut, there can be little doubt that the guardians of Islam erased female rebellion from the pages of history as ruthlessly as they eradicated it from the world in which they lived. They doubtless considered it their duty.

Uthman, the third caliph (644–56), allowed Muhammad's wives to go on pilgrimage and revoked Omar's arrangement for separate imams. Men and women once again attended mosque together, although women now gathered in a separate group and left after the men (Ibn Sa'd, 5:17). Uthman's restoration of some liberties to women, however, only briefly stayed a tide that was moving inexorably in the reverse direction. Aishah still took an active and eventually public role in politics, though acting out a part that in reality belonged to a dying order. When Uthman was murdered, she delivered, veiled, a public address at the mosque in Mecca, proclaiming that his death would be avenged. She proceeded to gather around her one of the two factions opposing the succession of Ali Ibn Abu Talib; the controversy over his succession gave rise eventually to the split between Sunni and Shi'a Muslims. Factional opposition culminated in the Battle of the Camel—named after the camel on which Aishah sat while exhorting the soldiers to fight and directing the battle, like her *jahiliyya* forebears. Ali, realizing her importance, had her camel cut down, causing her army to fall into disarray. The victorious Ali (who became the fourth caliph, 656–61) treated Aishah magnanimously. Nevertheless, the important role that she had played in this controversial battle—the first in which Muslims shed Muslim blood—earned her the reproach of many. Charges that the opposition had made from the start—that Aishah's going into battle violated the seclusion imposed by Muhammad, who had ordered his wives to stay at home, women's proper place in this new order—seemed more fully vindicated by her defeat.[48]

We have surveyed key moments in the shaping of Islamic marriage, as well as in the elaboration of the mechanisms of control that the new relationship between the sexes necessitated, and we have seen the participation and independence of women in the society in which Islam arose and the diminution of their liberties as Islam became established. *Jahiliyya* women were priests, soothsayers, prophets, participants in warfare, and nurses on the battlefield. They were fearlessly outspoken, defiant critics of men; authors of satirical verse aimed at formidable male opponents; keepers, in some unclear capacity, of the keys of the holiest shrine in Mecca; rebels and leaders of rebellions that included men; and individuals who initiated and terminated marriages at will, protested the limits Islam imposed on that freedom, and

mingled freely with the men of their society until Islam banned such interaction.

In transferring rights to women's sexuality and their offspring from the
woman and her tribe to men and then basing the new definition of marriage
on that proprietary male right, Islam placed relations between the sexes on a
new footing. Implicit in this new order was the male right to control women
and to interdict their interactions with other men. Thus the ground was
prepared for the closures that would follow: women's exclusion from social
activities in which they might have contact with men other than those with
rights to their sexuality; their physical seclusion, soon to become the norm;
and the institution of internal mechanisms of control, such as instilling the
notion of submission as a woman's duty. The ground was thus prepared, in
other words, for the passing of a society in which women were active participants in the affairs of their community and for women's place in Arabian
society to become circumscribed in the way that it already was for their
sisters in the rest of the Mediterranean Middle East.

Marriage as sanctioned or practiced by Muhammad included polygamy and the marriage of girls nine or ten years old. Qur'anic utterances
sanctioned the rights of males to have sexual relations with slave women
(women bought or captured in war) and to divorce at will. In its fundamentals, the concept of marriage that now took shape was similar to that of
Judaic marriage and similar, too, in some respects to Zoroastrian marriage,
practiced by the ruling Iranian elite in the regions bordering Arabia.[49] Not
surprisingly, once the Islamic conquests brought about an intermingling of
these socio-religious systems, Islam easily assimilated features of the others.

So far I have focused on the practices of the first community with respect
to women and marriage, omitting from consideration the broad ethical field
of meaning in which those practices were embedded—that is, the ethical
teachings Islam was above all established to articulate. When those teachings
are taken into account, the religion's understanding of women and gender
emerges as far more ambiguous than this account might suggest. Islam's
ethical vision, which is stubbornly egalitarian, including with respect to the
sexes, is thus in tension with, and might even be said to subvert, the hierarchical structure of marriage pragmatically instituted in the first Islamic
society.

The tensions between the pragmatic and ethical perspectives, both forming part of Islam, can be detected even in the Qur'an, and both perspectives
have left their mark on some of the formal rulings on women and marriage
made in the ensuing period. Thus some Qur'anic verses regarding marriage
and women appear to qualify and undercut others that seemingly establish

marriage as a hierarchical institution unequivocally privileging men. Among the former are the verses that read: "Wives have rights corresponding to those which husbands have, in equitable reciprocity" (2:229). Similarly, verses such as those that admonish men, if polygamous, to treat their wives equally and that go on to declare that husbands would not be able to do so—using a form of the Arabic negative connoting permanent impossibility—are open to being read to mean that men should not be polygamous. In the same way, verses sanctioning divorce go on to condemn it as "abhorrent to God." The affirmation of women's right to inherit and control property and income without reference to male guardians, in that it constitutes a recognition of women's right to economic independence (that most crucial of areas with respect to personal autonomy), also fundamentally qualifies the institution of male control as an all-encompassing system.

Thus while there can be no doubt that in terms of its pragmatic rulings Islam instituted a hierarchical type of marriage that granted men control over women and rights to permissive sexuality, there can be no doubt, either, that Islamic views on women, as on all matters, are embedded in and framed by the new ethical and spiritual field of meaning that the religion had come into existence to articulate.

CHAPTER IO

Aishah's Legacy: The Struggle for Women's Rights within Islam

Amina Wadud

Amina Wadud was born into a Methodist family in Bethesda, Maryland, USA, in 1952. In 1972 she converted to Islam while attending the University of Pennsylvania, a decision that is said to have been shaped by her experiences as an African-American woman.[1] She went on to get a PhD in Islamic Sciences and Arabic from the University of Michigan in 1988 and then joined the Department of Islamic Revealed Knowledge and Heritage in the International Islamic University in Malaysia. It was here that she first published her seminal work, Qur'an and Women. *In 1992 she accepted an appointment at Virginia Commonwealth University, where she is currently an Associate Professor of Islamic Studies.*

Over the last decade or so, Wadud has emerged as one of the most influential—and also controversial—voices of Islamic feminism. Wadud's hermeneutic focus has been on the proper reading of the Qur'an, more specifically on "what the Qur'an says, how it says it, what is said about the Qur'an, and who is doing the saying."[2] In so doing she explores the Qur'an's conceptualization of gender and gender relations, which, properly contextualized and understood, are highly liberating for both men and women. For Wadud, this "gender Jihad" is not simply an academic question. It is also personal. In August 1994, she delivered a Friday prayer sermon at a mosque in Cape Town, South Africa, and in March 2005 she led a Friday prayer congregation in New York. Both events earned her the condemnation of conservative Muslims and led to calls for her removal from her university post.

In the brief essay that follows, Wadud argues that both the Qur'anic teachings of Islam and its early manifestation at the time of the Prophet Muhammad were liberating for women as well as men. The essay appears here through the author's kind permission.

I converted to Islam during the second-wave feminist movement in the 1970s. I saw everything through a prism of religious euphoria and idealism.

Within the Islamic system of thought I have struggled to transform idealism into pragmatic reforms as a scholar and activist. And my main source of inspiration has been Islam's own primary source—the Qur'an.

It is clear to me that the Qur'an aimed to erase all notions of women as subhuman. There are more passages that address issues relating to women—as individuals, in the family, as members of the community—than all other social issues combined.

Let us start with the Qur'anic story of human origins. "Man" is not made in the image of God. Neither is a flawed female helpmate extracted from him as an afterthought or utility. Dualism is the primordial design for all creation: "From all (created) things are pairs" (51:49).

Therefore, when the proto-human soul, self or person (*nafs*) is brought into existence, its mate (*zawj*) is already a part of the plan. The two dwell in a state of bliss: the Garden of Eden. They are warned against Satan's temptation but they forget and eat from the tree. When the Qur'an recounts the event in the Garden, it uses the unique dual form in Arabic grammar showing that both were guilty. The female is never singled out and chastised for being a temptress.

Ultimately, the two seek forgiveness and it is granted. They begin life on earth untainted by a "fall" from grace and with no trace of original sin. On the contrary, in Islam the creation story for humans on earth begins with forgiveness and mercy as well as a most important promise or covenant from God. He/She/It will provide guidance through Revelation. Adam is the first prophet.

Furthermore, the Qur'an is emphatic that since Allah is not created then He/She/It cannot be subject to or limited by created characteristics, like gender. That Arabic grammar carries gender markers has led even the best Arab grammarians erroneously to attribute gender to the thing referred to. Modern feminist studies have analyzed this gender bias in language.

Islam brought radical changes regarding women and society, despite the deeply entrenched patriarchy of seventh-century Arabia. The Qur'an provides women with explicit rights to inheritance, independent property, divorce and the right to testify in a court of law. It prohibits wanton violence towards women and girls and is against duress in marriage and community affairs. Women and men equally are required to fulfill all religious duties, and are equally eligible for punishment for misdemeanors. Finally, women are offered the ultimate boon: paradise and proximity to Allah: "Whoever does an atom's weight of good, whether male or female, and is a believer, all such shall enter into Paradise" (40:40).

In the period immediately following the death of the Prophet, women were active participants at all levels of community affairs—religious, political, social, educational, intellectual. They played key roles in preserving traditions, disseminating knowledge and challenging authority when it went against their understanding of the Qur'an or the prophetic legacy.

The Prophet's favorite wife Aishah, from whom the Prophet said we should learn "half our religion," was sought after as an advisor to the early jurists. In the famous Battle of the Camel she was an army general. The Prophet even received Revelation while resting his head on her lap. Unfortunately, this period passed before it could establish a pattern sustainable as historical precedent. And the name of Aishah cannot erase what was to happen to the status of women in the following thousand years.

During the Abbasid period, when Islam's foundations were developed, leading scholars and thinkers were exclusively male. They had no experience of Revelation first hand, had not known the Prophet directly, and were sometimes influenced by intellectual and moral cultures antithetical to Islam.

In particular, they moved away from the Qur'an's ethical codes for female autonomy to advocate instead women's subservience, silence, and seclusion. If women's agency was taken into consideration it was with regard to service to men, family, and community. Women came to be discussed in law in the same terms as material objects and possessions. (This is today reflected in Pakistan's rape laws, which treat the offense as one of theft of male private property with no consideration for the woman's rights.)

Not until the post-colonial twentieth century would Muslim women re-emerge as active participants in all areas of Islamic public, political, economic, intellectual, social, cultural, and spiritual affairs.

Today Muslim women are striving for greater inclusiveness in many diverse ways, not all of them in agreement with each other. At the Beijing Global Women's Conference in 1995, nightly attempts to form a Muslim women's caucus at the NGO forum became screaming sessions. The many different strategies and perspectives just could not be brought to a consensus. On the Left were many secular feminists and activists who, while Muslim themselves, defined Islam on a cultural basis only. Their politics was informed by post-colonialist and Marxist agendas of nationalism. Concrete issues of women's full equality—standards of education, career opportunities, political participation, and representation—were understood in Western terms. The cultural imposition of veiling was to them a symbol of women's backwardness; for them full entry into the public domain and other indicators of liberation were reflected in Western styles of dress.

On the far Right, Muslim male authorities and their female representatives, known as Islamists, spearheaded a reactionary, neo-conservative approach. They identified an ideal Islam as the one lived by the Prophet's Companions and followers at Medina. All that was required today was to lift that ideal out of the pages of history and graft it on to modernity, adopting a complete *Sharia* state, unexamined and unquestioned and opposed to modern complexity. Then life would be perfect. There were no inequities towards women because the law was divine and the matter of patriarchal interpretation was irrelevant. Female Islamists representing this viewpoint handed out booklets (written by men) with titles such as "The Wisdom behind Islam's Position on Women." Although the arguments were not intellectually rigorous or critically substantial, they held a substantial sway. Ironically, these arguments would also form part of the rhetoric used by secular feminists to discredit human-rights and social-justice advocates who were in the middle ground, who insisted on fighting from within an Islamic perspective, or who happened to wear *hijab*.

As the term "Islamic feminism" gained currency in the 1990s through scholars and activists, it would clarify the perspective of a large number of women somewhere between Islamists and secular feminists. While they would not give up their allegiance to Islam as an essential part of self-determination and identity they did critique patriarchal control over the basic Islamic worldview. Islamic feminism did not define these women, and many still reject the term. However, the term helped others to understand the distinction between them and the two dominant approaches for Muslim women's rights.

Today more women are active in the discussion and reformation of identity than at any other time in human history. By going back to primary sources and interpreting them afresh, women scholars are endeavoring to remove the fetters imposed by centuries of patriarchal interpretation and practice. By questioning underlying presumptions and conclusions they are creating a space in which to think about gender. Drawing upon enduring principles of human rights, enshrined in the text, they extract meanings that can interact with the changing moral and intellectual circumstances of the reader. And women scholars and activists are also busy constructing a system of legal reforms that can be implemented today for the full status of women as moral agents at all levels of human society.

This moral agency is a mandate of the Qur'an and cannot be restricted by any amount of historical precedent, social custom, or patriarchal aspiration. The long-term success of this project lies in the fact that it is all happening within Islam. And the rationale for change comes from the most trustworthy and reliable source of Islam itself—the Qur'an.

CHAPTER II

Muslim Women and Fundamentalism

Fatima Mernissi

Fatima Mernissi is perhaps the most renowned feminist in the contemporary Muslim world. Born in Fez, Morocco, in 1940, she studied political science at the Sorbonne and later at Brandies University, where she earned a doctorate. As a Professor of Sociology at Muhammad V University in Rabat, Mernissi quickly established herself as a leading authority on the position of women in Islam and in Muslim societies. To date she has written 16 books in French, English, and Arabic, some of which include Forgotten Queens of Islam, Scheherazade Is Not a Moroccan, Islam and Democracy: Fear of the Modern World, Beyond the Veil: Male-Female Dynamics in Modern Muslim Society, *and,* The Veil and the Muslim Elite: A Feminist Interpretation of Women's Rights in Islam. *Since retiring from her post at the university, Mernissi has devoted herself to full-time writing and scholarship and to exploring issues of social empowerment and civic engagement. She also maintains the* www. mernissi.net *website.*

Most of Mernissi's earlier writings explored the historical development of Islamic thought and its contemporary manifestations, particularly in relation to the position of women. In The Veil and the Muslim Elite, *for example, she engaged in a detailed historical investigation of some of the* ahadith *used to justify the* hijab *and the social segregation of women, questioning their validity, and offering alternative, "feminist" interpretation instead. In more recent years, Mernissi's interests have turned increasingly towards questions of civic engagement, social responsibility, and democracy, and, more recently, towards the influences of globalization and information technology on developing societies.*

The essay that appears here, adapted from the introduction to Beyond the Veil, *originally appeared in, Fatima Mernissi, "Muslim Women and Fundamentalism," Middle East Report, no. 153 (July–August 1988), pp 8–11.*

When analyzing the dynamics of the Muslim world, one has to discriminate between two distinct dimensions: what people actually do, the decisions they make, the aspirations they secretly entertain or display through their patterns of consumption, and the discourses they develop about themselves, more specifically the ones they use to articulate their political claims. The first dimension is about reality and its harsh time-bound laws, and how people adapt to pitilessly rapid change; the second is about self-presentation and identity building. And you know as well as I do that whenever one has to define oneself to others, whenever one has to define one's identity, one is on the shaky ground of self-indulging justifications. For example, the need for Muslims to claim so vehemently that they are traditional, and that their women miraculously escape social change and the erosion of time, has to be understood in terms of their need for self-representation and must be classified not as a statement about daily behavioral practices, but rather as a psychological need to maintain a minimal sense of identity in a confusing and shifting reality.

To familiarize you with the present-day Muslim world and how women fit into the conflicting political forces (including religion), the best way is not to overwhelm you with data. On the contrary, what is most needed is some kind of special illumination of the structural dissymmetry that runs all through and conditions the entire fabric of social and individual life— the split between acting and reflecting on one's actions, the split between what one does and how one speaks about oneself. The first has to do with the realm of reality; the second has to do with the realm of the psychological elaborations that sustain human beings' indispensable sense of identity. Individuals die of physical sickness, but societies die of loss of identity, that is, a disturbance in the guiding system of representations of oneself as fitting into a universe that is specifically ordered so as to make life meaningful.

Why do we need our lives to make sense? Because that's where power is. A sense of identity is a sense that one's life is meaningful; that, as fragile as a person may be, she or he can still have an impact on his or her limited surroundings. The fundamentalist wave in Muslim societies is a statement about identity. And that is why their call for the veil for women has to be looked at in the light of the painful but necessary and prodigious reshuffling of identity that Muslims are going through in these often confusing but always fascinating times.

The split in the Muslim individual between what one does, confronted by rapid, totally uncontrolled changes in daily life, and the discourse about an unchangeable religious tradition that one feels psychologically compelled to elaborate in order to keep a minimal sense of identity—this, as far as I am concerned, is the key point to focus on in order to understand the dynamics of Muslim life of the late 1970s and the 1980s.

If fundamentalists are calling for the return of the veil, it must be because women have been taking off the veil. We are definitely in a situation where fundamentalist men and non-fundamentalist women have a conflict of interest. We have to identify who the fundamentalist men are, and who are the non-fundamentalist women who have opted to discard the veil. Class conflicts do sometimes express themselves in acute sex-focused dissent. Contemporary Islam is a good example of this because, beyond the strong obsession with religion, the violent confrontations going on in the Muslim world are about the two eminently materialistic pleasures: exercise of political power and consumerism.

Fundamentalists and unveiled women are the two groups that have emerged with concrete, conflicting claims and aspirations in the post-colonial era. Both have the same age range—youth—and the same educational privilege—a recent access to formalized institutions of knowledge. But while the men seeking power through religion and its revivification are mostly from newly urbanized middle- and lower-middle-class backgrounds, unveiled women by contrast are predominantly of middle-class urban backgrounds.

As a symptom, the call for the veil tells us one thing. Telling us another thing is the specific conjuncture of the forces calling for it—that is, the conservative forces and movements, their own quest, and how they position themselves within the social movements dominating the national and international scene.

Trespassing

Islam is definitely one of the modern political forces competing for power around the globe. At least that is how many of us experience it. How can a "medieval religion," ask Western students raised in a secular culture, be so alive, so challenging to the effects of time, so renewable in energy? How can it be meaningful to educated youth? One of the characteristics of fundamentalism is the attraction Islam has for high achievers among young people. In Cairo, Lahore, Jakarta, and Casablanca Islam makes sense because it speaks about power and self-empowerment. As a matter of fact, worldly self-enhancement is so important for Islam that the meaning of spirituality itself has to be seriously reconsidered.

What was not clear for me in the early 1970s was that all the problems Muslims have faced in recent decades are more or less boundary problems, from colonization (trespassing by a foreign power on Muslim community space and decision making) to contemporary human-rights issues (the political boundaries circumscribing the ruler's space and the freedoms of the government). The issue of technology is a boundary problem: how can we integrate Western technological information, the recent Western scientific memory, without deluging our own Muslim heritage? International economic dependency is, of course, eminently a problem of boundaries: the International Monetary Fund's intervention in fixing the price of our bread does not help us keep a sense of a distinct national identity. What are the boundaries of the sovereignty of the Muslim state vis-à-vis voracious, aggressive transnational corporations? These are some of the components of the crisis that is tearing the Muslim world apart, along, of course, definite class lines.

Naive and serious as only a dutiful student can be, I did not know in 1975 that women's claims were disturbing to Muslim societies not because they threatened the past but because they augured and symbolized what the future and its conflicts are about: the inescapability of renegotiating new sexual, political, economic, and cultural boundaries, thresholds, and limits. Invasion of physical territory by alien hostile nations (Afghanistan and Lebanon), invasion of national television by *Dallas* and *Dynasty*, invasion of children's desires by Coca-Cola and special brands of walking shoes—these are some of the political and cultural boundary problems facing the Muslim world today.

However, we have to remember that societies do not reject and resist changes indiscriminately. Muslim societies integrated and digested quite well technological innovations: the engine, electricity, the telephone, the transistor, sophisticated machinery and arms, all without much resistance. But the social fabric seems to have trouble absorbing anything having to do with changing authority thresholds: freely competing unveiled women, freely competing political parties, freely elected parliaments, and, of course, freely elected heads of state who do not necessarily get 99 percent of the votes. Whenever an innovation has to do with free choice of the partners involved, the social fabric seems to suffer some terrible tear. Women's unveiling seems to belong to this realm. For the last 100 years, whenever women tried or wanted to discard the veil, some men, always holding up the sacred as a justification, screamed that it was unbearable, that the society's fabric would dissolve if the mask was dropped. I do not believe that men, Muslims or not, scream unless they are hurt. Those calling for the re-imposition of the veil surely have a reason. What is it that Muslim society needs to mask so badly?

The idea one hears about fundamentalism is that it is an archaic phenomenon, a desire to return to medieval thinking. It is frequently presented as a revivalist movement: bring back the past. And the call for the veil for women furthers this kind of misleading simplification. If we take the Egyptian city of Asyut as an example, we have to admit that it is a modern town with a totally new cultural feature that Muslim society never knew before: mass access to knowledge. In our history, universities and knowledge were privileges of the elite. The man of knowledge enjoyed a high respect precisely because he was a repository of highly valued and aristocratically gained information. Acquisition of knowledge took years, and often included a period of initiation that compelled the student to roam through Muslim capitals from Asia to Spain for decades. Mass access to universities, therefore, constitutes a total shift in the accumulation, distribution, management, and utilization of knowledge and information. And we know that knowledge is power. One of the reasons the fundamentalist will be preoccupied with women is that state universities are not open just for traditionally marginalized and deprived male rural migrants, but for women as well.

Persons under 15 years of age constitute 39 percent of Egypt's and 45 percent of Iran's total population.[1] The natural annual population increase in Egypt and Iran is 3.1 percent.[2] The time span for doubling the population is 22 years for Egypt and 23 for Iran. Secondary school enrollment in Iran is 35 percent for women and 54 percent for men. In Egypt 39 percent of women of secondary school age are in fact there, as compared to 64 percent of men.[3] The same trend is to be found in other Muslim societies.

Centuries of women's exclusion from knowledge have resulted in femininity being confused with illiteracy until a few decades ago. But things have progressed so rapidly in our Muslim countries that we women today take literacy and access to schools and universities for granted. Illiteracy was such a certain fate for women that my grandmother would not believe that women's education was a serious state undertaking. For years she kept waking my sister and me at dawn to get us ready for school. We would explain that school started exactly three hours after her first dawn prayer, and that we needed only five minutes to get there. But she would mumble, while handing us our morning tea, "You better get yourself there and stare at the wonderful gate of that school for hours. Only God knows how long it is going to last." She had an obsessive dream: to see us read every word of the Qur'an and to answer her questions demanding an explanation of a verse. "That is how the *qadis* [Muslim judges] get all their power. But knowing the Qur'an is not enough to make a woman happy. She has to learn how to do sums. The winners are the ones who master mathematics." The political dimension of education was evident to our grandmother's generation.

While a few decades ago the majority of women married before the age of 20, today only 22 percent of that age group in Egypt and 38.4 percent in Iran are married.[4] To get an idea of how perturbing it is for Iranian society to deal with an army of unmarried adolescents, one has only to remember that the legal age for marriage for females in Iran is 13 and for males 15.[5] The idea of an adolescent unmarried woman is a completely new idea in the Muslim world, where previously you had only a female child and a menstruating woman who had to be married off immediately so as to prevent dishonorable engagement in pre-marital sex. The whole concept of patriarchal honor was built around the idea of virginity, which reduced a woman's role to its sexual dimension: reproduction within early marriage. The concept of an adolescent woman, menstruating and unmarried, is so alien to the entire Muslim family system that it is either unimaginable or necessarily linked with *fitna* (social disorder). The Arab countries are a good example of this demographic revolution in sex roles.

Space and sex roles

Young men, faced with job insecurity or failure of the diploma to guarantee access to the desired job, postpone marriage. Women, faced with the pragmatic necessity to count on themselves instead of relying on the dream of a rich husband, see themselves forced to concentrate on getting an education. The average age at marriage for women and men in most Arab countries has registered a spectacular increase. In Egypt and Tunisia the average age at marriage for women is 22 and for men 27. In Algeria it is 18 for women and 24 for men. In Morocco, Libya, and Sudan women marry at around 19 and men at around 25. The oil countries, known for their conservatism, have witnessed an incredible increase in unmarried youth; age at marriage for women is 20 and for men 27. And of course nuptiality patterns are influenced by urbanization. The more urbanized youth marry later. In 1980, in metropolitan areas of Egypt, the mean age of marriage was 29.7 for males and 23.6 for females. In the urban areas of upper Egypt, where the fundamentalist movement is strong, the mean age at marriage was 28.3 for men and 22.8 for women.[6]

The conservative wave against women in the Muslim world, far from being a regressive trend, is on the contrary a defense mechanism against profound changes in both sex roles and the touchy subject of sexual identity. The most accurate interpretation of the relapse into "archaic behaviors," such as conservatism on the part of men and resort to magic and superstitious rituals on the part of women, can be defined as anxiety-reducing mechanisms in a world of shifting, volatile sexual identity.

Fundamentalists are right in saying that education for women has destroyed the traditional boundaries and definitions of space and sex roles.

Schooling has dissolved traditional arrangements of space segregation, even in oil-rich countries where education is segregated by sex: simply to go to school women have to cross the street! Streets are spaces of sin and temptation, because they are both public and sex-mixed. And that is the definition of *fitna*: disorder!

Fundamentalists are right when they talk about the dissolution of women's traditional function as defined by family ethics; postponed age of marriage forces women to turn pragmatically towards education as a means for self-enhancement. If one looks at some of the education statistics, one understands why newly urbanized and educated rural youth single out university women as enemies of Islam, with its tradition of women's exclusion from knowledge and decision making. The percentage of women teaching in Egyptian universities was 25 percent in 1981. To get an idea of how fast change is occurring there, one only has to remember that in 1980 the percentage of women teaching in American universities was 24 percent, and 25 percent in the former Democratic Republic of Germany.[7] Even in conservative Saudi Arabia, women have invaded sexually segregated academic space: they constitute 22 percent of the university faculty there. Women constitute 18 percent of the university faculty in Morocco, 16 percent in Iraq, and 12 percent in Qatar.[8]

What dismays the fundamentalists is that the era of independence did not create a new all-male class. Women are taking part in the public feast. And that is a definite revolution in the Islamic concept of both the state's relation to women and women's relation to the institutionalized distribution of knowledge.

CHAPTER 12

Islam, Justice, and Politics

Chandra Muzaffar

Chandra Muzaffar (b. 1947) is considered one of Malaysia's most prolific and respected Islamic philosophers. He obtained his PhD from the University of Singapore in 1977 and for several years taught at Universiti Sains Malaysia in Penang. He held his last academic position as Professor and Director in the Center for Civilizational Dialogue at the University of Malaya. In 1977, Muzaffar was one of the principal founders of Aliran Kesedaran Negara (ALIRAN)—a multi-ethnic social reform group that sought to raise public awareness about issues pertaining to democracy and ethnic relations in Malaysia—and subsequently he led the organization for 14 years. He currently presides over the International Movement for a Just World (JUST), while also working with a number of other international NGOs concerned with social justice and civilizational dialogue, having in the process received a number of international academic and human-rights awards.

Chandra Muzaffar's focus on political activism in recent years has not slowed down the pace of his prolific scholarship. In addition to having published several books in Malay, he has written or edited a number of books and journal articles in English, including: Universalism of Islam *(editor),* Islamic Resurgence in Malaysia, Human Rights and the New World Order, Dominance of the West over the Rest *(editor),* Human Wrongs *(editor), and* Alternative Politics For Asia: A Buddhist–Muslim Dialogue *(together with Sulak Sivaraksa).*

In the following essay Chandra Muzaffar concentrates on the importance accorded to "justice" in the Qur'an, and on some of the main obstacles that justice currently faces in the Muslim world and in the rest of the globe. The essay originally appeared in: Chandra Muzaffar, Rights, Religion and Reform: Enhancing Human Dignity through Spiritual and Moral Transformation *(London: RoutledgeCurzon, 2002), pp 173–96.*

The ubiquitous commandments in the Qur'an to act in accordance with justice create a positive obligation on Muslims to stand for social reform and the creation of just societies.

We sent afore time
Our apostles with Clear Signs
And sent down with them
The Book and the Balance
Of Right and Wrong, that men

May stand forth in Justice (57:25).

Justice is the real goal of religion. It was the mission of every prophet. It is the message of every scripture.

Justice in the Qur'an

The Holy Qur'an abounds with references to justice. Its importance is emphasized in a whole variety of human situations—in inter-personal relationships, within the family, within the community, in the interaction between communities and nations, in the interface between the human being and nature.[1] There is justice to kith and kin, to the orphan, to the destitute, to the slave, to the wayfarer, to the needy.[2] There is justice that is humanly attainable. There is justice that is only divinely possible. In the words of an Islamic scholar:

> The demand for providing justice at every level of society features very promi-
> nently in the Quran. At every level, be it personal or public, in dealing with
> friends or foes, Muslims and non-Muslims, both in words and deeds, the
> Muslims are urged to be fair and just. Justice is an integral part of the faith
> and upholding the principle of justice is not confined to the courtroom envi-
> ronment or to a set of formal injunctions but commands a high priority in the
> order of Islamic moral and spiritual values.[3]

So central is justice to the Islamic value system that Muslims are reminded that it transcends an individual's most precious bond—the bond to oneself. As the Qur'an puts it:

> O ye believe! Stand out firmly For justice as witnesses To God, even as against
> Yourselves, or your parents, Or your kin, and whether It be (against) rich or
> poor; For God can best protect both. Follow not the lusts (Of your hearts), lest
> ye Swerve, and if ye Distort (justice) or decline To do justice, verily God is well
> acquainted With all that you do (3:135).

If any further proof is needed of the singular significance of justice in Islam it is provided by that well-known Qur'anic call, "Be just; that is Next to Piety" (5:8).

To find out what is actually meant by justice one has to probe a little the verses in which the term appears. From these verses, it seems that the Qur'an is concerned with different types of justice, including adjudicative justice, retributive justice, distributive justice, and, of course, divine justice. Calls to "judge fairly" would fall within the first category; punishments for certain kinds of wrongdoing would come within the second category; the practice of *zakat* and rules on inheritance would belong to the third category; and God's judgment in the hereafter would qualify for the fourth category.

Justice: our duty

The Qur'an not only gives us an indication of what justice is: it also emphasizes over and over again our responsibility as human beings to strive relentlessly for justice. We have already mentioned verses in the Qur'an which exhort us to "stand out firmly for justice" and to "be just." In numerous other places too, it asks us to uphold justice. For instance, we are told that, "God doth command you To render back your Trusts To those to whom they are due And when ye judge Between man and man That ye judge with justice" (4:58). In another verse we are advised, "When you speak (make sure that you speak) with justice" (6:152).

Upholding justice is undoubtedly one of the human being's primary duties. It is a duty that he must perform as the bearer of God's trust, as the vicegerent of God, the Khalifah Allah.

To assist and guide the human being in the performance of this duty, God has revealed to him a message, an eternal message, which has been affirmed and reaffirmed through the ages, the quintessence of which is embodied in the Qur'an. It is through realization of the values and principles, the precepts and practices which constitute this message that the human being will fulfill his trusteeship as Khalifah Allah. It is by bringing the Qur'anic truth into fruition that justice will triumph.

The power and the potential to achieve this lies with all human beings—especially those who have accepted the Qur'anic truth. Every human being can, in order to bring about justice, "enjoin what is right and forbid what is wrong [*al-amr bil-ma' ruf wan-nahi an al-munkar*]" (3:104). And what is right and what is wrong is lucidly articulated in the Qur'an and reflected in the *sunna*, the words and deeds of the Prophet Muhammad.

Justice: knowing the Qur'an

But to discharge one's responsibilities as a Khalifah Allah determined to join what is right and forbid what is wrong, one has to know the Qur'an and the *sunna*. To know the Qur'an in particular means to gain direct access to it, to read it, to understand it, to absorb it, to internalize its ideas and its ideals, its values and its vision. It must be emphasized over and over again that understanding the Qur'an is a task that the individual must undertake on his own and not through someone else. For in Islam there is no intercessor. The relationship with God is direct. The word of God in its final form was made available to the whole of humanity through the last of God's prophets. We may seek the guidance of those who are well versed in the Qur'an as we try to learn God's Word, but the responsibility of understanding and applying it to our lives is our own. There is another reason why the study of the Qur'an is the individual's own obligation. The Qur'an itself asks us to shoulder this responsibility. We are challenged to

> Read! In the name of thy Lord and Cherisher who created—Created man, out of A (mere) clot of congealed blood. Proclaim! And thy Lord is Most Bountiful—He Who taught (the use of) the Pen—Taught man that Which he knew not (96:1–5).

Though the Qur'an beseeches the human being to "read," to "write," to "know," the vast majority of Muslims today have no direct knowledge of the Qur'an for the simple reason that illiteracy is rampant in the Muslim world.[4] It is a sad reflection of the tragic state of affairs within the *Ummah* that the one religion which places greatest emphasis upon the acquisition of knowledge should have the largest number of illiterates as its followers! This is why our first and foremost challenge if we want to create a responsible *Ummah* committed to the transformation of the Qur'anic ideal of justice into reality is the total eradication of illiteracy within the Muslim world. Perhaps the Organization of Islamic Conference (OIC), with its vast material resources, could make this its primary objective—to be accomplished by the year 2010! If Muslim countries can spend so much on producing World-Cup-class football teams, surely they can do something about helping each and every male and female to read and understand the Qur'an.

This leads us to a second point. There are a lot of Muslims who are literate but do not know the Qur'an because they have memorized it in a language they do not understand. One should therefore learn Arabic, which is a praiseworthy thing to do, or, alternatively, study the Qur'an in one's own native language so that one will at least comprehend its contents. After all, good translations of the Qur'an are available in almost every language used by people today.

Understanding the language of the Qur'an alone is not enough. One should try to empathize with the Qur'an as God's eternal message, which means being able to distinguish what is fundamental in it from what is peripheral, what is universal from what is contextual. In other words, we must grasp the dynamic spirit of the Qur'an. There is no doubt that eternal values and principles demand new interpretations as they manifest themselves in new forms from epoch to epoch. For instance, if the underlying principle in the question of slavery—which the Qur'an alludes to in a number of places—is connected to the problem of control and domination of one individual, group, community, or nation by another, then the verses on slavery are still relevant to contemporary society, since the same phenomenon of control and domination persists in new forms to this day.

Our inability to interpret and understand the Qur'an at a more profound level has resulted in an obsession with superficialities. Instead of seeing the Qur'an and the *sunna* in a holistic manner, we have adopted a selective, sectarian approach which in itself is an injustice to God's Revelation. This is why the Qur'an's fundamental proclamation of justice and compassion is sometimes lost in a cacophony of trivialities. An example or two will illustrate this point.

When an Islamic government was established in a Muslim country that had just defeated a foreign aggressor after a long and bloody conflict, one of its first moves was to coerce Muslim women to wear the *hijab* in public. This was a country where there was no law and order, everything was in chaos, and contending factions were preparing for a civil war. From an Islamic point of view, there were a thousand and one other issues related to life and death which demanded urgent attention and action. But the superficial mind fascinated by form could only focus on the *hijab*.

Another Muslim government determined to Islamize society as quickly as possible decided that it would appoint "custodians of prayers" in all state institutions who would make sure that Muslims performed their prayers at the prescribed times. Since a Muslim is expected to pray of his own volition, this new edict made little sense. Besides, poverty, hunger, and disease were—and still are—rampant in that country. It is a country where there are about 15 million child laborers, living and working in the most inhuman conditions imaginable. Shouldn't a just Islamic government regard the emancipation of these oppressed children as its cardinal goal?

The type of Islamization undertaken by many Muslim states convinces us that there should be a serious attempt to develop a better understanding of Islam and the Qur'an within the *Ummah*. Towards this end, there should be a gigantic transnational effort to translate into as many languages as possible the writings of illustrious Muslim thinkers and reformers. The main criterion should be whether the writings in question help to convey that sense of justice, that feeling of compassion which constitutes the kernel of Islam. On that basis, the works of Shah Walliyullah, Muhammad Iqbal, Kalam Azad, Ali Shariati, Ayatollah Taleghani, Baqer Sadr, Fazlur Rahman, and Muhammed Natsir, among others, would be worth considering.

At the same time, since visual communication—rather than written communication—has a much more pervasive and penetrative impact in today's world, we should make better use of both television and cinema to convey the real message of the Qur'an. Certain social themes could be developed from certain verses in the Qur'an, and sketches and stories could be constructed on the basis of these themes. For example, Sura 2:177 tells us what righteousness really means.[5] Our compassion for the orphan, the needy, the wayfarer, and not just the act of turning our faces towards east or west, define our piety. There are elements in the Sura which could be harnessed for formulating some powerful visual images. The same could be said for Sura 90:10–20, which shows what it is to struggle up the "steep path," and Sura 107:1–7, which exposes the hollowness of worshippers bereft of a sense of justice and compassion.[6]

Justice: the role of government

To organize a transnational translation program, and to utilize the electronic media effectively for Islamic education centered around justice and compassion, one needs both money and human power. If there was a government in the Muslim world committed to reformist Islam, it could take the lead. It should be a government that feels very strongly about the legitimacy of Qur'anic justice and has a good track record of protecting the dignity and welfare of its people. We emphasize the role of government in this because we know that without political power it will not be possible to put into practice the values and principles of justice contained in the Qur'an.

A government that wants to implement these values and principles will create space in society for individuals and groups seeking "to enjoin what is right and forbid what is wrong." In fact, the Qur'an itself expects groups to come together for this purpose.[7] As an aside, this shows that the Qur'an, through Sura 3:104, has, in fact, given real meaning to two of the three basic civil and political rights contained in the Universal Declaration of Human Rights, namely, the freedom of expression and the freedom of association.

A just Islamic government will go further. It will ensure that citizens who are fighting for justice have easy access to both the written and electronic media. The media itself should be free of government control and should not be dominated by vested interests of whatever variety.

Again in consonance with Islamic values the government will protect and preserve the independence of the judiciary. It is significant that the inspiration for an independent judiciary comes from Qur'anic values about judging in a fair manner without being swayed by passions and prejudices.[8] Using those values as guidelines, the fourth caliph, Ali Ibn Abu Talib, exhorted his officials to ensure that the judiciary was, "above every kind of executive pressure or influence, fear or favor, intrigue or corruption." [9]

Just as an independent judiciary is an important cornerstone of an upright and ethical administration, so is the concept of *shura* (consultation) fundamental to an Islamic political system. The Qur'an asks the Prophet as the head of the Islamic state of Medina, "to consult them in the conduct of their affairs" (3:159). It also notes, "they manage their affairs by mutual consultation" (42:38). Both these verses suggest that people should have a say in shaping their own destiny. The process of decision making should be democratic.

While freedom of expression, the right of assembly, an unfettered media, an independent judiciary, and *shura* are political principles which reinforce the concept of justice in the Qur'an, there is yet another idea in the Holy Book that is relevant to government and yet permeates the whole of Islam, indeed the entirety of creation. As it should be obvious by now, God is at the very heart of the Islamic political system. In the loftiest metaphysical sense it is God that rules, that governs, that administers. God is the ultimate authority. God is the final repository of power.

What this means in concrete terms is that the power and authority of government is limited by the power and authority of God. No Islamic government—however great its popular support—can introduce legislation that challenges those values, principles, and laws that are part of God's Revelation. For instance, an Islamic government cannot—whatever else it may do—legalize gambling or the consumption of liquor or adultery or bribery even if 100 percent of the electorate want these changes. It is this that makes an Islamic government different from most other forms of government. It is a government that can make laws and devise policies but only within the framework established by God's Word or what is described in Islamic jurisprudence as the *Sharia*.

The recognition of God's authority over men and governments and the whole of creation is what Islam is all about. Islam is an affirmation of God's "majesty, His sovereignty, His power and His absolute Oneness in transcendence." [10] This Oneness in transcendence, or *tawhid*, is "the knowledge of Allah as the one and only divine sovereign Lord." [11]

Tawhid, as faith and idea, is intimately linked to the quest for justice in politics and society. The Oneness of God is the creative, spiritual foundation for the oneness, the unity of the Muslim *Ummah*, and indeed, of the whole of humankind. It is a unity based upon righteousness and piety. *Tawhid* recognizes that unity of humankind is possible only when there is

justice within the human family. Indeed it is only by striving for justice that
tawhid, a spiritual idea, can be transformed into *tawhid* a living social reality.[12]

In the quest for a just, united society guided by *tawhid*, the worship
of the one God, leaders have a particularly important role to play. Islamic
political thought has always lauded leaders who submit totally to God and,
in the process, cultivate the noble attributes of humility, of love for the
people, and of compassion blended with a strong commitment to justice. It
is only when leaders possess these qualities and work selflessly for the well
being of ordinary men and women that justice will prevail and society will
be at peace. This was the view of illustrious scholars like al-Farabi, Mawardi,
al-Ghazali, and Ibn Khaldun.

The emphasis given by these and other scholars to the role of leaders in
the creation of a just social order was influenced no doubt by the example
of the noble Prophet. He offered a leadership model that was without precedent and is without parallel in the whole of human history. In the course
of his life he performed a variety of formal and informal leadership roles—
he was a herdsman and trader, a missionary and an orator, an organizer
and a mobilizer, an administrator and a politician, a judge and a military
commander, and of course both Prophet and Head of State—apart from
being a good husband and a good father. This explains why in almost every
field of human activity, the Prophet comes across to the *Ummah* as a model
of exemplary conduct.

The righteous caliphs such as Abu Bakr as-Siddiq, Omar ibn al-Khattab,
and Ali Ibn Abu Talib were also utterly selfless, totally sincere individuals with extraordinary leadership qualities. Once when there was a severe
famine in a part of his empire, Omar decided that he would go without food
until the "least of the least" of his subjects had something to eat. Like Omar,
Ali was also a staunch defender of the poor and powerless. In a well-known
letter to one of his governors he reminded him that,

> God listens to the voice of the oppressed and waylays the oppressor. It is the
> common man who is the strength of the State and of the Religion. It is he who
> fights the enemy. So live in close contact with the masses and be mindful of
> their welfare.[13]

There were a number of rulers—after the period of the righteous
caliphs—who also upheld Qur'anic justice and who, in certain respects,
were paragons of virtue. The Ummayyad caliph, Omar Ibn-Abdul Aziz, was
one such person. On the whole, these good rulers subjected themselves to
the *Sharia* and limited the powers of the state. In this regard, it is important to emphasize that, contrary to the view expressed in certain circles,

the *Sharia* for most of Muslim history "functioned basically as a protective shield in defense of the rights and liberties of the citizen against arbitrary power." [14]

Justice: the internal threat

Nonetheless, there is evidence to show that now and then Muslim rulers transgressed the *Sharia* and the basic tenets of the Qur'an and *sunna*. These transgressions took place whenever factional feuds developed as a result of succession conflicts. They also tended to occur when rulers became obsessed with wealth and luxury and began to lead decadent lives.

Factional feuds have a long history in Islam. Invariably, they were linked to the politics of power and position. In fact, factionalism began soon after the death of the Prophet. The followers of Ali, the Prophet's cousin and son-in-law, felt that he should have been the rightful successor of the Prophet and never really accepted the leadership of the first three caliphs. The intrigues and manipulations which ensued resulted in open, bloody conflict. The followers of Ali became the Shi'a (a party or faction) and have remained a minority within the Muslim family—though they are the inheritors of a glorious tradition of struggle and sacrifice.

Shi'a bitterness against the majority who came to be known as the Sunnis reached its zenith when the Ummayyad ruler, Yazid, massacred Ali's son, Husayn, and his small band of followers in the tragic battle of Karbala. According to one writer:

> It [the massacre at Karbala] created an unbridgeable gulf between the Shiites and the Ummayyads and the Sunnis, despite the fact that the Sunnis themselves were horrified by the cruel desecration of ahl-Bait [the family of the Prophet]. [15]

The Shi'as continued to challenge the Ummayyads and eventually defeated them. The rise of the Abbasids, led by a Shi'a, however, did not end the Shi'a–Sunni conflict. Though the Shi'a–Sunni divide remains the most serious cleavage within the *Ummah*—a cleavage that has been reduced some-what in recent decades—there have also been other splits among Muslim groups at various points in history. Within the three most powerful empires of the latter period—the Safavids in Iran, the Mughals in India, and the Ottomans in West Asia, North Africa, and Europe—there were occasions when dissension and conflict threatened peace and stability. Sometimes these conflicts resulted in wanton discrimination against the followers of a particular group or sect. At other times, a ruler might choose to arbitrarily execute supporters of his rival.

While factionalism rooted in succession conflicts sapped, to some extent, the energies of Muslim empires of the past, a greater threat to the integrity of the religion came from the greed and corruption of the ruling classes. Very often, it was the love of luxury, the desire for grandeur that drove rulers to accumulate wealth through illegal and immoral means. Since institutional controls upon their power were minimal, they could, if they chose to, set aside the moral constraints imposed by the *Sharia* and acquire all the riches in the world with very little regard for ethical values and principles.

Here again, the tendency towards venality expressed itself early in Muslim history. From most accounts, Uthman, the third caliph, lacked the moral rectitude of his two predecessors and his immediate successor.[16] Muawiyya, the founder of the Umayyad caliphate, was guilty of an opulent lifestyle. He allowed his cronies to acquire huge tracts of land at the expense of the public. Other Umayyad caliphs "used the *Baitul-Mal* [treasury] funds indiscriminately to favor their friends and relatives, manipulated grants of pensions and gave these to undeserving persons, and generally ignored the rules."[17]

In the empires that emerged after the Ummayyad caliphate, there were also rulers who succumbed to the glitter of gold. Indeed, some of these empires—insofar as rectitude and decadence were concerned—appeared to conform to the pattern of rise and fall that Ibn Khaldun had observed in his study of society. In the initial stages when an empire is beginning to establish itself, the first few rulers always evince lofty moral values. They are simple, honest, and selfless. After the empire expands and grows prosperous, the later caliphs tend to become materialistic and develop a taste for luxury. Corruption sets in. The moral fiber of the ruling class weakens. Eventually, the empire disintegrates, declines, and disappears.

If we reflected upon both these diseases of the Muslim empires of the past in the light of factionalism and division on the one hand and corruption and decadence on the other hand, we would conclude that Muslim polities today are still not healthy. It is undeniably true that the *Ummah* is deeply divided and hopelessly disunited. Succession disputes may not be the root cause any more, but power is as vital a factor as ever. Often it is the desire to perpetuate one's power whatever the costs and consequences that causes dissension and conflict. Sometimes, it is the determination of a dissident group to acquire power by whatever means which is the problem. More likely than not, tussles for power are linked to ideology. It is becoming increasingly clear that a "secular state versus Islamic opposition" is looming large on the horizon. And what exacerbates the situation is the active involvement of Western powers, bent on preserving their own interests, in these conflicts. Indeed, they have played a diabolical role for a long while now in keeping the *Ummah* divided so that it will remain perpetually weak and at their mercy.

In the midst of all this there are Muslim ruling elites who wallow in vulgar opulence and indulge in crude extravagance—helped no doubt by their oil wealth. Some of them have kept huge segments of their people poor and ignorant while they feed their fantasies with all that money can buy. There is not an iota of justice in these semi-feudal monarchies, which are almost always dependent upon Western military and political support for their survival.

Justice: the global obstacle

Disunity and decadence within the Muslim world have become issues of grave concern to thinking, feeling Muslims everywhere. For unlike the past, the *Ummah* today is confronted by a global system which is not only prejudiced against Muslims but whose interests and orientations are inimical to Islamic notions of human dignity and social justice. What this means, in other words, is that the world today has become a much more difficult place for Muslims to achieve their concept of justice. And by the "world today," what we mean essentially is a whole system of political, economic, and cultural relationships which have grown out of the 200 years of Western domination of the planet. To put it in another way, it is the world as defined and determined by the West that challenges Islam and Muslims today.

Part of that challenge is the prejudice that exists within mainstream Western society against Islam and the Muslims. This, in itself, is a terrible injustice. Conditioned by the Muslim conquest of Europe, on the one hand, and Western subjugation of Muslim lands, on the other, and colored by the crusades, the politics of oil and imperialism, among other factors, prejudice against Islam is deeply embedded in the Western psyche. It continues to manifest itself through a variety of political and non-political events in contemporary society. "Islamic militancy," "Islamic terrorism," and "Islamic fundamentalism" are but the latest attempts to derogate and denigrate a community and a religion with which Western society has always been uncomfortable.

Fair-minded Western scholars and writers themselves have decried the pervasiveness and persistence of this negative attitude towards Islam and the Muslims. As the Irish writer Erskine Childers put it,

> With the exception of culturally liberated sociologists and social anthropologists, a relative handful of historians, and a small minority of contemporary religious and lay public commentators, a systematically biased outlook upon Islam has permeated the Western world.[18]

The consequence of this has been a reluctance on the part of the West to try to understand some of the underlying causes of Muslim reaction to Western domination and control. That the Muslim reaction may in fact be a cry for justice, a plea for a more equitable relationship with the West, is something which has not occurred to most Western political and economic elites and media commentators.

It is very unlikely that a better understanding of the Muslim world will develop in the foreseeable future. For mainstream Western society and Islam are, in one sense, moving further and further away from one another. As the West renews its faith in its "secular worldview" through what it regards as the triumph of Western democracy, it has less and less tolerance for the religious outlook on life represented by Islam. Moreover, Islam makes no distinction between religion and politics, since the moral values and ideals of the religion are expected to inform one's political behavior. The West, with its own unique history of separation of church and state finds such an attitude unacceptable and even "medieval." In the words of a Western scholar who is generally critical of the West's treatment of Islam,

> Modern, post-Enlightenment secular language and categories of thought distort understanding and judgement. The modern notion of religion as a system of personal belief makes an Islam that is comprehensive in scope, with religion integral to politics and society, "abnormal" insofar as it departs from an accepted "modern" norm, and nonsensical. Thus Islam becomes incomprehensible, irrational, extremist, threatening.[19]

There is another reason why it is going to become even more incomprehensible in the future. In many Muslim societies, as we have hinted, Islamic resurgence is getting stronger and stronger. As more and more Muslims become more and more Islamic, they will discover that on many fundamental issues pertaining not just to politics but also to economics, culture, education, health, the community, the family, and the environment, Islam and the post-Enlightenment secular West are diametrically opposed to one another. Muslims will then realize that unless they transform the secular world of the West, that vision of justice embodied in the Qur'an will never become a reality.

Besides, from whatever point of view, Islamic or non-Islamic, the present Western-led global system is so palpably unjust that any human being with even an atom of commitment to social justice would want to change it for the good of human beings everywhere. It is a system which concentrates political, military, economic, social, and cultural power in the hands of a privileged few located largely in the North. It is this concentration of power that enables those who manage the global system to wage wars, occupy foreign territories, impose economic sanctions, usurp natural resources, perpetuate crippling debts, control information flows.

More specifically, within this global system, the poor South (which is the home of the vast majority of the world's Muslims) had to "pay" the rich North something like $132 billion in debt servicing in 1988. It has been estimated that 650,000 children die across the Third World each year because of debt repayments.[20] It should also be noted that "in 1960, 20 per cent of the world's people who live in the richest countries had 30 times the income of the poorest 20 per cent—by 1995, 82 times as much income."[21] What is even more distressing,

> the world's 225 richest people have a combined wealth of over $1 trillion, equal to the annual income of the poorest 47% of the world's people (2.5 billion). The three richest people have assets that exceed the combined GDP of the 48 least developed countries.[22]

These statistics are just the tip of the iceberg—and only the economic iceberg at that! If we examined the data on other structures—from resource control and technology to information and entertainment—we would be shocked that such severe iniquities have been allowed to persist for so long at the global level. For Muslims, the colossal injustices of the global system constitute a clear violation of Qur'anic teachings. According to the distinguished Islamic scholar, the late Fazlur Rahman,

> The economic disparities were most persistently criticised, because they were the most difficult to remedy and were at the heart of social discord.[23]

He also points out that,

> The Quran's goal of an ethical, egalitarian social order is announced with a severe denunciation of the economic disequilibrium and social inequalities prevalent in contemporary commercial Meccan society.[24]

It is not just the stark inequalities within the global system that Muslims denounce. Many Muslims would argue that the system is unjust because it has caused tremendous pain and suffering to Muslims in particular. What is worse, it is a system which is neither willing nor capable of overcoming their pain and suffering. As proof, they will point to Bosnia-Herzegovina—the tens of thousands who were killed, raped, tortured—and remind us of the utter impotence of the UN and of those who manage the global system in stopping the Serbian slaughter of the Muslim population.[25] They will point to Iraq where, according to certain sources, 5,000 children were dying every month as a result of unjust economic sanctions (prior to the 2003 US invasion), which should have been abrogated as soon as the Iraqi army was forced out of Kuwait.[26] They will point to Libya, where a few hundred innocent people have died as an indirect consequence of limited sanctions imposed by the US-led UN Security Council to punish Libya for its alleged involvement in the bombing of an American and a French airliner. And they will of course point to Palestine, where since 1948 thousands of Palestinians fighting to free their motherland from Zionist occupation have been brutally massacred by a regime that has the full support of the USA. As they look at each of these situations, Muslims are bound to ask, Why are we suffering so much? Why are we the victims of such horrific injustices? Is it because we are Muslims?

Some Muslims would highlight certain other recent episodes to show that they are undeniably the victims of injustice, or more specifically, of bias and discrimination. As a case in point, an Islamic party which was about to win the first ever general election in Algeria in 1992 was crushed mercilessly by the military, and yet the US and other Western governments and the Western media acquiesced in what amounted to an outrageous rape of democracy. In Sudan an independent-minded Islamic government came to power through a coup in 1989, and alarm bells have been ringing in every major Western capital ever since. In Iran the commitment to independence and autonomy, so fundamental to Islam, is still as strong as ever 27 years after the Islamic Revolution, and the US and some of its allies are worried. It is not surprising, therefore, that the US continues its campaign of vilification against Iran. Though this campaign abated somewhat as a result of the ascendancy of President Mohamed Khatami and the strengthening of the reformist trend within Iran (1997–2005), the country is still being projected, through the mainstream Western media, as a terrorist state, spreading the ideology of fundamentalism to Muslim lands all over the world. Here again, as some Muslims reflect on each of these episodes they begin to wonder: has the phobia of Islam within the West reached a new, more dangerous level? Has Islam become the new ideological adversary of Western "market-democracy" now that the communist system has collapsed?

If we located the pain endured and the discrimination suffered by the various Muslim states and societies mentioned in this discussion within the larger context of an unjust global system, which has always exhibited bias and prejudice against Islam and the Muslims, it is only too obvious that the religion and its followers are going to be confronted by a formidable challenge in the twenty-first century. But it is important to remember, in this connection, that what is unfolding before our eyes is not a simple West versus Islam confrontation. There will always be Muslim states which the West will regard as its strategic allies. These states, in turn, for a variety of reasons, will choose to stick with the West. At the same time, there will also be non-Muslim states which will be the targets of dominant Western political and economic interests. And within this scenario, it is quite conceivable that Muslims must first get rid of their exclusiveness—both in their approach to Islam and their attitude towards problems facing the *Ummah*. Nonetheless, at the most fundamental ideological and political level there is no doubt at all that the centuries-old Western antagonism towards Islam, often latent, sometimes blatant, is beginning to intensify again.

Justice: the future challenge

In this situation, the choice before the *Ummah* is clear. If we are honest to our faith and committed to the goal of justice embodied in the Qur'an, we must, as we have suggested, seek to transform the world. But how will we transform the world when Muslims are only 21 percent of the world's population and are so badly divided among themselves?

Muslims must first get rid of their exclusiveness—both in the approach to Islam and in their attitude towards problems facing the *Ummah*. They must learn to present the essence of the Qur'an as a truly universal message meant for the whole of humanity. What this demands is re-articulating with renewed vigor and vitality the central doctrine of the Qur'an and indeed of all divine Revelations since the beginning of time—namely the faith in the oneness of God (*tawhid*). Let us demonstrate that *tawhid* can emerge as the unifying worldview of the whole of humanity, of every community and every nation regardless of its religious affiliation.

As a unifying worldview, *tawhid* contains at least five important beliefs:

1. A belief in the common spiritual origin, mission, and destiny of the whole of humanity.
2. A belief in the organic unity of existence—of the immanent and the transcendent, of life and death, of this world and the hereafter, of man and nature, of individual and community, of man and woman, of the material and the spiritual.
3. A belief in the human being as God's vicegerent or trustee.
4. A belief that there are universal moral values and principles which are beneficial to the whole of humankind.
5. A belief that the human being, both at the individual and at the collective level, possesses universal rights and responsibilities, roles and relationships which help to nurture and nourish a holistic way of life.

These beliefs, as the essentials of an alternative *tawhidic* worldview, challenge the dominant secular, materialistic Western worldview. The Muslim,

who is conscious of *tawhid* as the foundation of Islam, would try to reconstruct life and society on the basis of these beliefs. In the process, as the
famous philosopher Muhammad Iqbal noted decades ago, the Muslim
"would alter the pattern of world politics." For the real "meaning and role of
Islam lies in the inevitable march of history towards world unity." [27]

But to convince people that world unity is possible through *tawhid*, we
must be able to show how its values and principles can help overcome the
injustices that confront humanity today. A worldview which cannot demonstrate in concrete, tangible terms its ability to deliver justice has little chance
of emerging as an alternative to the present global system.

In this regard, it would be worthwhile to remind ourselves that it was
Islam's proven ability to ensure justice that led to its phenomenal growth
from the early seventh century onwards. Within 100 years of the *Hijrah*
(the Prophet's migration from Mecca to Medina) it had spread eastwards to
China and westwards to Spain. The expansion of Islam during that period
was the most rapid ever accomplished by any faith or ideology in history.
And the power behind it—if we may repeat—was justice in its most comprehensive Qur'anic sense.

Can the Qur'anic message of justice repeat its great historical feat? Can
the universal values derived from the belief in the oneness of God re-emerge
as guiding principles in humanity's quest for justice in the twenty-first
century?

If the question of justice is linked to some of the severest challenges
facing humankind today, we will begin to appreciate the relevance of the
Qur'anic message of *tawhid* to our times.

First, at the most private, intimate level, is this message not relevant to
the strengthening of male–female ties, to the restoration of the family as the
basic unit of a harmonious society—especially when AIDS, promiscuity,
homosexuality and drugs have desecrated inter-personal relationships and
destroyed the moral fabric of many a community?

Second, is it not true that *tawhid*, demonstrated by the practices of the
Prophet and some of the great caliphs, offers brilliant insights into ethnic
relations? Is it not because of the Qur'anic exhortations on unity within
the human family, and the living example of the Prophet, replicated by so
many other rulers right through Muslim history, that Islamic civilization
can proudly proclaim to the world that of all civilizations known to man,
it has the best record on inter-community harmony? And, in a world where
ethnic violence and racism have become more widespread and more virulent
than ever before, does Islam not provide some real, workable solutions?

Third, is it not true that the prohibition on *riba* (usury), and the curbs on exploitation, corruption, accumulation of wealth, extravagance, wastage and hoarding and the emphasis on *zakat* (wealth tax), the equitable distribution of wealth, the reduction of disparities, the utilization of natural resources for the benefit of all, the provision of the basic needs of the poor, and the dignity of labor, serve to strengthen the sinews of a *tawhidic* economy or economy of unity—which is precisely what the world is crying out for today, given the wide chasm that divides North and South, rich and poor, strong and weak?

Fourth, is it not true that the Qur'anic teaching on *tawhid* regards nature "as an integral part of man's religious sharing in his earthly life" and as "the theophany which both veils and reveals God" and for that reason preserves and protects the integrity of the environment? If such an attitude towards the environment was a dominant element in the worldview of Western man in the last two centuries, wouldn't we have been spared such a colossal environmental crisis that today threatens the very survival of the human race?

Finally, if politics had as its overriding principle the service of humanity and not the tussle for power, it is certain that justice would have triumphed much more in both domestic and international affairs in the last few decades. And what can control the lust for power but a deep and abiding awareness of an authority higher than man, of a power greater than the human being? For if man does not submit to God, he surrenders to his own ego. It is to check that danger that the Qur'an, like all other Revelations before it, makes *tawhid* the single most important principle of life.

The struggle for justice in politics is the struggle to translate that principle into policy. Each and every one of us will have to participate in that struggle in our own way. And on the Day of Judgment, each and every one of us will have to testify on "how we stood forth in justice."[28]

CHAPTER 13

Facts and Values: An Islamic Approach

Hasan Hanafi

Born in Cairo in 1935, Hasan Hanafi has emerged as one of Egypt's most influential scholars and a renowned philosopher of Islam throughout the Muslim world. He acquired a doctorate degree in philosophy from the Sorbonne in 1966 and is currently Professor of Philosophy at the University of Cairo. The author of some 30 books on the topics of modernism, tradition, fiqh, and hermeneutics, Professor Hanafi has served as the Secretary General of the Egyptian Philosophical Society since 1976 and as the Vice President of the Arab Philosophical Society since 1983.

The basic tenets of Hanafi's thoughts have remained consistent over the span of a long and distinguished academic career. This has been the case whether he has approached his subject of inquiry from the perspective of hermeneutics, as he did early on in his career, or more of a social scientist, as was the case in the 1980s and the 1990s, or as a social critic of Egyptian society, which is how he might best be described today. Throughout, his intellectual preoccupations have revolved around one or a combination of three inter-related themes: "the examination of the Islamic heritage and its relationship with renewal and modernity;" "using the conceptual and faith resources of the Islamic heritage and transforming them into an Islamic revolutionary theology," or, as he has put it, "going from dogma to revolution;" and, providing "a thorough analysis of Western heritage from a perspective that is not Western in its own origin and, in this way, provides a basis for a more comprehensive understanding of the relationship between Islam and the West, especially in the context of modernity."[1]

In the following essay, Hanafi argues that, properly understood and practiced, in Islam there is no fundamental separation between "facts" and "values." The essay originally appeared in, Hassan Hanfi, "Facts and Values: An Islamic Approach," in M.C. Doeser and J.N. Kraay (eds), Facts and Values: Philosophical Reflections from Western and Non-Western Perspectives *(Dordrecht: Martinus Nijhoff Publishers, 1986), pp 161–70.*

The apparent duality between facts and values, between description and evaluation, *sein* and *sollen*, may insinuate a separation of the two. The conjunction "and" is just an external connection but it tends to suggest the separation. Moreover, this separation is legalized by the logical distinction between judgment of fact and judgment of value.

Since Islam is not only religion but also culture, this contribution will give an example or a model of the fact–value problem in a religious culture based on identity more than on separation. An Islamic approach means primarily the analysis of Islamic data in the philosophical classical sciences and in the Qur'an, the first source of Islam. A comparative study with Western ethics as system of reference would facilitate the understanding of Islamic data.

There are four major Islamic sciences: theology, philosophy, mysticism, and jurisprudence. Each transforms the new given, namely Revelation, to an object of science. Theology formulates a creed, philosophy expands it to a worldview, mysticism describes the *itinerarium mentis Deum*, jurisprudence deduces particular judgments from primary norms of behavior. In spite of the distinction between these four disciplines, they all agree on one intuition, the complete identity of fact and value. A fact is a realized value, and a value is a potential or an ideal fact.

Theological identity of facts and values: God as value

The creed is structured on eight articles. All of them evince the identity of *is* and *ought*, not only as an ideal and possible identity, but also as a real description of man's place in the world; not only as a hope, a wishful thought expressed in the subjunctive mode but also as a reality, expressed in the indicative mode. The first four articles contain the theory of the essence, attributes, and acts of God; the second four are related to eschatology in a wider sense including prophecy, resurrection, faith and works, and the state. While the first four are rational and apodictic, the second are scriptural and hypothetic. There is no certainty without an argument of reason.

1. The proofs of the existence of God precede the description of his essence—man, living in the world, can see it changing; this observed contingency in the world leads to the notion of necessary being. Meditation on facts leads to the discovery of values. Contingency, affirmed by change, is a fact; the existence of God is a value. The cosmological and the physico-teleological arguments effectuate this passage from fact to value. The essence of God, identical to his existence, reveals the unity of fact and value. The ontological argument is not only epistemological but also axiological. This unity is the first attribute of the essence. The eternity of God (God has neither beginning nor end in time—second and third attributes of the essence) reveals

the universal value for all peoples from the beginning of mankind till the end. The transcendence of God (he has no place or resemblance—fourth and fifth attributes) indicates the formal value or the categorical imperative. The unity of God (the sixth attribute) refers to the unity of value. In the hierarchy of values God appears as the supreme value.

2. God *per* se has these six attributes. God *per aliud* has seven other attributes: omniscience, omnipotence, life, hearing, sight, speech, and will. The first three indicate that life has two reasons: pure reason (science) and practical reason (power). Hearing and sight stress the experimental type of science. Will is a concretization of power. Life is a value–fact attribute. If science is a value, power is the attribution of this value in a fact; hearing and sight would be also one actualization of science as value in experience. If power is value, will is the realization of this value as fact in the world.

Moreover, God has 99 holy names which are indeed models of human values and norms of behavior. They have to be assimilated and transformed to actual life. Some of them are: Creator, Inventor, Wisdom, Expert, Giver, Faithful, Compassionate, Pardoner, Sublime, Holy, Container, High, Strong, Just, Judge, etc. Some are theoretical, such as Wisdom; others are practical, such as Giver and the third group, such as Just, is related to judgment.

3. and 4. This theory of essence and attributes is described as the theory of unity (*tawhid*). The theory of acts is a theory of justice. Unity becomes a value and justice is a fact. The only value of unity is its realization in justice as fact. The theory of justice (theodicy) implies the freedom of man and the autonomy of his reason. Man is capable of action. His moral actions are based on his free will. Since moral actions require perception of good and bad, man is not only free but also rational. Reason is the foundation of freedom. Both freedom and reason are value-facts or fact-values. They are factualized values or "valuable" facts.

5. God spoke. His words are communicated to mankind through prophets. The Word of God is a value, prophecy is a fact. God spoke several times in different periods, according to the degree of development of human consciousness. Every prophet liberates human consciousness from one or more kinds of oppression, natural, social, political, moral, etc. He destroys and maintains at the same time (compare the double meaning of *Aufheben* in Western thought). The accomplishment of prophecy is not only a historical fact but also a moral value. It means the total liberation of human consciousness from all hindrances in finally gaining the evidence of reason and the

autonomy of the will. Miracles are not proofs of a true prophet. Even if they were historical facts they are not a moral value. They tend to contradict two well-established values: evidence of reason and autonomy of will. Reason conceives natural law and the will uses it to dominate nature and perform action in the world. Moreover, once Revelation becomes a historical fact it is transmitted as a value from generation to generation by word of mouth or in writing. Revelation becomes a source of norms, a standard of behavior.

6. Eschatology, as in every religion, is a theology of hope, a desire to transcend the events of the time and to overcome injustice in the world. Since hope is a value, it requires an actualization into fact and reaches towards future events such as resurrection, judgment, justice, worth (*istihgag*), reward, and punishment. The power of hope as a value creates eschatology as a fact. However, the description of the last judgment is metaphorical. A metaphor is a common figure in the language of persuasion. The analogy between the future event and the present event comes from the power of conviction in a moral law.

7. Faith is a value, action is a fact; since faith without action is void and vain, a non-actualized value becomes abstract and formal. The purpose of this unity between faith and action, words and deeds, thoughts and feelings, ideas and emotions is the creation of an autonomous personality, in which value and fact are one.

8. The head of the state is chosen according to values embodied in him, such as knowledge, justice, power, piety, etc. Only such moral values make him eligible for political leadership. A mere political leadership without these conditional values becomes a usurpation of power. Heredity or designation are not means of nomination because they are not moral values. Heredity is blood relationship, and designation is an authoritarian decision. Both are against free choice as a value. If the leader becomes a mere fact without a value he receives detailed advice. If the advice is not enough a formal order to follow the values is issued. If neither means are sufficient a real revolt of the masses is necessary to overthrow him. If in the course of time there is a general and gradual degradation of leadership, the value becoming less and mere factuality increasing, primitivism, revivalism, or a movement of "return to the roots" becomes necessary to regain the original model, namely the unity between fact and value in political leadership.[2]

Philosophical identity of description and evaluation (reason as value)

The identity of fact and value appears also in philosophy. After the transmission of Greek philosophy as a fact, it was assimilated, restructured, and expressed as a value. The parts were completed in the whole, the imperfect became perfect, and the extraneous was reshaped to a just measure.

Philosophy contains three major parts: logic, physics, and metaphysics. Sometimes physics and metaphysics become one science and a third part would be anthropology (ethics, sociology, politics, and history), the study of man and society.

Logic is a normative science. It protects human thought from errors in reasoning. Logic is an *ought* which controls thought which is an *is*. Logic plays the same normative role in thought as Revelation does in faith and action. Historical knowledge through narratives is included as a part of the data of demonstration (second analytics). It carries Revelation as a fact to be embodied into logic as a value.

Physics and metaphysics are conceived in a hierarchical way, ranging from absolute imperfection to absolute perfection. Matter is not only a fact but also and at the same time a value. According to the famous theory of emanation, the world as a fact proceeded from the perfection as a value. Factual gradation in the process amounts to a hierarchy of values. The first emanation has more value than the second. The supra-lunar world has more value than the sub-lunar one. In the sub-lunar world, composed of form and matter, man appears at the top of perfection. Downward come the animals, the plants, the four elements, and finally the minerals. Even the four elements are unequal in value according to their movement upward (fire and air) or downward (water and earth). The plant soul has less value than the animal soul and both are less in value than the human soul. In the human soul cognition is more perfect than inclination and movement, which are shared with the animal. Both are more perfect than nutrition, growth, and generation, which are shared with the plant soul. The hierarchy of Being is identical to the hierarchy of Value.

The theory of communication between active intellect and passive intellect symbolizes the double transfusion between fact and value. The passive intellect is a fact. It becomes a value when it receives its knowledge from the active intellect which is always a value-fact. In this theory metaphysics as value and physics as fact are unified.

In ethics, the soul has three powers: reason, feeling, and volition. Since each one is a fact it has its own value. The three facts correspond to three values, namely, wisdom, courage, and continence. The harmony between these three powers creates a fourth fact which is the health of the body and a fourth corresponding value which is justice. Human life is not only a fact but also a value. It is not only physical life but also ethical life.

In the ideal society conceived by philosophers, the philosopher-king is a symbol of this unity between fact and value. Leadership is a fact, a necessity for any social group. Wisdom is a value necessary for virtuous leadership. Society collapses when leadership as a fact is separated from wisdom as a value. In that case the virtuous city disappears and the ignorant or vicious city takes over.

Emotional identity of fact and value (pathos as a value)

In mysticism the same identity between fact and value appears both in its birth and in its structure. Mysticism was born when fact and value were separated in political leadership and in daily behavior. Even a revolutionary struggle led by an ideal leadership did not succeed in unifying again fact and value in daily life. The resistance became hopeless. Mysticism appeared to escape from the mundane fact and to maintain value, creating from it a new fact. The concentration on the ideal creates its own real. In a crisis things appear on an emotional level. The concentration on the heart creates its own object.

Mysticism as structure is a way to God, a road to divinity. The final goal would be the unity of the mystic with God. God is value, the whole world, including the mystic, is a fact. Mysticism is the annihilation of this separation between God and the world, between value and fact. The world without God is a mere fact. It has no significance. In the beginning there was an intimate tie between value and fact even before the creation of man. Because of the misuse of human freedom, the fall occurred. Mysticism tries to abolish this fall, to effectuate a counter-movement of return through spiritual exercises to bridge this distance between fact and value.

Historically, mysticism traversed three stages: moral (second and third century AH), psychological (third and fourth century), and metaphysical (fifth and sixth century). Mysticism began as normative behavior according to ideal standards of conduct, as science of ethics. Afterwards it turned from the outside to the inside, from the external world to the internal one, from the science of the organs to the science of the heart. Mysticism switched from ethics to psychology. Subsequently it turned once more, from the interior to the superior, from psychology to metaphysics. Mysticism as a historical course went from the exterior to the interior and from the interior to the superior. Mysticism as a road to God follows the same path. The mystic begins with ethics, moves on to psychology, and ends in metaphysics, culminating in the union with God.

The most important stage of the three is the second, the psychological one. The road to God is characterized by several double psychological states which are neither values nor facts but something in between, passive and active. The mystic goes from the passive to the active in one round. This goes on for seven, nine, 11, or 13 rounds. The number is always uneven, symbol of the singularity and the unity of God. These double psychological states are such as: fear-hope, stupor-awareness, absence-presence, estrangement-familiarity, loss-gain, etc. This dialectic between negation and affirmation ends in a state of unity which is the complete absorption in God, the complete annihilation of human existence, a kind of Nirvana called *fana*.

The step (*maqam*) is the transition from one round to another. If the psychological states are not under men's control the steps to be taken are. If the first are gifts from God, signs of his Grace, the second are obtained by human effort. Such steps are: repentance, poverty, asceticism, piety, patience, reliance, resignation, gratitude, etc. Most of them are passive values in order to prepare one's self for a gradual and complete annihilation. Once the world becomes a fact and is lost as a value, a substitute-value comes in, God, and becomes a substitute-fact in the mystic's heart. Once the journey comes to an end, not only divine science appears in the heart of the mystic but God Himself. God as a value-fact becomes inherent in the mystic as a fact-value. The unity between God and man or the world symbolizes the unity between value and fact.

Practical identity of fact and value (praxis as value)

Jurisprudence unites fact and value in practical life. The law is based on a double structure: intentions and actions. Since the law is given by God to man, both intentions and actions are either universal (divine) or particular (human). Universal intentions are concretized in the preservation of five value-facts or fact-values in human life, namely: life, reason, truth (religion), honor, and wealth. Life is at the same time a fact and a value. That is why alcoholism is forbidden. Truth, i.e., religion, is also a value-fact. There is something to be known with certitude and as universal knowledge which does not differ from man to man, from time to time, or from place to place. That is why paganism, polytheism, skepticism, agnosticism, relativism etc. are all pseudo-knowledge to struggle against. Both honor and wealth are also fact-values, one eidetic and the other material. That is why insults are prohibited, being assaults on one's honor. Theft is also prohibited, as is trespassing on one's property.

Individual intentions are more simple. Intention is the value and action is the fact. Action as a fact is conditioned by its intention as a value. That is why all forms of casuistry are forbidden. An action based on bad conscious-ness is only a fact without a value. The bad will is never a source of a good action. Kant's ethics find here their full application.

Rituals are not only factual gestures but also moral purifications of the heart. The five pillars of Islam are not simple movements of the tongue or the hand or of the body but they carry values. The declaration of the unity of God, "no gods except God" (*La ilaha ilia Allah*), is not only an utterance with the tongue but a double act of consciousness: first, the negation of all pseudo-gods which prevent the freedom of consciousness; second, the affir-mation of the unity and the transcendence of a Universal Principle. Praying is not a factual movement of the body but a concentration of the heart on a value. Fasting is not a simple abstention from nutrition during the day for health reasons, but a moral affirmation of the existence of the poor. Sharing one's possessions is not only a material redistribution of wealth but a moral re-edification of the rich. Finally, pilgrimage is not only a journey towards a place in time but an annual meeting of human beings to share common experiences and to issue collective decisions.

Universal actions (prescriptions and proscriptions) are those that are lawful and done in the name of God. In other words, they reveal the structure of the law as positive law established in the world. Every action is structured in reality on five foundations: reason (cause), condition, obstacle (hindrance), capacity (idealistic or realistic forms of action), and authenticity. The reason is the purpose for which a law is decreed. Loss of life, for example, would be the reason of the death penalty. The condition is a prerequisite of any action before performance, for instance, maturity as a condition for moral responsibility. The obstacle is a hindrance which prevents the application of the law in case of *force majeure*, such as permission to drink alcoholic bever-ages or to eat non-ritually slaughtered animals in case of danger of death caused by thirst or by hunger. The capacity is the measure according to which the action is performed. No action can be performed beyond human physical capacity. In the case of full and normal capacity the idealistic and normative act is performed. But in the case of feeble capacity or disability, a realistically acceptable form of act is performed. Such acceptable forms are: shortening the prayer during a journey or breaking the fast in case of illness. Finally, an authentic action is performed in good faith while an inauthentic action is performed in bad faith, such as making a journey to break one's fast. In all these five foundations of positive law the value is anchored in fact. The affirmation of values cannot be on account of fact. A value is a value because it maintains life as primary fact.

Individual acts are performed according to five levels of behavior. The hierarchy of values corresponds to the hierarchy of acts as practical facts in deontic logic. The levels are these:

1. The necessary positive act, *wajib*, is an absolute must, a compulsory deed according to a positive, imperative "do." In case of performance it generates a reward, but in case of failure it generates a punishment. Reward and punishment are not only in the other world but also in this world, as gains in the case of doing and as loss in the case of not doing,

2. The possible positive act, *mandub*, is an optional deed rendered probable by positive recommendations. If it is done it generates a reward; if it is not done it does not generate any punishment. If the first act is a universal code, the second is a particular one chosen freely according to one's aptitudes. It makes room for competition and individual difference in the accomplishment of moral values.

3. The necessary negative act, *nuhorran*, is an absolute must not, a negative imperative "do not." Contrary to the first act, if it is done it generates punishment, and if it is not done, it generates reward. Sanctions are due, given the effort in the case of doing or in the case of not doing.

4. The possible negative act, *nakruh*, is an optional act rendered probable by negative recommendations. If it is done no punishment is required; if it is not done it generates a reward due to the effort of abstaining. It is the counterpart of the second action, the possible positive act.

5. The neutral act, *halal, muhab*, is a natural act finding its legal status in the nature of things. It requires neither punishment nor reward whether in the case of doing or in the case of not doing. Man can behave naturally. In natural behavior value and fact are unified. Religious law is not only positive law but also natural law.[3]

Aesthetic unity between fact and value (image as value)

The Qur'an unifies in advance description and evaluation. There is no pure description of the world without evaluation. The creation of the world means contingency in life and consequently the dialectic between life and death culminating in resurrection. Since Revelation was sent to mankind regardless of degrees of education, the best means of expression was the image where fact and value are unified. The image resembles the fact but at the same time it carries a value. God, the world, man, society, etc.—everything can be expressed in images. In the aesthetic dimension, informative and ethical languages are unified. Images are usually means of expression of the unseen world.

However, even in the description of the visible world description is at the same time evaluation. In the theory of perception, sensation is only an organic impression and becomes perception by the awakened consciousness. This is not only a description but an evaluation, not only material observation but also a moral judgment. Evaluation is not external to description if the fact itself is a value.

The affirmation of the unseen world is not only a factual judgment but also a moral one. Transcendence is not only an attribute of God but also an attribute of man. God transcends all human images and descriptions; man transcends his own perceptive world. Both God and man are not mere existence but also values.

The descriptions of history are evaluations of previous people's experiences. The purpose of narratives is not to give historical information about facts and events but to draw the lesson for the present generation to remember and to be reminded of. Historical laws are indeed moral laws. The end of the era of miracles is a recognition of natural laws and of the necessary events in nature. It is also a value: the power of reason to understand and to discover, the power of the will to dominate laws and to use them for the benefit of mankind. The end of despotism is not only a political fact but also a moral value. Human consciousness aware of its freedom shakes the foundation of despotism.

The unity between fact and value appears in the Qur'an, but cannot be found in a review of Indo-Christian ethics regarding two doctrines, that of the Jewish Covenant and of Christian monasticism.

The Jewish Covenant is a fact but without moral value. A unilateral covenant in which only one side, namely God, gives everything and the other side, the people, does not commit itself to anything, a material covenant in which God gives land, city, temple, victory, and nutrition, and not a spiritual one—a collective covenant offered to the people saved thanks to the remnant, not to the individual who saves himself by his own actions—such a covenant may be a fact, not a value. On the contrary, a contractual covenant in which each party is committed to fulfill the clauses of the contract from his side, a conditional covenant which can be broken from one side (God) if the other side breaks it, an individual covenant in which everyone is responsible for himself and accountable for his own deeds, such a covenant is a moral covenant in which man is committed to virtue and moral law. Only in such a covenant are fact and value unified.

Christian monasticism is one of the highest values in any ethical code but it is not a common fact, a common norm of behavior and a usual style of life. Monasticism is only for heroes, not for the rest of us mortals. Islam prefers the intrusion of monasticism in daily life, the unity between fact and value.[4]

Conclusion

The unity between fact and value is not something given in advance, a *fait accompli* without human effort, but a project, an ideal to be realized through human action. The Unity of God, the *tawhid*, is an active noun, not a substantive; it means an activity, a process of unification between two things, not a ready-made unity.

Therefore the classical distinction in Western ethics between *sein* and *sollen*, as if they are two different judgments, is based on a primordial and original duality as an assumption. In praxis, there is no such separation between fact and value. The origin of this separation is purely historical—idealism in the eighteenth century and positivism in the nineteenth century. Kant separated *sein* from *sollen*, pure reason from practical reason, one for science and the other for ethics, one for facts and the other for values. The purpose was to destroy knowledge in order to build faith.[5] As a reaction the opposite view was taken, keeping the separation between fact and value, but this time destroying the value and retaining the fact. This happened in nineteenth-century Europe with the birth of positivism which opposed the older idealism on this point and chose for objectivism over against subjectivism. It is, then, a historical or a circumstantial separation, not an eidetic one.

Nicolai Hartmann and Max Scheler may have approximated the Islamic approach, the first by attributing to the value an ontological status, the second through the affirmation of the ethics of material value (*Materielle Wertethik*).

CHAPTER 14

Reason, Freedom, and Democracy in Islam

Abdolkarim Soroush

Abdolkarim Soroush is one of the most well-known intellectual figures in Iran today. Born in 1954, he attended the University of Tehran and later studied history and philosophy of science in England. Active in post-revolutionary politics in the immediate aftermath of the 1978–79 Revolution, he later taught Islamic mysticism at the University of Tehran and, in 1990, became a member of Iran's Academy of Sciences. A prolific writer and a frequent speaker on various university campuses, his calls for the democratization of contemporary Islamic philosophy and hermeneutics resulted in his dismissal from Tehran University in 1996 and he was forced to leave Iran. Having held Visiting Professorships at Harvard, Yale, and Princeton Universities, he later returned to Iran and currently resides there, although he is subject to frequent harassment by the authorities.

A compelling and gifted speaker with an impressive command of Persian poetry, Soroush's speeches to university students throughout Iran were once as much a staple of the reformist discourse in Iran as were his journal articles and books. As the 1990s wore on, the physical attacks on Soroush and his audiences became more frequent and more violent. Today he gives fewer speeches and, instead, prefers to communicate his ideas through journal articles and essays, spending most of his time outside Iran. Nevertheless his books, perhaps the most influential of which is Qabz va Bast-e Te'orik-e Shari'at *(The Theoretical Contraction and Expansion of the Sharia), continue to be widely read and influence the evolution of the ongoing discourse of religious reformism in Iran.*

For Soroush, it is not Islam but rather the human understanding of it that needs to change in order to strike a synchronicity between its eternal principles and the ever changing world. In the following essay, which was originally delivered at Tehran's Shahid Beheshti University in 1991, Soroush demonstrates the essential compatibility between Islam, reason, and freedom. The essay is taken from Mahmoud Sadri and Ahmad Sadri (eds), Reason, Freedom, and Democracy: The Essential Writings of Abdolkarim Soroush *(Oxford: Oxford University Press, 2000), pp 88–104.*

Reason and freedom

> In the name of God the Beneficent, the Merciful.
> There is no might or power save that which flows from the most high,
> the most expansive.

It is heartening as well as liberating to freely attend a meeting of the free-dom-seeking brothers and sisters of the university community in order to address the noble and worthy topic of freedom. We have all at least reflected on this important problem. Some of us have gone beyond thinking to fight in the cause of freedom in the course of the revolution. We are not the first to join this issue. Nor can we ever say or think enough about freedom. What Rumi said about love is true of freedom as well:

> As much as I enlarge on love,
> I am ashamed when I come to Love.
> Renditions of tongue reveal the core,
> But silent love reveals more.

No matter how well we articulate this theme, upon reaching the truth, the essence and the worth of freedom for the spiritual life of humanity, we shall find that words fail us. I hope we can reach a height at which we may advance beyond the explanation of freedom and its essence.

The title of my discussion is the relationship between reason and free-dom. Our sages have found a number of binary divisions in reason. They have divided reason into the pure (*Nazari*) and practical (*Amali*), the innate (*Fetri*) and acquired (*Kasbi*), and the particular (*Jozvi*) and universal (*Kolli*). They have counterpoised reason to madness, idiocy, love, and wrath. They have alternately applied the concept of reason to the faculty of reasoning or to its contents. The latter has meant the apprehension of either self-evident or the acquired truths. The neo-Platonists consider reason an external entity rather than an internal faculty. In the West, "rationality" used to be associ-ated with metaphysics, but now it is more or less connected to experiment and quantity. It is also somehow related to the analytical and logical quali-ties of thought. It used to defy relativity, but today it has become relative. Any of these intricacies is deserving of investigation.

The same is true of the concept of freedom. It has been divided into civil and philosophical, external and internal. Some have observed the differ-ences between the social and spiritual varieties of freedom, between "free-dom from" and "freedom to" or "negative" and "positive" liberties. Freedom is contrasted to submission to the divine will, human bondage, or the law. There is even a distinction between freedom and the feeling of freedom. Freedom is compared and contrasted to such opposing concepts as tyranny and democracy; at other times it is used as a synonym of democracy. Some have looked at it as a right, others as a reality. Hegel viewed it as the goal towards which the absolute spirit is advancing. Some have tried to reconcile freedom with equality and justice; others have despaired of achieving this aim. Freedom has been equated with rebellion as well as subordination. Existentialists identify it as the essence of humanity. Suggestive as these leads are, it is not possible to follow all of them in a single lecture.

My speech is about the kind of reason that serves as a dynamic faculty for thinking and seeking the truth; it is about the kind of freedom that is required by reason *qua* reason. Therefore we will seek to clarify the relationship between reason and freedom. We will ask whether reason and freedom help or hinder each other. We shall thus talk about the freedom for exercising the faculty of reason, that is the freedom of thinking.

1. We are sympathetic to freedom and demand it because we are rational. Freedom and unfreedom are a matter of indifference to creatures deprived of reason. We cannot speak of freedom in the case of either the superhuman angels or the subhuman beasts. We are impassioned about freedom and consider it the *sine qua non* of humanity because reason and freedom are inextricably intertwined. The absence of one would vitiate the existence of the other. Freedom belongs to the rational human beings. Reason requires the company of its close kindred spirit: freedom.

2. We can have two visions of reason: reason as destination and reason as path. The first sees reason as the source and repository of truths. The second sees it as a critical, dynamic, yet forbearing force that meticulously *seeks* the truth by negotiating tortuous paths of trial and error. Now, if we identify reason only by its dynamic movement and sifting quality, we will be obligated to provide the requisite environment for its existence and growth. Considering it as a mere repository of truth will require a different treatment.

3. The vision of reason as a treasure trove of truths is not conducive to thinking about the origin and the manner of arriving at the truths. But viewing reason as a truth-seeking, sifting, and appraising agent entails as much respect to the method of achieving the truth as it does to the truth itself. Here it is not enough to attain the truth; the manner of its attainment is equally important. While the former is indifferent to freedom, the latter depends on it.

Reason as storehouse entails a notion of enforced truth; the dynamic view of reason would prefer the methodically acquired error, for it contains the kind of flow that is the only guarantor of the life and longevity of reason. The advocates of administered truth need no room for questioning and doubt; dynamic reason would see such an environment as stifling and stupefying. Realizing the difference between the two views of reason may help us to understand the motives of those who feign interest in freedom but end up castigating and denouncing it, ostensibly out of concern for peace and humanity, but actually out of fear that errors might contaminate the stock of truths stored in the warehouse of reason.

Here we are not talking about those who praise violence, who have never spent any time on ideas, thinking, and its requirements. These use opposition to freedom as a front for opposing reason itself. Rather, we are talking about those who are truly concerned about the people and sincerely care about the truth while advocating limits on freedom, arguing that if we allow freedom of thought, false opinions might gain currency. Obviously this view is only compatible with the warehouse—or fortress—view of reason. But for those who prefer methodically adduced errors to imposed truths, truth must be chosen from among competing false opinions. Our mission as rational human beings is to search actively for the truth. This view attaches more value to earning a modest living in a small trade than to finding a treasure in the wilderness. The second version of reason employs a method that can be exercised by everyone, while the first version depends on luck and fate, thus benefiting only the elite. Systems that have sought to dictate the truth have abused humanity more than those open to the possibility, indeed the necessity, of making errors as a precondition.

Some scholars have argued that freedom must be denied to those who indulge in philosophical questions concerning human nature, happiness, and destiny because of the attendant confusing multiplicity of views that arise from such speculation. They have suggested a screening process for filtering out harmful ideas. Yet these same scholars have sanctioned unconditional freedom of thought in the natural and empirical sciences, presumably because these sciences are based on solid foundations that preclude such controversies. What a preposterous distinction this is! We need more freedom where there is darkness and conflict of views, not less. Where the issue is in doubt, we are more in need of others' views. Freedom is there not only for people to say their piece and blow off steam. It is there because they need each others' help against darkness and falsehood. The initial darkness is the pathway for reaching the final light. History teaches us that the conditions of freedom have prevailed wherever problems have been resolved.

Truths that are taken for granted today have not been acquired easily; they, too, have passed through the crucible of criticism, appraisal, and controversy.

If we choose the dynamic vision of reason as our guiding light, we shall not fear errors as a menace to freedom. Nor will we condemn freedom of thinking or the clash of ideas. We shall gain a new respect for the blend of tastes and colors and learn to search for the sweet truth in the midst of the bitter errors: "All the sweetness in this world and beyond / Do shrouds of bitterness ever surround."[1] We prefer the fecund hardships of the dynamic reason that benefits everyone to the drowsy clutch of the static reason.

4. Those who shun freedom as the enemy of truth and as a possible breeding ground for wrong ideas do not realize that freedom is itself a truth (haq).[2] It is as though these people do not consider freedom as a blessing, a truth, or virtue. They act as if it is so much hot air, an illusion or a myth, failing to recognize that the realization of freedom leads to the strengthening of the truth and the weakening of the falsehood. The world is the marketplace for the exchange of ideas. We give and take, and we trust that the ascendance of the nobler truths is worth the sacrifice of an occasional minor truth: "As the barrel of wine shall last, let the occasional chalice break."

Only those who are in love with their own feeble ideas will fear freedom, while the lovers of truth cannot help but love freedom as much. Freedom might upset personal convictions, but it cannot possibly offend the truth except for those who presume to personify the absolute truth. Barring those who suffer from self-adulation and megalomania, no one will be harmed by freedom.

5. According to the Commander of the Faithful,[3] "justice is spacious. One who feels confined by justice shall find injustice even more confining."[4] Flight from justice leads only to injustice, where there is even less in the way of liberty, rights, and growth. Just as there is no happy medium between justice and injustice, so there is none for reason, logic, and their opposites. Reason has a certain expansiveness, the alternative to which is the narrowness and the darkness of ignorance. And the same is true of freedom: anyone who finds it frustrating will find the alternative even more so. Some well-wishers of humanity (I am not talking about the malicious, the ignorant, and those who glorify violence and wage war against reason) may make the mistake of resenting freedom because it may allow the forces of darkness and corruption to surround righteousness. This group must realize that denouncing freedom is itself an evil worse than any they might wish to fight. No

one who is blessed with foresight and wisdom would rely on evil in order to establish the reign of the good. Such an endeavor is based on the misguided idea that the ends justify the means. No end is completely detached from the means. Means are constitutive of the end as much as the premises determine the final conclusions. Besides, reaching the truth in an open environment is essentially different from attaining it in a closed one. In fact these are two different species of truth that are acquired in two different ways. If truth is fragile in an open environment, it is even more so in a closed one. Freedom provides a range and dynamism for the truth that is absent in unfreedom. It is true that freedom can make falsehoods bolder. But this lesser evil may be condoned in view of the greater good that freedom makes possible.

6. If the naked truth were to reveal itself easily to us, we would not spurn it and would prefer even imposed truth to methodically derived errors. But the entire experience of mankind shows us that truth is never naked but is often concealed a hundredfold. If truth were naked and easy, the word "discovery" would not arise or acquire so much veneration. Discovery means uncovering the truth, which is a public, prolonged, and difficult task.

The fact is that freedom is not a currency with which we bribe people so they may feel better, but a necessary tool they need to uncover the truth. Only those who consider themselves to be directly inspired by God, who profess to possess the absolute truth, and who find their reason above benefiting from the assistance and consultation of others, will refuse the gifts of freedom. Others will find themselves in serious need of the freedom that allows public participation and discourse. Freedom is the slogan of the humble and the needy; it is the catchword of those who are aware of the penury of their own reason. Human beings still need the light of a star even if they have reached the sun; they cannot afford to turn down a jar of water even in the midst of the sea:

> In the midst of the ocean I settle
> Craving still the water in the kettle
> Like David, possessing calves, ninety
> I covet the rival's calf to increase my bounty.

7. Emotionalism breeds devotees, while reason fosters autonomous individuals. The lightning of emotions dazzles the eye of reason. In emotional upheavals, when reason is paralyzed, rational analysis is replaced with the urge to act out of blind devotion, which often leads to remorse. Of course, we cannot advance without leaning on the staff of emotions, but without seeing through the eyes of reason we might stumble into the gutter of fanaticism. Those emotions that slay reason just as easily slaughter free-

dom. Rational discourse among human beings must not be replaced by emotional harangues. Emotionalism alone cannot support a social system save one based on blind devotion to a master. Emotions dim or douse the light of reason and dissolve human autonomy. It is true that reason causes conflict, but its main product is autonomy. By fostering independence of the mind, reason prevents the dissolution of the individual personality, which is essential for preservation of freedom. Emotional subservience is even more tragic and devastating when it is manipulated by a corrupt authority. Such affective states as anger and lust, which shackle reason from within, also limit one's external freedom. We are indebted to those philosophers and theologians who have fed the fire of reason, even if they have indulged in speculative controversies, focusing people's attention on trivial and often misleading problems. Otherwise the world would have been enveloped by darkness, bereft of love, reason, and order. It is hardly surprising that hatred of reason rises under tyranny and dictatorship. Fascists found a friend in the passions of youth and a foe in the rationality of the mature. Nazis despised democracy and public deliberation because they carried the aroma of reason; worshipping Hitler was encouraged because it was based on blind and brutish obedience. The death or degradation of rational discourse might give rise to ultra-rational states of mind or mystic lovesickness among the rarified elites. It is, however, much more likely that in such a situation utter idiocy and competition over devotees[5] will prevail, precluding the use of the small allotment of practical reason that is available to the people.

I shudder every time I evoke the impassioned poetry of Rumi and Hafez in my lectures, lest their ecstatic odes to love and their contempt for reason be used as a weapon by the enemies of reason and freedom. I am afraid this will lead us to spurn the small measure of reason that we have been granted at the sight of a mirage. The august words of these sages are to be revered, but I ask you: how many of their audience have ascended to the peak of spiritual heights? Humanity takes pride in the few who have reached those lofty peaks. Indeed we love humanity for the sake of these few exemplars. But the rest of us who are not so blessed must use our God-given gift of reason and engage in rational discourse. Freedom is liberating, but it also implies responsibility. The idle, who are content to live a life without the trouble of freedom and responsibility, are delighted to jettison them, using the pretext of mystic intoxication. Let us not ignore our divine gifts. Let us not direct the blessed instructions of our sages to support base intentions by indolently parroting:

One should trade reason for innocence;
Insanity is the path to the lofty trance.

I have explored the ways of providence in reason.
I have resolved to choose the path of unreason.[6]

Let us remember that reason has two rivals: love and stupidity. Love is the share of the virtuosi. The rest must know what is left for them. Eric Fromm, in his explanation of the success of fascism in Nazi Germany, argues that those who sing the praises of freedom shun it in practice because it is a heavy burden to carry. They would sooner prostrate themselves to the authority of another human being than face the responsibilities of being free. Reason elevates us, diminishes the fires of anger and lust, and creates the serenity needed for internal freedom. In Rumi's words:

He said I shall die where two roads are crossed,
The path of anger and that of lust.
Who can resist the forces of lust and anger?
In search of such a man I ever meander.[7]

And this cannot be accomplished except by strengthening reason. So much for internal freedom. Let me tell you that the same obtains in the case of external freedom: strengthening reason rids us of all kinds of bondage and oppression. As Rumi says: "There is no blight worse than lack of knowledge." It is not possible to strengthen reason without creating a free environment for reasoning. Individual reason can, in Rumi's words, secrete passions and be enthralled by emotions. But collective reason is free from such enslavement. Individual desires and prejudices nearly vanish when reason is made universal. "Oh gallant man, passion is the contrary of reason! What unleashes passions, cannot be called reason."[8]

8. Can reason be enslaved by ideology? Here the word ideology is not used in its common usage to imply a school of thought (e.g. "Islamic ideology" or "Marxist ideology"). Rather *ideology* in the present context connotes its exact and precise meaning: those ideas that have causes but no reasons. In this sense ideology is the veil of reason; it is the enemy of rationality and clarity. It contradicts objectivity and forces one to see the world through a single narrow aperture, even if the result is a distorted view of the world. Idealism and dogmatism often accompany an ideology, but its core is the quality that conceals its falseness by placing it above rational discourse. One can only dote on an ideology or be infatuated by it; one can never rationally evaluate it.

No reasons can be properly adduced for a false idea. If we try to find rational grounds or reasons for ideologies, they too must be flawed. The only thing to do at this juncture is to look for the causes and the origins of various groups insofar as they constitute the causes of certain ideas. This points to the ideological nature of ideas or, in Marxist parlance, to their "class origins." With this definition the fight against ideology cannot be a rational one because ideology is by definition anti-rational. To fight an ideology, then, becomes an actual and concrete struggle. Because ideology has no rational grounds, any effort to eliminate its causes must be extra-rational and ideational.

The view of freedom espoused by a school of thought hinges on whether it considers human reason a prisoner of ideologies. The history of Marxism is a case in point. If you share the Marxist belief that people's views are distorted and that their rationality is flawed (as eyes that may be myopic) by objective causes (not subjective reasons), then you would not waste time on convincing the believers of the error of their ways. In order to set them straight, you would have to perform like a surgeon, not a teacher. Everything depends on you, the sole possessor of the right reason. For communists, giving free rein to public reasoning is a laughable idea. Instead, they favor building an infirmary for the sick, ideology-addled minds. They blame the prevalence of ideology on the class system.

Ideology consists of the systematically generated errors of mind, the basic malfunctioning of the scales of reason. But it does not follow that freedom from ideology is the same as immunity to error. In the latter case making a mistake is not a systematic result but a random occurrence. The extent to which freedom and reason require each other must be apparent from the preceding. To view reason as a permanent slave of ideology entails hostility to freedom, while accepting error as an accidental yet correctable by-product of reason generates respect for free and public discourse, which is the only way errors may be eliminated.

9. I started out by emphasizing that we pursue freedom with such unfailing devotion because we possess a precious gem: reason. A spirit from a different world; in the words of Rumi, a "totally other."[9] Reason is by nature a free zone. Some philosophers have used the chain of causality to make a case for determinism. They say the feeling of freedom is but an illusion because we are confined by causality: we are born into a particular family, among the followers of a specific religion, and under the domination of a given government. Everything is inculcated in us during childhood. We are indebted to others for everything. How can we begin to talk about freedom when we are the products of genetics or environment? Consider the position of Bertrand Russell: "Newtonian physics and scientific laws have left no elbowroom for human agency, volition and freedom. Only the recent introduction of quantum mechanics has broken certain links in the chain of causality

and opened up some space for freedom." The following is an example of how these philosophers contrast causality to freedom and human volition. Russell asks, how can I claim to be free when the very movements of my lips are already determined?

But I would argue that even if we accept these arguments (despite many reservations), the realm of reason remains free. If causality does amount to an ineluctable chain, reason is free from this chain; if it does not, reason is free in every direction. Reason is not an "essential nature;" it is not bound by the chain of causality. It can be penetrated only by "reasons." Our emotions are bound to the chain of causality, and thus they can bring us difficulties and even bondage. Reason is by definition impervious to force. Thus the intrusion of any non-rational element (such as ideology, passion, or anger) disturbs its purity and impairs its liberty. The freedom of pure reason does not imply freedom from logic, which is the very nature of reason. To remain free and pure, reason needs a free range. By providing external freedom, we help individual reasons to join forces, lose all traits of their isolation, and become even more pure and radiant. Another condition for the purification of reason is resisting the temptations of the flesh, mastering the passions, and taming the wild beast of anger:

> Hide from the strangers, not friends of the inner ring
> Coats are made for the winter, not the bloom of spring.
> If reason joins forces with reason seeking delight,
> Light shall prevail and the Path will be bright.
> Should desire couple with desire and trade,
> Darkness will descend and the Path shall fade.[10]

> Reinforce reason with the help of reason.
> Invoke the "consultation verse" for every season.[11]

10. Freedom feeds only on freedom, as reason feeds only on reason. This is one of the pleasant points of convergence of these two blessings (the other being the expansiveness provided by reason and freedom, compared to the narrowness resulting from their absence). This feedback serves us in two areas: self-correction and proficiency. In order to become proficient in reasoning, we must reason; in order to catch the mistakes of reason, we must seek the assistance of reason. The same is true of freedom. In order to discover and correct the problems of freedom, we need freedom. In order to better utilize freedom, we need to be free and exercise our freedom. We cannot prepare for public freedom by practicing in private. This is a machine that is fueled by its own products.

11. Some of our orators have made disparaging comments about "those who have elevated freedom to a principle." Of course, why should it not be the main principle? Freedom is essential. Even those who adopt the path of religion and submission are valued because they have chosen this path freely. True submission is predicated upon the principle of freedom; indeed, they are one and the same. Is there any merit in an imposed religion or forced prayers? Have we forgotten the Qur'anic verse: "Let there be no compulsion in faith." [12] Have we not read the following statement by Noah in the Holy Qur'an: "Shall we compel you to accept it when ye are averse to it?" [13] Did not Pharaoh taunt his repentant sorcerers thus: "Believe ye in Him before I give you permission?" [14] Who would want to emulate Pharaoh and make people's beliefs contingent upon his decree? Religion is, by definition, incompatible with coercion. Freedom has two virtues: it endows life and the choices we make in it with meaning.

12. No seeker of justice can be indifferent to the question of freedom. If we define justice as the realization of all rights, it would be an affront to justice to neglect the right to be free. The antinomy some have supposed between freedom and justice (under the guise of the contrast between democracy and socialism) is a false one. Freedom is one of the components of justice. The seeker of freedom is partly in pursuit of justice, and the seeker of justice cannot help pursue freedom as well. Without freedom, justice is incomplete. Why, then, should we shy away from choosing freedom as a principle, especially when it is freedom that complements justice and constitutes the very meaning and soul of laws? The value of freedom is so fundamental that even the enemies of freedom need it to express their opposition. Why should we not embrace freedom as our principle when it, like God, does not begrudge its benefits even to its enemies? The right to liberty is a component of justice and is included in it. At the same time, the discussion and illumination of justice requires freedom, which is, in this sense, the forerunner of justice.

13. Freedom and reason have yet another similarity: they can both be dismissed because of their imperfections or accepted in spite of them. We see both of these attitudes in our society. Some use the slightest excuse to squelch freedom, while others do everything possible to expand its reign. To be sure, freedom has its undesirable consequences, and the same is true of reason. The question is whether you are a friend or foe of freedom and reason at heart. As a friend, you will forgive the faults of freedom and strive to correct its errors. As a foe, you will use a single shortcoming to abandon freedom altogether. "He is a false lover of flowers who deigns not to bear its

thorns' pains."[15] Anyone who speaks about freedom must answer this question: are freedom, human dignity, and reason worth their occasional failings? Is the flower of freedom to be trampled because it has a few thorns?

The same holds for reason. Has reason been always the harbinger of righteousness, commonweal, and bliss for mankind? Even the advocates of reason accept that many are misled by their own reason. Have we not heard of the demonic as well as divine reason?[16] Doesn't our reason often find itself at the mercy of temptations? Does it not stumble and err? As in the case of freedom, we have two possible approaches. There are sophists (and occasionally the Sufis) who argue that for exactly these reasons we must jettison reason to avoid being beguiled and deceived by it. And there are rationalists who say that as lovers of reason we must find a way to "de-thorn" this flower. The sophists reject reason because of its rare lapses. Those who oppose freedom because of its occasional faults and afflictions are the sophists of the world of politics. We must understand that nothing can replace reason and freedom. We need freedom and reason even if we intend to reform and rectify them. How can we spurn such generous healers? To indulge in sophistic rejection of freedom and reason will bring us certain harm and condign punishment for refusing our divine legacy. The beauty, enchantment, and bliss of freedom and reason impel us to retain them at any cost.

The defenders of freedom are well aware of its problems, but they do not think that these problems could be remedied by turning their backs on freedom. The supporters of reason do not assume that all false religions are valid or that the temptations and the squabbles of the disbelievers are acceptable. Defending freedom is not the same as defending any obscenity, falsehood, or iniquity. Rather it is like defending a sun that shines on everything—even the waste—or a holy fire that may consume even the sacred pages of *Mathnavi*.[17] Freedom is a noble fortune that may bring an occasional loss, a method and a tool that may be occasionally wielded by the corrupt and the wicked. Defending the flower is not the same as defending the thorn; but what can we do if flowers grow on thorny branches? After all, we are not entrusted with the administration of the world: we were neither allowed to invent this world nor consulted about its ways. Thus we must develop a systematic and comprehensive point of view. The sages have held a similar view on the problem of evil in the world: if fire decides to abide our will and burn only the bad and spare the good, it will no longer be fire. Fire will then become "un-fire." Fire is what it is; it cannot change its nature in order to accommodate our wishes.

It is true that the emergence of any deception or corruption stabs at the heart of lovers of freedom, but even this is beneficial. In the parlance of the metaphysicians, the intrusion of evil and corruption into the scheme of divine ordination or into the realm of freedom is accidental: they are the unintended by-products of reason and freedom. These unsavory elements can be best repelled in the light of freedom and reason. If you allow reason to remain free, someone like Ibn Kamouneh will emerge to introduce doubt about the Oneness of God[18] and garner the title of "the pride of the devils" from Mulla Sadra[19] as if all the disciples of Satan glorify him for throwing such a stumbling block in the path of the faithful. This is the nature of reason. Rumi did not overstate the case when he said, "The trustworthy and blissful soul has perceived / That cunning in Satan, and love in Man were conceived." The prevalence of cunning will bring forth the likes of "the pride of the devils" to insinuate a Satanic doubt and cause a great Shi'a scholar (the late Aqa Hussein Khansari) to say, "if the Lord of Time[20] should appear, my first request to him would be to settle this question." This is one of the consequences of the cunning of reason. But is it true that defending reason amounts to defending every doubt and scandal? The defender of reason is well aware that all of the consequences of rational discourse will not conform to one's wishes. But the antagonistic consequences of reason must also be resolved by reason: "I escape to you, from you." The question of Ibn Kamouneh must be examined and rebuffed by reason. This was done by Sadr al-Din Shirazi. The same is true of freedom. As we said earlier, freedom and reason feed on each other: we cannot help freedom by tyranny nor save reason by ignorance. Reforming freedom and reason cannot be accomplished by shutting them down.

14. Freedom is a contest. Internal freedom is achieved by liberating oneself from the rein of passion and anger. External freedom consists in emancipating oneself from the yoke of potentates, despots, charlatans, and exploiters. The prerequisite for achieving external freedom is participation in the contest of freedom, which is a public process based on rules and regulations. Some people think that freedom means throwing caution to the winds and instigating anarchy, insanity, and disorder. But freedom is far from a synonym for irresponsibility and anomie. To remain free and to protect freedom is a duty of the free-minded. "One must tolerate the enemies, except the enemies of tolerance." An ignorant critic of this wise maxim has said that this constitutes an unwarranted exception to the maxim of freedom. Indeed, this is not an exception but the main rule of the game. This judgment is a consequence of refusing to view freedom as a contest. The contest of freedom eliminates the masters of mediocrity, the pompous windbags, and the incompetent overlords. It honors responsibility and courage. In a

closed and oppressive system, there is no contest between the people, so the government arbitrarily promotes some to the positions of leadership. People do not get to compete, and truths do not get a chance to shine against falsehoods. Rather the distribution of rewards is determined by the dominant will of one group: the same "masters of mediocrity" who would surely lose in a fair contest. But there is no victory without the competition. Those who wish to rest on their laurels without participating in the game use any excuse to disrupt the game and would not hesitate to use force to do so. The law contradicts neither a rule-governed contest nor freedom. It is the disruption of the rules of the game that contradicts freedom. Violence must be applied only to those who refuse to play according to the rules.

As I said, the game is restricting because it has set and constraining rules. But if you leave the game you would be more restricted because lawlessness, or what Durkheim termed "anomie," is still more undesirable. The violation of freedom and law will turn justice to injustice and promote the incompetent. Conversely, to view freedom as a game allows all to participate and accept responsibility for it. If some violate the rules of the game or withdraw from it, they can no longer complain of the proliferation of problems. Freedom is not there to accommodate the particular interests of a particular group.[21] Freedom must be revered for its own sake. The game of freedom must be spirited and continual if its benefits are to spread to all.

15. This game, like any other, improves with practice. There is no doubt that in the beginning there will be a great deal of loss and waste, but there is no shorter or better way to learn the game. It is impossible to become a good player without actually playing. This is the meaning of our earlier assumption that "freedom only feeds on itself." A soccer player becomes a champion only by playing the game. The game of freedom is no less demanding.

16. Is truth more powerful than falsehood? In my estimation those who (in good faith, not for self-serving reasons) hold freedom in contempt and reject it, fearing that falsehoods may find a foothold, harbor two misgivings. For one thing, they suspect that human reason is weak and servile. For another, they do not have much faith in the stamina of the truth; they fear it will falter in an open clash with mendacity.

I am not sure about the origins of these two misgivings, but there is no doubt about their implications. Where both reason and the truth are held to be weak, freedom cannot be cultivated. But we find a different story in the Holy Qur'an. When Moses was fearful that the Pharaoh's sorcerers would put a spell on the rational faculties of the people and turn them away from the right path, God firmly admonished him: "Fear not, for thou hast indeed the upper hand."[22] This is not addressed only to Moses, but to all Moses-like noble souls throughout the ages: they must not fear but rest assured that they are superior to the legions of the Pharaoh.

I am not arguing that because of our confidence in the strength of the truth, we must deliberately promote falsehoods. Rather I am saying that we must not exaggerate the power of those who peddle lies and worry that they may vanquish the truth. We must perform our duties, struggle and wage *Jihad* against falsehoods, and put our trust in God. We must know that fraud will not succeed nor the iniquitous prevail. This is the meaning of *tavakkol* (trust in God).

17. In addressing the relationship between truth and freedom, I have already rejected the assumption that pursuit of truth and freedom are mutually exclusive. Only when all opinions have been aired can one recognize the truth. This is the meaning of "hearing all and choosing the best."[23] So seeking the truth does not exclude loving freedom; the two depend on each other.

The fact is that what is opposed to the truth is not freedom but power. It is a mistake to think that repressing falsehoods would promote truths. Has it not occurred to us that the corruptive consequences of power are far more harmful than those of any falsehood? Those who rhapsodize about the dangers of freedom choose not to speak about the dangers of despotic power. This is the result of complacency, lack of historical vision, disregard for the blessings of reason and its requisite climate, craving for power, and, last but not least, a political culture deeply influenced by centuries of tyranny.

What about the blights of power? Would an oppressive regime tolerate the propagation of truths that were not conducive to its reign? Would it not attempt to monopolize the sphere of ideas in order to establish its own legitimacy? A dominant regime considers itself to be the measure of all truths. Even if we assume that such a regime acts in good faith, there is evidence to suggest that it will not always be successful in discriminating between truth and falsehood. Is it not true that tyrannies attract a considerable retinue of corrupt panegyrists and sycophants? What is this but moral and social corruption? Is it a wonder that those who miss few occasions to deliver a litany against the evils of freedom refuse to put two words together about the evil of absolute power? "Eyes and ears open, and intellect in such a bind? / Lord be praised who allows the closing of the mind."[24] What is inconsistent with the search for freedom is the hunger for power, even the power that arrogates to itself the right to seek the truth and vanquish all falsehoods. It is not enough to have good intentions. Method is essential here. The Holy Qur'an states: "That House of the Hereafter we shall give to those who intend not high-handedness or mischief on earth: and the end is (best) for the righteous." [25]

It is amusing to listen to the reasoning of those who say "freedom allowed someone like Marx to propagate atheism. Then someone else cultivated this seed in Russia, whose people suffered for more than 70 years before repenting in disgrace." What unctuous sophistry! What caused Marx's ideas to take root in the foreign soil of Russia, the truth of his theory notwithstanding? Was it freedom or power, right or might? Would his ideas have lasted so long if freedom of conscience, expression, and the press prevailed there? Would the buds of truth blossom in a climate where all intellectual and political dissent were suppressed or confined to mental hospitals, prisons, and work camps? Is this regime not the very quintessence of falsehood and the most harrowing form of depravity? The wrong must be challenged, but only with the methods that are themselves right. The right must be propagated, but never with the machinations of the wrong. The method of the wrong consists in suppression of freedom. Marx deserves the castigation implied in the following question: would he be allowed to express himself in an ideal society of his own design as well as he did in London?

The problem of the enemies of freedom is that they think that power has caused corruption only because it has been wielded by others. They think that power in their hands would magically retain its charms but lose its blemishes. They do not seem to realize that "absolute power has only one logic: to subdue the truth; to turn it into its handmaiden." They do not seem to realize that power controls the man, not the other way around. They do not know that when they attain absolute power, they will no longer be what they used to be. This is a steed that transforms its rider. They do not seem to realize that power greatly magnifies human frailties. They do not understand that striving to curb absolute power is the most exalted of all good deeds, or that a political order without a system of checks and balances is nothing more than an ineffective and ruthless order. One of the most important shortcomings of Marxism was its lack of a system of harnessing power. The Marxists thought that the state would wither away. In reality, however, it gained in power and stature and increased its repression, injustice, and tyranny. So the loss of Marxism must be billed to the ledger of absolute power, not that of freedom of conscience. With freedom of conscience, autonomy of truth, and respect for reason, few of these moral and social corruptions would have taken root.

Therefore, it should not be said that if we guaranteed freedom of expression, another Marx will appear and lead humanity astray. While such a society may permit a Marx-like figure to emerge, it will surely allow his opponents to confront and defeat him. Do not assume that only your enemies err and wallow in falsehoods while your minds are the overflowing fountainheads of pure, unadulterated truth. Allow your own errors to be exposed as well. Do not assume that the truth and falsehood are so clearly delineated in absence of a free sphere. What caused all that corruption was the intellectual guardianship of Marx and Engels, and the same will ensue wherever such guardianship exists.[26]

18. The dull-witted, the sluggish, the crooked, and the indigent are afraid of entering a marketplace rife with bright and brisk merchants. In the words of Rumi, "Hatred of the light is the pretenders' blight / The pure gold adores the daylight."[27] Only those who lack in ideas need fear the marketplace of ideas. Because of their own penury, they curse the marketplace and view the wealthy merchants with bitterness. Here I engage in a forthright genetic and motivational analysis because most of the enemies of freedom do not argue in good faith or according to the rules of rational discourse. In order to hide the fact that their coffers are empty, some elevate themselves above the truth and would sooner sacrifice it than confess their own bankruptcy. Their defense of the truth and religion is only an excuse. Their threadbare mantles merely cloak their flaws; their seclusion is due to lack of proper garments.

These people must acquire worth and wealth instead of shutting down the market. They must gain enlightenment and allow the lights to remain lit: "Do not burn the rug to spite a flea / Do not waste your day on a fly's plea."[28] Why choose the illicit course of deception, character assassination, intimidation, cant, calumny, and destruction when acquiring virtue is a lot easier and more legitimate? Is it not better to adopt scholarly modesty, bow at the altar of truth, and humble oneself to God, the creator of all truths? Instead of abolishing the contest, is it not easier to train and prepare to win it? Why close the mosque when it is better to join the ranks of its worshippers?

19. No blessing is more precious for mankind than the free choice of the way of the prophets. Nothing is better for humanity than submission based on free will. Blessed are those who are guided in this manner, who freely choose the way of the prophets and are awash in a cascade of divine grace: "For those who believe and work righteousness is (every) blessedness and a beautiful place of (final) return."[29] But in the absence of this state of

grace, nothing is better for humankind than the possession of freedom. All free societies, whether they are religious or non-religious, are humane. But totalitarian societies abide neither divinity nor humanity. All that remains is ruthlessness and brutishness. The free societies are closer to the prophets than the totalitarian ones. Our thinkers have so far been more afraid of falsehood than of power. It is high time we put excessive power at the top of the list of falsehoods and reflect on its enormous potential to breed corruptions.

20. We need both internal and external freedom. Our wise predecessors were more concerned with internal freedom. Rumi said:

> Oh honorable ones, we have slain the external foe,
> A more forbidding enemy lurks down below.
> Dislodging it. Intellect and reason would not dare;
> The inner lion is not the play-thing of a hare.
> It is a common lion who breaks the legion's rows.
> The true lion is he who breaks the inner foes.[30]

This is all true, except for the part about slaying the external foe. Our sages had not slain the external foe, nor were they concerned with real foes. They did not care who ruled them—the Mongols, the Abbasid caliphs, or the Saldjuqid dynasty. This venerable sage and many others like him are only concerned with inner challenges. This is a worthy but incomplete enterprise because the external enemy can easily divert our attention from the internal battle. The inner battle is contingent upon overcoming the external enemy; sometimes the two conflicts are one and the same. Living under tyranny plunges the whole society into such iniquity and causes such legitimation and institutionalization of corruption that fighting the internal enemy becomes impossible.

Conversely, contemporary Westerners have entirely forsaken the internal battle. The battle against desires has vanished from their discourse. Their concern in words and deeds revolve around the external enemy. "Liberty, Equality, and Fraternity" was the slogan of the French Revolution. which sought liberation from the king, the church, the nobility, and unfair taxation. Liberation from passions and ambitions were not at issue. The truth is that if the internal and external freedom are not combined, both will suffer. In Rumi's exultant parlance, those who have not tasted internal justice and moderation will never appreciate external justice. Those who are not free from internal tyrants shall, at the slightest provocation, sell out the external freedom as well. Those who have not beheaded their own tyrannical desires are unable to recognize the external tyrants: "The art of separating the unjust from the just he will acquire / who beheads the inner tyrannical desire." [31]

Thus in the Western world we see injustice, colonialism, and arrogance towards other countries alongside the pursuit of liberty. There is external freedom, but no one is interested in internal freedom. Internal freedom can be achieved only by the light of submission and through following the guidance of the divine messengers. Those who are deprived from this beacon of guidance cannot fully embrace either kind of freedom.

What we desperately need today is to take our cue from the seekers of freedom and from our own religious and mystic culture, to combine external and internal freedoms: the freedom predicated on submission and the submission predicated on freedom. We must tie these two together and desire them at once. We must not elevate one at the expense of the other. The bird that has been flying on one wing must be blessed with two wings in order to reach the nest of bliss. [32] And peace is upon you.

Notes

Chapter 1. Introduction: Reformist Islam in Comparative Perspective

1. Albert Hourani, *Arabic Thought in the Liberal Age 1798–1939* (Cambridge: Cambridge University Press, 1962), p 67.

2. For more on these and some of the other reformist thinkers not included here see, John Cooper, Ronald Nettler, and Mohamed Mahmoud (eds), *Islam and Modernity: Muslim Intellectuals Respond* (London: I.B.Tauris, 1998); John L. Esposito and John O. Voll, *The Makers of Contemporary Islam* (Oxford: Oxford University Press, 2001); Taji-Farouk (ed), *Modern Muslim Intellectuals and the Qur'an* (Oxford: Oxford University Press, 2004); and Suha Taji-Farouk and Basheer M. Nafi (eds), *Islamic Thought in the Twentieth Century* (London: I.B.Tauris, 2004).

3. Oliver Roy, *Globalized Islam: The Search for a New Ummah* (New York: Columbia University Press, 2004), pp 18–19.

4. James Bill and Robert Springborg, *Politics in the Middle East*, 5th ed (Reading, MA: Addison-Wesley, 2000), p 43.

5. Issa Boullata, *Trends and Issues in Contemporary Arab Thought* (Albany, NY: SUNY Press, 1990), p 154.

6. Roy, *Globalized Islam*, pp 5–6.

7. Oliver Roy calls this "re-Islamization:" "The quest for authenticity is no longer a quest to maintain a pristine identity, but to go back to and beyond this identity through an ahistorical model of Islam. ... Re-Islamization means that Muslim identity, self-evident so long as it belonged to an inherited cultural legacy, has to express itself explicitly in a non-Muslim or Western context" (*Globalized Islam*, p 23).

8. In the words of Fouad Ajami, "in the simplified interpretation we have of that civilization [meaning Muslim civilization], the young had taken to theocratic politics; they had broken with the secular politics of their elders." Fouad Ajami, *The Dream Palace of the Arabs: A Generation's Odyssey* (New York: Pantheon, 1998), p 7.

9. Data supplied by Mr Walid Alshoab, Ministry of Islamic Affairs, State of Kuwait, private correspondence, November 12, 2005.

10. Data supplied by Mr Salahuddin Alghanim, Ministry of Islamic Affairs, Kingdom of Saudi Arabia, private correspondence, November 16, 2005.

11. *Ibid.*

12. By the late 1980s, in Egypt the Islamic investment companies (IICs) held deposits estimated at between $2 and $3 billion from some half a million investors. The top four IICs had funds amounting to 14 percent of the total commercial bank deposits and 21 percent of deposits held by public-sector commercial banks. See Abdel Monem Said Aly, "Privatization in Egypt: The Regional Dimensions," in Iliya Harik and Denis J. Sullivan (eds), *Privatization and Liberalization in the Middle East* (Bloomington, IN: Indiana University Press, 1992), pp 52–4.

13. Data collected from www.islamonline.net/arabic/politics/2002/2/article3.shtml. Accessed on November 28, 2005.

14. *Ibid.*

15. Dale Eickelman. "Inside the Islamic Reformation," *Wilson Quarterly*, vol. 22, no. 1 (winter 1998), p 85.

16. Nor, it is important to point out, is this the only way to conceptualize the multiple divisions that tend to characterize contemporary manifestations of Islam in the modern world. For alternative categorizations see William Shepard, "Islam and Ideology: Toward a Typology," *International Journal of Middle East Studies*, vol. 19, no. 3 (August 1987), pp 305–35.

17. Hourani, *Arabic Thought in the Liberal Age*, p 68.

18. *Ibid.*, p 136.

19. Janet Afary, *The Iranian Constitutional Revolution, 1906–1911* (New York: Columbia University Press, 1996), p 44.

20. For the radicalization of Algerian students and their increasing attraction to Islam around this time, for example, see Severine Labat, "Islamism and Islamists: The Emergence of a New Type of Militant," in John Ruedy (ed), *Islamism and Secularism in North Africa* (New York: St Martin's, 1996), pp 107–8.

21. Oliver Roy, *The Failure of Political Islam*, trans Carol Volk (Cambridge: Harvard University Press, 1994).

22. *Ibid.*, p 60.

23. Since the organization could not secure government permission, Muslim Brotherhood candidates ran as independents.

24. Emad Eldin Shahin, *Political Ascent: Contemporary Islamic Movements in North Africa* (Boulder, CO: Westview, 1998), p 100.

25. Newspapers and journals serve as another form of "middle-class shelter," through which Islamist ideas are formulated and conveyed to intended audiences, a function that books play as well, though to a somewhat lesser extent owing to their narrower circulation and readership.

26. Carrie Rosefsky Wickham, "Islamic Mobilization and Political Change: The Islamic Trend in Egypt's Professional Associations," in Joel Beinen and Joe Stork (eds), *Political Islam* (Berkeley, CA: University of California Press, 1997), pp 121–2.

27. John Entelis, "Political Islam in the Maghreb: The Nonviolent Dimension," in Lisa Anderson, et al (eds), *Islam, Democracy and the State in North Africa*

(Bloomington, IN: Indiana University Press, 1997), pp 59–61.

28. Shahin, *Political Ascent*, p 155.

29. Beverley Milton-Edwards, *Islamic Politics in Palestine* (London: I.B.Tauris, 1999), pp 116–18.

30. Barry Rubin, *Islamic Fundamentalism in Egyptian Politics* (New York: Palgrave Macmillan, 2002), p 35.

31. Sayyid Qutb (1906–66), often called "the ideological father of contemporary fundamentalism," defined *Jihad* thus: "If anyone adopts the attitude of resistance [to Islam], it would then be obligatory on Islam to fight against him until he is killed or he declares his loyalty and submission. Scholars of defeatist and apologetic mentalities, while expressing their views on the subject of 'Jihad' in Islam, trying to wash this 'blot,' intermingle two things and thus confuse the issue; first, this religion forbids imposition of belief by force ..., while on the other hand, it annihilates all those political and material powers that stand between the people and Islam, which makes one people bow before another and prevent them from the servitude of Allah—these two principles are quite apart and have no mutual relevance, nor is there any room for intermixing them." Sayyid Qutb, "War, Peace, and Islamic Jihad," in Mansoor Moaddel and Kamran Talattof (eds), *Modernist and Fundamentalist Debates in Islam: A Reader* (New York: Palgrave Macmillan, 2002), p 227.

32. Mark Juergensmeyer, *Terror in the Mind of God: The Global Rise of Religious Violence* (Berkeley, CA: University of California Press, 2003), p 61.

33. *Shirk* could also be translated as "association"—a "theological term referring to the association of someone or something with God, that is, putting someone or something in the place of God, thus deviating from monotheism." John Esposito, *The Oxford Dictionary of Islam* (Oxford: Oxford University Press, 2003), p 293. For an insightful and concise analysis of the different interpretations of *tawhid* in Islam, especially by fundamentalists, see Mir Zohair Husain, *Global Islamic Politics*, 2nd ed (New York: Longman, 2003), pp 81–5.

34. Husain, *Global Islamic Politics*, pp 85–91.

35. *Ibid.*, p 90.

36. Juergensmeyer, *Terror in the Mind of God*, p 79.

37. Roy, *Globalized Islam*, pp 51–4.

38. Hugh Kennedy, "Intellectual Life in the First Four Centuries of Islam," in Fardad Daftary (ed), *Intellectual Traditions in Islam* (London: I.B.Tauris, 2000), pp 18–19.

39. *Ibid.*, p 25.

40. *Ibid.*, pp 27–8.

41. Oliver Leaman, "Scientific and Philosophic Enquiry: Achievements and Reactions in Muslim History," in Fardad Daftary (ed), *Intellectual Traditions in Islam*, pp 33–4.

42. Esposito and Voll, *Makers of Contemporary Islam*, p 9.

43. *Ibid.*, p 15.

44. *Ibid.*
45. Basheer M. Nafi and Suha Taj-Farouki, "Introduction," in Suha Taj-Farouki and Basheer M. Nafi (eds), *Islamic Thought in the Twentieth Century*, p 7.
46. *Ibid.*
47. These are alternative designations offered by William Shepard, though his conceptualization of each category is slightly different from that offered here. See William Shepard, "The Diversity of Islamic Thought: Towards a Typology," in Suha Taj-Farouki and Basheer M. Nafi (eds), *Islamic Thought in the Twentieth Century*, p 63.
48. *Ibid.*
49. *Ibid.*, p 84.
50. See, for example, Seyyed Hossein Nasr, *Living Sufism* (London: Mandala, 1980).
51. Robert D. Lee, *Overcoming Tradition and Modernity: The Search for Islamic Authenticity* (Boulder, CO: Westview, 1997), p 14.
52. Akbar Ahmed, *Postmodernism and Islam: Predicament and Promise* (London: Routledge, 1992), p 109.
53. *Ibid.*, pp 117–18.
54. Mehrzad Boroujerdi, *Iranian Intellectuals and the West: The Tormented Triumph of Nativism* (Syracuse, NY: Syracuse University Press, 1996), p 160.
55. Tomas Gerholm, "Two Muslim Intellectuals in the Postmodern West: Akbar Ahmed and Ziauddin Sardar," in Akbar S. Ahmed and Hastings Donnan (eds), *Islam, Globalization and Postmodernity* (London: Routledge, 1994), p 197.
56. Quoted in *ibid.*, pp 196–7.
57. Born in Egypt in 1926 and currently based at the University of Qatar, al-Qaradawi has recently emerged as one of the most influential theologians in the Arab world, thanks largely to his popular television show on the Al-Jazeera channel. He was one of the first Muslim scholars to condemn the attacks of September 11, though, as mentioned above, he has refused to condemn suicide bombings in the Palestinian–Israeli conflict. A prolific author with some 42 books, he also heads the European Council for Fatwas and Research. For the text of one of al-Qaradawi's interviews with BBC Television on the subject of suicide bombings see http://news.bbc.co.uk/2/hi/programmes/newsnight/3875119.stm (available as of November 20, 2005). Al-Qaradawi's views on other topics are available in English on www.islamonline.net, an Internet site behind which he is a central figure.
58. Farzin Vahdat, *God and Juggernaut: Iran's Intellectual Encounter with Modernity* (Syracuse, NY: Syracuse University Press, 2002), p 209.
59. The issue of women has generally received scant and at best uneven attention by Muslim thinkers. Of the male thinkers included in this volume, Talbi has paid perhaps the greatest attention to the issue of women, as have Shahrour and Abu Zaid. For more on this topic see, Hibba Abugideiri, "On Gender and Family," in Suha Taj-Farouki and Basheer M. Nafi (eds), *Islamic Thought in*

the Twentieth Century, especially pp 250–1.

60. Derek Hopwood, "Introduction: The Culture of Modernity and the Middle East," in John Cooper, Ronald Nettler, and Mohamed Mahmoud (eds), *Islam and Modernity: Muslim Intellectuals Respond* (London: I.B.Tauris, 1998), p 9.

61. Suha Taji-Farouk, "Introduction," in Suha Taji-Farouk (ed), *Modern Muslim Intellectuals and the Qur'an,* p 1.

62. Abdullah Saeed, "Fazlur Rahman: A Framework for Interpreting the Ethno-Legal Content of the Qur'an," in Suha Taji-Farouk (ed), *Modern Muslim Intellectuals and the Qur'an,* p 43.

63. Quoted in John L. Esposito and John O. Voll, *Islam and Democracy* (Oxford: Oxford University Press, 1996), p 29.

64. Abdullahi Ahmed An-Na'im, *Toward an Islamic Reformation: Civil Liberties, Human Rights, and International Law* (Syracuse, NY: Syracuse University Press, 1996), pp 28–9. An-Na'im is currently Professor of Law at Emory University in the United States.

65. Quoted in Esposito and Voll, *Makers of Contemporary Islam,* p 82.

66. Hasan Hanafi, "Contemporary Islamic Philosophy," in Brian Carr and Indira Mahalingam (eds), *Companion Encyclopedia of Asian Philosophy* (London: Routledge, 1997), p 1039.

67. Charles Kurzman, "The Globalization of Rights in Islamic Discourse," in Ali Mohammadi (ed), *Islam Encountering Globalization* (London: RoutledgeCurzon, 2002), p 133.

68. Quoted in Ronald L. Nettler, "Mohamed Talbi on Understanding the Qur'an," in Suha Taji-Farouk (ed), *Modern Muslim Intellectuals and the Qur'an,* p 233.

69. Suha Taji-Farouk, "Introduction," p 20.

70. Hopwood, "Introduction: The Culture of Modernity and the Middle East," p 8.

71. Abdulaziz Sachedina, *The Islamic Roots of Democratic Pluralism* (Oxford: Oxford University Press, 2001), p 135.

72. *Ibid.,* p 17.

73. *Ibid.,* pp 138–9.

74. An-Na'im, *Toward an Islamic Reformation,* p 171.

75. *Ibid.,* p 170.

76. Hugh Goddard, "Perceptions of Christians and Christianity," in Suha Taj-Farouki and Basheer M. Nafi (eds), *Islamic Thought in the Twentieth Century,* pp 306–7.

77. Nettler, "Mohamed Talbi on Understanding the Qur'an," p 226.

78. Goddard, "Perceptions of Christians and Christianity," pp 310–11.

79. Laith Kubba, "Faith and Modernity," in Larry Diamond, Marc F. Plattner, and Daniel Brumberg (eds), *Islam and Democracy in the Middle East* (Baltimore, MD: The Johns Hopkins University Press, 2003), p 265.

80. *Ibid.,* p 266.

81. Mahmood Monshipouri, "Islam and Human Rights in the Age of Globalization," in Ali Mohammadi (ed), *Islam Encountering Globalization,* p 103.

82. Esposito and Voll, *Makers of Contemporary Islam*, p 81.
83. Farzin Vahdat, "Post-Revolutionary Islamic Modernity in Iran: The Interpretive Hermeneutics of Mohamad Mojtahed Shabestari," in Suha Taji-Farouk (ed), *Modern Muslim Intellectuals and the Qur'an*, p 213.
84. *Ibid.*, pp 213–14.
85. Kurzman, "The Globalization of Rights in Islamic Discourse," p 133.
86. Esposito and Voll, *Makers of Contemporary Islam*, p 16.
87. Taji-Farouk, "Introduction," p 15.
88. Kurzman, "The Globalization of Rights in Islamic Discourse," p 141.
89. Esposito and Voll, *Makers of Contemporary Islam*, p 20.
90. Jon W. Anderson. "The Internet and Islam's New Interpreters," in Dale F. Eickelman and Jon W. Anderson (eds), *New Media in the Muslim World*, 2nd ed (Bloomington, IN: Indiana University Press, 2003), p 47.
91. For an incisive discussion of the notion of reformation in Islam in both Western and Islamic scholarship see Charles Kurzman and Michelle Browers, "Comparing Reformations," in Michelle Browers and Charles Kurzman (eds), *An Islamic Reformation?* (Lanham, NJ: Lexington, 2003), pp 1–17.
92. Under great pressure both domestically and internationally, Aghajari's death sentence was initially commuted to life imprisonment, and, after serving five years in prison, he was released. For more on his case see Pourya Hajizadeh and Pardis Hajizadeh, *Aqajari* (Aghajari) (Tehran: Jameh Daran, 1382/2003). Some of Aghajari's own views are outlined in Hashem Aghajari, "Kalbod Shekafi-e Enqelab, Khosunat va Eslahat" (Autopsy of Revolution, Violence and Reforms), *Aftab*, vol. 1, no. 3 (1380/2001), pp 10–22; and Hashem Aghajari, *Hokumat-e Dini va Hokumat-e Demokratik* (Religious Government and Democratic Government) (Tehran: Zekr, 1381/2002).
93. Eickelman, "Inside the Islamic Reformation," p 82.
94. Dale Eickelman, "The Coming Transformation of the Muslim World," *Current History* (January 2000), p 20.
95. Eickelman, "Inside the Islamic Reformation," p 84.
96. Muhammad Qasim Zaman, *The Ulama in Contemporary Islam: Custodians of Change* (Princeton, NJ: Princeton University Press, 2002), pp 144–51. Zaman does note, however, that the state often becomes just as dependent on the religious establishment for its legitimacy and the ability to enact certain public policies, especially in a country like Egypt, where the Al-Azhar can exercise significant institutional autonomy.
97. Zaman, *The Ulama in Contemporary Islam*.
98. The Gülen schools—which include elementary and high schools as well as college preparatory institutions, dormitories, and universities—were reported to number around 300 by the late 1990s and can be found in 50 different countries. See Thomas Michael, "Fethullah Gülen as Educator," in M. Hakan Yavuz and John L. Esposito (eds), *Turkish Islam and the Secular State: The Gülen Movement* (Syracuse, NY: Syracuse University Press, 2003), pp 69–84.

99. Briefly, in 1992 Professor Abu Zaid applied for promotion to the rank of full professor at Cairo University's Department of Arabic Studies. During the ensuing review process, his reformist arguments and his writings were said to suffer from "cultural AIDS" by an influential colleague who also happened to be a Friday preacher at a Cairo mosque. The sentence of apostasy passed on Abu Zaid was subsequently confirmed by Cairo's Court of Appeals, and he was decreed divorced from his wife. Abu Zaid currently lives and teaches in the Netherlands. For a detailed account of his drama see Fauizi Najjar, "Islamic Fundamentalism and the Intellectuals: The Case of Nasr Hamid Abu Zayd," *British Journal of Middle Eastern Studies*, vol. 27, no. 2 (2000), pp 177–200.

100. Taken from the title of a recent *New York Times* bestseller: Irshad Manji, *The Trouble with Islam Today* (New York: St Martin's Griffin, 2003).

101. Carool Kersten, "Collateral Damage: The Marginalization of (Post) Modernist Muslim Thinkers," paper presented at the International Conference on Religion and Globalization, Payap University, Chiang Mai, Thailand, 2003.

102. Tariq Ali, *The Clash of Fundamentalisms: Crusades, Jihad and Modernity* (London: Verso, 2002).

Chapter 2. Present-Day Islam Between Its Tradition and Globalization

1. Roger Pol Droit, *Philosophie et démocratie dans le monde* (Paris, 1995), p 22.
2. *Ibid.*, p 24.
3. *Ibid.*
4. On connections between philosophy, anthropology, and other social sciences, see the works of P. Bourdieu, notably his latest title, *Méditations Pascaliennes* (Seuil, 1997).
5. Benjamin R. Barber, *Jihad vs. McWorld: How Globalism and Tribalism are Reshaping the World* (New York, 1996); French trans, *Djihad vs. McWorld: Mondialisation et integrisme contre la démocratie* (Paris, 1996).
6. I refer to the works of Ilya Prigogine, *La fin des certitudes* (Paris, 1995), Claude Allegre, *La Defaite de Platon* (Paris, 1996) and Alain Finkelkraut, *La Defaite de la pensée* (Paris, 1988). The abundant literature on this theme expresses at the same time the anguish of our time in face of the errancy of our history and the will to clarify new conditions of reflection to prevent as much as possible other totalitarian adventures.
7. C. Edmund Bosworth, *The New Islamic Dynasties: A Chronological and Genealogical Manual* (Edinburgh, 1996).
8. See especially C. Geertz, *Islam Observed* (Chicago, 1968).
9. Mohammed Arkoun, *Lectures du Coran* (Paris, 1982), pp 69–86.
10. Hourani, *Arabic Thought in the Liberal Age, 1798–1939*.
11. I evoke here a distinction of anthropological scope between learned written culture and oral culture termed "popular;" the first is linked to all statist formations from the appearance of writing, the second applies particularly to segmentary societies in tension with centralizing powers. The bibliography on

the subject is vast; the best introduction remains the work of J. Goody, *The Interface Between the Oral and the Written* (Cambridge, 1987). See the application which I make of it in "Transgressor, Deplacer, Depasser," *Arabica*, 43 (1996), pp 28–70.

12. I do not overlook the great religions of Asia, but owing to a lack of sufficient competence, I cannot pronounce on the linguistic status of their founding discourses.

13. My friend Daryush Shayegan has already reflected upon the general problem of religious revolution in *Qu'est-ce qu'une révolution religieuse?* (Paris, 1982).

14. Mohammed Arkoun, "L'Islam actuel devant sa tradition," in *Aspects de la foi de l'Islam* (Brussels, 1985); also M. Arkoun, *Penser l'Islam aujourd'hui* (Algiers, 1993).

15. In 1957 I published in the Tunisian periodical *al-Fikr* a first programmatic text entitled *Maghza ta'rikh shamal Ifrikiya*. Morocco and Tunisia had just regained their independence and the Algerians pursued a tragic struggle which was to last until March 1962. I had already the naivety to believe that the rights of critical knowledge, bearing on vital subjects which the ideology of battle seizes upon, ought to be respected and integrated in the liberation struggle which derived its better legitimacy in the promises of liberty lavished on intellectuals, artists, creators, and thinkers. All North Africans of my generation shared enthusiastically this naive vision. Today the destiny of liberties and rights of the spirit in all societies molded by the Islamic fact is such that there is no longer any place for naive projects driven by plausible Utopia; but the ever current project of a critical re-reading of the entire North African past inseparable from its African and Mediterranean dimensions does not allow us to dispose of either the social frames capable of supporting and putting it to advantage, or the research duly formed for conducting several sites of exploration and writing with the tools of thought and scientific competency required by what I have called the emerging reason, different from all types of reason bequeathed by all types of tradition, including the reason of the Enlightenment.

16. Shlomo D. Goitein, *Studies in Islamic History and Institutions* (Leiden, 1966).

17. F. Braudel, *Civilization and Capitalism, 15th to 18th Century* (London, 1981–84), and J. Habermas, *The Philosophical Discourse of Modernity*, trans F. Lawrence (Cambridge, 1987).

Chapter 3. The Way (*Al-Sharia*) of Islam

1. The mere fact that I have referred to this notion has caused some researchers to cast doubt on my works. In so doing, they do not take into account how I define it, or how I propose we should approach the subject. They simply, and often maliciously, "surf" the very negative images that are widespread among the general public in order to dismiss any approach to it, without taking the time to study it or discuss its principles, its logic, and the perspectives it may have to offer.

2. Is this not an innovative, or at least self-contradictory, phrase?

3. There has been much discussion of the question "Who is a Muslim?" as much because scholars have differed in their opinions as out of the need to discuss the sectarian approaches of some movements that claim that they alone are the true "Muslims." In my view, all the women and men are Muslims who see themselves as such and have pronounced the *shahada*, which is the decisive factor in belonging to Islam. The question of practice and behavior falls within the responsibility of those who accept the consequences without this calling into question their being recognized as "Muslim." This is the opinion of many scholars, including almost naturally the women and men who are concerned about faithfulness in their practice and daily life because it is for them especially that life in the West is sometimes a problem and often a challenge.

4. Attempts have often been made to oppose the intimate "mystical Way" (Sufism) to the "legal Way" (the *Sharia*). In the redefinition of concepts that is proposed here, this opposition becomes meaningless: the intimate "mystical Way" is at the heart (it is the heart) of the "path towards the spring." Spirituality is the first requirement of faithfulness. There is no faithfulness without spirituality.

5. Upon reading the texts, one discovers that these prohibitions are not numerous, even though in some areas they are very precise.

6. It is sometimes useful to remind certain intellectuals in the West of these truths when they forget that, although the principles of democracy are identical, the models of democracy in Europe and also in the United States vary widely. Often they demand that the Muslim world adhere to a particular model of democracy, while the heart of the debate lies in discovering whether or not Muslims oppose democratic principles. As far as the model is concerned, each society should be free to find one that is most appropriate to its history, its culture, and its collective psychology.

7. This explains the differences between the ways of life of Muslims in Europe, Africa, and Asia and on the continent of America. Their creed and the body of principles they hold to are the same (this is what is meant by one Islam, one and the same religion), but their cultures differ and are integrated into their way of being in the world insofar as this does not run counter to an accepted boundary. It is with regard to this cultural aspect that one may speak of an African, Asian, American, or European Islam, without having to use the plural when referring to "Islam:" the universality of the latter accommodates the diversity of the former.

8. Some traditionalist and literalist trends do not make this differentiation: to follow the Prophet means to dress like him. The essence of the principle is subsumed into its historical application. The difference of approach in this is the most easily observed expression of the divergence between these trends and the reformist school.

9. This recalls the humility of origin.

10. *Istislah* is the tenth form of the root *sa-lua*, which is also the root of *maslaha*.

11. Abu Hamid al-Ghazali, *Al-mustasfa min ilm al-usul* (Baghdad: Muthanna, 1970).

12. Cf. *Al-mustasfa min ilm al-usul*, vol. I, pp 286–7. See also Muhammad Khalid Masud's interesting book, *Shatibi's Philosophy of Islamic Law* (Islamabad: Islamic Research Institute, 1995), pp 139–40.

13. Apart from the ulama of the Zahirite school, who did not even recognize the concept of *maqasid*.

14. *Al-masali al-daruriyya* are requirements upon which people's lives depend, as well as the protection of the meaning of their worship of God. Later some ulama added *al-ird* (honor).

15. *Al-masali al-hajiyya* are requirements related to difficult situations. We find in this category rules concerning, for example, the sick and the old, and dispensations (*rukhas*) related to prayer and fasting.

16. *Al-masali al-tahsiniyya* may deal with, for example, cleanliness and moral virtues, which may lead to an improvement in religious practice and be a means of attaining what is desirable.

17. Thus it was considered that there was no room for speaking of *istislah*, since the *Sharia* itself and all its injunctions were founded on *al-masali*, which represent both the content and the objective of the revealed laws.

18. Al-Shatabi expains, in his analysis in *Al-Itisam*, that the two sources of Islam are the Qur'an and the *sunna*, whose injunctions are based on *al-maslaha* (he agrees on this point with Ibn Hazm); but he is clear that we have to refer to our reason when the texts contain no indication (according to al-Shatibi, this was once done by means of *ijma* or *qiyas*). So, when the texts are silent, *al-maslaha* is the point of reference and acts as an independent source in light of the Qur'an and the *sunna*.

19. This was the view of al-Ghazali, who, by subordinating the method of reasoning based on *al-maslaha* to *qiyas*, linked the sources in order to avoid a purely rational formulation that might be remote from any reference to the sources.

20. The meaning of *mursala* has been discussed by numerous scholars, and it would be pedantic and unprofitable to discuss it here. The classification "undetermined" gives the meaning generally admitted and legally appropriate.

21. Subhi Rajab al-Mahmasani, *Falsafat at-tashri fil-islam* (Leiden: Brill, 1961), p 117, cited in Mohammad Hashim Kamali, *Principles of Islamic Jurisprudence* (Cambridge: Islamic Texts Society, 1991), p 276.

22. Such was the case when some ulama wanted to justify usury and bank interest (*riba*) in the name of the common good. There can be no *maslaha mursala* here because this matter is the subject of clear and indisputable directions in the Qur'an (*qati al-thubut wa-qati al-dalala*—indisputable with regard to both transmissions and meaning) and the *sunna* (*zanni al-thubut wa-qati al-dalala*—conjectural with regard to transmission and disputable with regard to meaning).

23. There are numerous other secondary conditions (for example, the *maslaha* must be reasonable (*maqula*) according to Malik, and indispensable (*daruriyya*) according to al-Ghazali). For more details and deeper analyses, see the specialized works already referred to by al-Shatibi (*Al-Itisam*), Khallaf, Hassab Allah, and Kamali.

24. Yusuf al-Qaradawi, *Al-ijtihad al-muasir, bayna al-indibat wa-al-infirat* (Cairo: Dar al-tawzi wa-al-nashr al-islamiyya, 1993), pp 66–77.

25. Qur'an, 7:157.

26. Qur'an, 10:57.

27. Qur'an, 2:219.

28. Ibn al-Qayyim al-Jawziyya, *Ilam al-muwaqqiin an rabb al-alamin*, vol. 3 (Cairo, n. d.), p 1.

29. We shall deal with various levels of "clarity" when we study the notion of *ijtihad*.

30. The vast majority of the ulama agree in saying that there can be no *ijtihad* (and hence no *maslaha*, no *qiyas*, no *istihisan*, and no need for *ijma*) as far as religious practice (*al-ibadat*) is concerned, for its judgments and modalities are known to us through Revelation and must be applied as they were revealed to the Prophet and taught and explained by him; similarly, when there are clear and detailed injunctions (though of course without neglecting a vision of the whole body of objectives of Islamic law and the social situation, as we have explained).

31. Qur'an, 2:185.

32. Muhammad Khalid Masud, *Shatibi's Philosophy of Islamic Law*, p 367.

33. Muhammad Hashim Kamali, *Principles of Islamic Jurisprudence*, p 366.

34. Muhammad Hamidullah, *The Emergence of Islam*, ed and trans Afzal Iqbal (Islamabad: Islamic Research Institute, 1993), p 97.

35. There are various opinions among the ulama as to the number of these verses and *ahadith*. For example, al-Ghazali and Ibn al-Arabi counted 500 verses, while Abd al-Wahlab Khallaf has listed about 228. Al-Shawkani, however, believed that such calculations were not reliable and definitive, since some verses can be variously interpreted according to the scholar and the context. One could say the same about the *ahadith al-ahkam*, even if Ibn Hanbal is supposed to have said that there are about 1,200 *ahadith* in this category. Cf. al-Shawkani, *Al-qawl al-mufid fi al-ijtihad wa-al-taqlid* (Cairo, 1975), chapter 2; and Abd al-Wahhab Khallaf, *Ilm usul al-fiqh* (Kuwait: Dar al-galam, 1978).

36. There are many other detailed classifications in the area of *ijtihad*, which are beyond the scope of this work. They are known by specialists in *usul al-fiqh* and are the subject of discussions and controversies among the ulama. An example is the "divisibility of *ijtihad*" (*al-tajza*), about which pages and pages of argument have been written. It is a very theoretical and secondary issue.

37. Al-Shatibi, *Al-muwafaqat fi usul al-sharia*, new ed, vol. 4 (Lebanon: Dar al-marifa, 1996), chapter "The conditions for *ijtihad*," pp 477ff.

38. This is what al-Shatibi himself calls the second quality. Having said that the first is the objective, he adds that "the second is the instrument" (*ibid.*, vol. 4, p 478).

39. Al-Shatibi, for example, was very demanding in this particular; he thought that no one could attain the true level of *ijtihad* without a deep knowledge of Arabic (*ibid.*, vol. 4, pp 590ff).

40. This recognition must also come from other scholars and from the Muslim community.

41. The ulama have set down various conditions for the *mujtahid mutlaq* (absolute) and the *mujtahid muqayyad* (limited) who are content to deduce judgments within the framework of a specific juridical school. The conditions required for the latter are certainly less demanding, and added to them is knowledge of the rules of deduction related to the juridical school in question.

42. For a detailed analysis of these historical reasons, see Muhammad Iqbal, *The Reconstruction of Islamic Thought* (Lahore: Ashraf, 1951), pp 149–52.

43. Al-Shatibi, *Al-muwafaqat fi usul al-sharia*, vol. 4, pp 595–602.

44. The ulama have often used the words *mujtahid* and *mufti* synonymously. However, the two functions are not exactly the same either in nature or in degree, even if the areas they cover overlap. The *mujtahid* works on the sources and tries to deduce legal judgments from them, while the *mufti* must give specific answers to questioners (whether this is an individual or a community) and so works downstream from the *mujtahid*. *Mufti* must have most of the qualities referred to earlier, unless their *fatwas* are restricted to a specific subject area (*juzi*). We shall deal with the various levels of *fatwas* later.

45. In this explanation, al-Shatibi identifies the *mufti* with the *mujtahid*.

46. Al-Shatibi, *Al-muwafaqat fi usul al-sharia*, vol. 4, pp 595–6.

47. Qur'an, 21:79.

48. Al-Shafii, *Al-risala* (Cairo: al-Amiriyya, 1926), p 128.

49. Cf. *Fatwas* of the European Council for Fatwas and Research, English translation (Islamic Foundation of Dublin, 2001).

50. Yusuf al-Qardawi, *Fi fiqh al-aqalliyyat al-muslima* (On Law and the Jurisprudence of Muslim Minorities) (Cairo: Dar al-Shuruq, 2001).

51. This position is entirely understandable, since he does not live in the West and his reflections accompanied the first stage in the establishment of Muslims in Northern societies.

52. This approach is also necessary in all majority-Muslim countries, as they are nowadays all in contact with Western culture.

53. For this see my preface of *Recueil de fatwas*, Tawhid edition (Lyon: Tawhid, 2000), pp 9–19, as well as the commentaries of the *fatwas*.

54. Critical and fruitful discussions with the anthropologist Abd al-Halim Herbert have fed and inspired the discussion developed in this section.

55. See *To Be a European Muslim*, part I, "The Birth of the Islamic Sciences."

56. This is not to deny some possibilities of harmonization but rather to remember that the obsessive desire to show links between contemporary science and

Qur'anic teachings tends to become very unhealthy and may even lead to serious reversals in conviction: the scientific truths of today may be considered erroneous tomorrow.

57. The "Islamic" sciences, as they are traditionally called, each have a methodology dependent on the areas of study of the revealed Book. All the other sciences also have varieties of methodologies differentiated on the basis of the object of study in the "open book" (the universe)—the book of nature.

58. We have chosen to include the most familiar sciences because the size of the table makes it impossible to mention them all.

Chapter 4. A Comparative Approach to Islam and Democracy

1. Abu Shuja' Shirawayh ibn Shahrdar al-Daylami, *Al-Firdaws bi-Ma'thur al-Khitab* (The Heavenly Garden Made Up of the Selection from the Prophet's Addresses) (Beirut: Dar al-Kurub al-Ilmiya, 1986), 4:300.

2. For the second part of the *hadith* see the sections "Nikah" (Marriage Contract) in Abu' Abdullah Muhammad ibn Ismail al-Bukhari (ed), *al-Jami' al-Sahih* (A Collection of the Prophet's Authentic Traditions) (Istanbul: al-Maktabat al-Islamiya, n. d.), chapter 45; "Birr wa-Sila" (Goodness and Visiting the Relatives) in Imam Abu Husayn Muslim ibn Hajjaj (ed), *Al-Jami' al-Sahih*, chapter 23; and for the first part see "Tafsir" (The Quranic Commentary) and "Manaqib" (The Virtues of the Prophet and His Companions) in Abu 'Isa Muhammad ibn 'Isa al-Tirmidhi, *Al-Jami' al-Sahih* (Beirut: Dar al-Ihya al-Turath al-'Arabi, n.d.), chapters 49 and 74. The original text in Arabic does not include the word "sisters" in the command. However, the masculine form used refers to both men and women, as is the rule in many languages. An equivalent in English would be "mankind," which refers to both men and women. By saying "O servants of God," the Prophet also means women, because both men and women are equally servants of God.

3. See Karl R. Popper, *The Poverty of Historicism*, trans Sabri Orman (Istanbul: Insan yayinlari, 1985)

4. 'Ala al-Din 'Ali al-Muttaqi al-Hindi, *Kanz al-"Ummal Fi Sunan al-Aqwal wa al-Af al* (A Treasure of the Laborers for the Sake of Prophet's Sayings and Deeds) (Beirut: Muassasat al-risala, 1985), 6:89.

Chapter 5. Religious Liberty: A Muslim Perspective

1. A. Yusuf Ali, *The Holy Qur'an: Text, Translation, and Commentary* (Leicester, UK: The Islamic Foundation, 1975), p 510, n.1480.

2. *Ibid.*, p 1407, n.4933.

3. It is important to recall that, from a Muslim perspective, *Jihad* is neither war nor holy war. This is an Orientalist's conception. The Arabic word *Jihad* literally means "effort." The *Jihad* consists in striving to fulfill God's purpose. Its highest form consists in fighting against our inner evil inclinations. It is for historical and contingent reasons that the wars fought by Muslims have more often than not been improperly called *Jihad*. It is impossible to give a bibliog-

raphy; the most recent book on this question is A. Morabia's doctoral thesis, *La Notion de jihad dans l'Islam médiéval, des origines à al-Gazali* (Université de Lille III, 1975). See also M. Arkoun, M. Borrmans, and M. Arasio, *L'Islam religion et société* (Paris, 1982), pp 60–2.

4. In the formulae of conversion to Islam it is explicitly mentioned that the convert has "freely chosen Islam, without fear, in complete security against danger, and without any kind of coercion." See Muhammad b. Ahmad al-Umawi al-ma'ruf bi-Ibn al-'Attar, *Kitab al-watha'iq was-l-sigillat*, ed P. Chalmeta and F. Corriente (Madrid, 1983), p 405; see also pp 409–10, 414, 415–16.

5. Mahmoud Taha was hanged by General Numeiri in Khartoum, Sudan, on January 18, 1985, at 10am, as an apostate. Dr 'Abd al-Hanrid 'Uways supported this enforcement of the law (see *al-Muslimun*, a Saudi weekly paper specializing in Islamic studies, March 23–29, 1985, p 15).

6. A *hadith* is called *mutawatir* when it is transmitted by several driving chains of reliable warrantors.

7. *Hadd* is legal penalty explicitly specified in the Qur'an.

Chapter 6. Freedom of Religion and Belief in Islam

1. Mehdi Ha'eri Yazdi, "Islam and the Universal Declaration of Human Rights," *The Yearbook of the Shi'ite School of Thought*, no. 4 (1963), pp 67–76.

2. In Twelver Shi'ism, the Prophet Muhammad, his daughter Fatima, and the 12 Shi'a imams are assumed to be infallible and are collectively called the "Fourteen Infallibles."

Chapter 7. The Divine Text and Pluralism in Muslim Societies

1. Andreas Christmann, "'The Form is Permanent, but the Content Moves': The Qur'anic Text and its Interpretation(s) in Mohamad Shahrour's *al-Kitab wal-Qur'an*," in Suha Taji-Farouk (ed), *Modern Muslim Intellectuals and the Qur'an*, p 269.

Chapter 8. The Nexus of Theory and Practice

1. Quoted in Navid Kermani, "From Revelation to Interpretation: Nasr Hamid Abu Zayd and the Literary Study of the Qur'an," in Suha Taji-Farouk (ed), *Modern Muslim Intellectuals and the Qur'an*, pp 175–6.

2. *Ibid.*, p 174.

Chapter 9. Women and the Rise of Islam

1. *The Qur'an: The Revelation Vouchsafed to Muhammad the Seal of the Prophets* (in Arabic and English), trans Muhammad Zafrulla Khan (London: Curzon Press, 1971; reprint, 1985). All quotations from the Qur'an in this chapter are from this translation.

2. W. Robertson Smith, *Kinship and Marriage in Early Arabia* (Cambridge: Cambridge University Press, 1885); W. Montgomery Watt, *Muhammad at Medina* (Oxford: Clarendon Press, 1956), pp 272–3.

3. Watt, *Muhammad at Medina*, p 375.

4. *The Translation of the Meanings of Sahih al-Bukhari* (in Arabic and English), 9 vols, trans Muhammad M. Khan (Medina: Dar al-fikr, 1981), 7:44. Here and below I have translated the Arabic rather than used the precise wording of Khan's rendering. Whenever possible, I have used works that give both Arabic and English texts.

5. Watt, *Muhammad at Medina*, pp 277–9, 376–7; Gertrude Stern, *Marriage in Early Islam* (London: Royal Asiatic Society, 1939), pp 61–2, 172–3.

6. Abu'l-Faraj al-Isfahani, *Kitab al-aghani*, 20 vols (Bulak: Dar al-kutub, 1868), 16:106; Stern, *Marriage in Early Islam*, pp 39–43. For a further discussion of marriage and divorce in pre-Islamic Arabia see Laila Sabbaqh, *Al-mar'a fi al-tarikh al-'arabi fi tarikh al-'arab qabl al-islam* (Damascus: Manshurat wizarat al-thaqafa wa'l-irshad al-qawmi, 1975), especially chapter 2.

7. Watt, *Muhammad at Medina*, p 384 (quotation); Muhammad Ibn Sa'd, *Biographien/Kitab al-tabaqat al-kabir*, 9 vols, ed Eduard Sachau (Leiden: E.J. Brill, 1904–40), 8:4. Ibn Sa'd is hereafter cited in the text.

8. *Sahih al-Bukhari*, 7:45–6.

9. See Nabia Abbott, *Studies of Arabic Literary Papyri*, 3 vols, Oriental Institute Publications, vols 75–7 (Chicago: University of Chicago Press, 1957–72).

10. *Sahih al-Bukhari*, 1:298; Ahmad ibn Muhammad ibn Hanbal, *Musnad*, 6 vols (Beirut: al-maktab al-islami lil-tiba'a wa'l-nashr, 1969), 6:42.

11. *Sahih al-Bukhari*, 1:1–4.

12. Khadija is described in the same text as a woman "of honor and power and a hirer of men" (Ibn Sa'd, 8:9).

13. Gertrude Stern, "The First Women Converts in Early Islam," *Islamic Culture*, 13, no. 3 (1939), p 293.

14. Watt, *Muhammad at Mecca*, pp 102–5.

15. 'Umar Ridda Kahhalah, *A'lam al-nisa: fi a'lami al-'arab wa'l-islam*, 3 vols (Damascus: Al-matba'a al-hashimiyya, 1940), 1:280; Stern, "First Women Converts," p 291.

16. 'Abd al-Malik ibn Hisham, *Al-sira al-nabawiyya*, 2 vols, ed Mustapha al-Saqqa, Ibrahim al-Ibyari, and Abdel Hafiz Shalabi (Cairo: Al-babi al-halabi, 1955), 1:356. I quote here from Alfred Guillaume's *Life of Muhammad: A Translation of Ishaq's Sirat Rasul Allah* (New York: Oxford University Press, 1955), p 161.

17. Ibn Hisham, *Al-sira al-nabawiyya*, 2:441.

18. Nabia Abbott, *Aishah, the Beloved of Muhammad* (Chicago: University of Chicago Press, 1942), p 3 (quotation); Maxime Rodinson, *Mohamad*, trans Ann Carter (New York: Penguin Books, 1971), p 55.

19. Stern, *Marriage in Early Islam*, p 34.

20. Ibn Hisham, *Al-sira al-nabawiyya*, 1:487.

21. *Ibid.*, 1:498–9.

22. William Muir, *The Life of Muhammad from Original Sources* (Edinburgh: J. Grant, 1923), pp 175–6, 201; Abbott, *Aishah*, pp 50, 68.

23. Ibn Hanbal, *Musnad*, 6:211.

24. Abbott, *Aishah*, pp 2, 7–8, 31–5.

25. *Sahih al-Bukhari*, 7:88; Watt, *Muhammad at Medina*, p 381.

26. Other women besides Khadija are mentioned in the early texts as trading in their own right, for example, Aishah's bint Mukhariba, in Ibn Sa'd, 8:220. See also Watt, *Muhammad at Medina*, p 290.

27. *Sahih al-Bukhari*, 4:85–6; Nabia Abbott, "Women and the State on the Eve of Islam," *American Journal of Semitic Languages*, 58 (1941), p 273. See also Ilse Lichtenstadter, *Women in the Aiyam al-Arab* (London: Royal Asiatic Society, 1935).

28. Stern, *Marriage in Early Islam*, pp 111ff.

29. Ibn Hanbal, *Musnad*, 6:271.

30. Abbott, *Aishah*, p 25.

31. *Encyclopedia of Islam* (Leiden: E.J. Brill, 1913–), s.v. "masdjid;" *Sahih al-Bukhari*, 1:257; Watt, *Muhammad at Medina*, p 285.

32. Henri Lammens, *Fatima et les filles de Mahomet* (Rome: Scripta Pontificii Instituti Biblici, 1912), pp 53–4.

33. *Encyclopedia of Islam*, new ed (Leiden: E.J. Brill, 1960–), s.v. "hidjab;" Stern, *Marriage in Early Islam*, pp 108–10; E. Abrahams, *Ancient Greek Dress* (Chicago: Argonaut Press, 1964), p 34; *Jewish Encyclopedia* (New York: Fund and Wagnalls, 1901), s.v. "veil."

34. Stern, *Marriage in Early Islam*, pp 114–15.

35. See also Abbott, *Aishah*, pp 45, 49–54; Stern, *Marriage in Early Islam*, p 114.

36. Abbott, *Aishah*, pp 56–8.

37. Abbott, "Women and the State on the Eve of Islam," pp 275–6.

38. *Ibid.*, pp 264–6.

39. Abbott, *Aishah*, pp 68–9.

40. Abbott, "Women and the State on the Eve of Islam," pp 279–80.

41. *Ibid.*, pp 281–4.

42. F. Beeston, "The So-called Harlots of Hadramaut," *Oriens*, 5 (1952), pp 16–17.

43. *Ibid.*, pp 16ff.

44. Wiebke Walther, *Woman in Islam*, trans C.S.V. Salt (London: George Prior, 1981), p 78.

45. Abbott, *Aishah*, pp 11, 84, 95–7.

46. *Encyclopedia of Islam* (1913–), s. v. "Omar ibn al-Khattab;" Abbott, *Aishah*, p 88; Stern, "First Women Converts," p 299.

47. See also Abbott, *Aishah*, p 94.

48. *Ibid.*, pp 160–9.

49. For an analysis of the strong parallels between Islamic and Judaic formulations of marriage see Judith Romney Wegner, "The Status of Women in Jewish and Islamic Marriage and Divorce Law," *Harvard Law Journal*, 5, no. 1 (1982), pp 1–33.

Chapter 10. Aishah's Legacy: The Struggle for Women's Rights within Islam

1. Asma Barlas, "Amina Wadud's Hermeneutics of the Qur'an: Women Rereading Sacred Texts," in Suha Taji-Farouki (ed), *Modern Muslim Intellectuals and the Qur'an*, p 99.
2. *Ibid.*, p 101.

Chapter 11. Muslim Women and Fundamentalism

1. *1983 World Population Data Sheet* (Washington, DC: Population Reference Bureau).
2. *Ibid.*
3. "People's Wallchart," *People Magazine*, vol. 12 (1985).
4. *Ibid.*
5. *Ibid.*
6. *World Fertility Survey*, no. 42, "The Egyptian Survey," November 1983.
7. *Annuaire Statistique* (Paris: UNESCO, 1980).
8. *Ibid.*

Chapter 12. Islam, Justice, and Politics

1. See, for instance, Qur'an, 4:58, 65, 105, 135; 7:29; 16:90; and 7:25.
2. Qur'an, 2:177.
3. Muhammad Hashim Kamali, "The Limits of Power in an Islamic State," *Islamic Studies Quarterly Journal*, vol. 28, no. 4 (winter 1989) (Islamabad: Islamic Research Institute, International Islamic University), p 329.
4. It is estimated that about 65 percent of the *Ummah* can neither read nor write.
5. The relevant Sura in full reads as follows: "It is not righteousness That ye turn your faces Towards East or West But it is righteousness—To believe in God And the Last Day And the Angels And the Book And the Messengers To spend of your substance, Out of love for Him, For your kin, For orphans, For the needy, For the wayfarer, For those who ask, And for the ransom of slaves; To be steadfast in prayer, And practice regular charity; To fulfill the contracts Which ye have made And to be firm and patient, In pain (or suffering) And adversity And throughout All periods of panic Such are the people Of truth, the God-fearing" (Sura 2:177).
6. Sura 107:1-7 in full reads: "Sees thou one Who denies the Judgement (To come)? Then such is the (man) Who repulses the orphan (With harshness) And encourages not The feeding of the indigent So woe to the worshippers Who are neglectful Of their Prayers Those who (want but) To be seen (of men) But refuse (to supply) (Even) neighbourly needs."
7. Sura 4:58. See also Suras 3:110 and 9:71.
8. See also Sura 38:26.
9. Imam Ali, *A Selection from Nahjul Balagha* (Houston, TX: Free Islamic Literatures Incorporated, 1978), p 15.

10. Mahmoud M. Ayoub, *Islam: Faith and Practice* (Ontario: The Open Press, 1989), p 25.

11. *Ibid.*

12. For a comprehensive study of the worldview of *tawhid* see Ayatullah Murtaza Mutahhari, *Fundamentals of Islamic Thought* (Berkeley, CA: Mizan Press, 1985).

13. *Concept of Islamic State* (London: Islamic Council of Europe, 1979), p 33.

14. Kamali, "The Limits of Power in an Islamic State," p 326.

15. *Ibid.*, p 66.

16. *Ibid.*, especially pp 54–5.

17. *Ibid.*, p 70.

18. Erskine Childers, "Amnesia and Antagonism," *Mimeograph* (1992), p 1.

19. John Esposito, *The Islamic Threat: Myth or Reality?* (Oxford: Oxford University Press, 1992), p 198.

20. Chandra Muzaffar, *Human Rights and The New World Order* (Penang: Just World Trust, 1993), p 20.

21. United Nations Development Program (UNDP), *Human Development Report 1998* (New York: UNDP, 1998), p 29.

22. *Ibid.*, p 30.

23. Fazlur Rahman, *Major Themes of the Qur'an* (Chicago: Bibliotheca Islamica, 1980), p 38.

24. *Ibid.*

25. *Ibid.*, chapter 9.

26. See *The New Straits Times*, April 12, 2000.

27. Quoted in Suroosh Irfani, "The Return of History," *Dawn* (Pakistan), Friday, January 4, 1991.

28. The phrase "stood forth in justice" is taken from Sura 57:25.

Chapter 13. Facts and Values: An Islamic Approach

1. John L. Esposito and John O. Voll, *Makers of Contemporary Islam*, pp 80–1.

2. Hasan Hanafi, *From Faith to Revolution* (Tokyo: United Nations University Publications, 1985).

3. Hasan Hanafi, *Les méthodes d'éxègese; La conscience active* (Cairo: University Press, 1965).

4. Hasan Hanafi, *Religious Dialogue and Revolution* (Cairo: University Press, 1977).

5. "I have therefore found it necessary to deny *knowledge*, in order to make room for faith." Immanuel Kant, *Critique of Pure Reason*, preface to the second ed, trans Norman Kemp Smith (London: Macmillan, 1963), p 29.

Chapter 14. Reason, Freedom, and Democracy in Islam

1. *Mathnavi*, Book I, verse 4157.

2. The Persian word *haq* connotes metaphysical truth and rightness, as well as civil and legal rights.

3. Shi'a Muslims reserve this title only for their first Imam, Ali, who was also the cousin and son-in-law of the Prophet Muhammad.

4. *Nahj al-Balaghah*, Sermon 15.

5. The Persian *morid bazi* refers to the corruption associated (primarily but not exclusively) with the abuse of the relationship between the devotees and the Sufi masters.

6. *Mathnavi*, Book I, verses 2332–6.

7. *Ibid.*, Book II.

8. *Ibid.*, Book IV, verse 2301.

9. Rumi (*Divan-e Kabir*, elegy 633) uses the phrase "totally other" to denote an ineffable and transcendental essence. "My sun, my moon, my sight, my hearing has arrived. My own silver framed one, my very gold mine has arrived. The intoxication of my head, the light of my eyes has arrived. If you wish a 'totally other,' my 'totally other' has arrived."

10. *Mathnavi*, Book II, verses 25–7.

11. *Ibid.*, Book V, verse 167.

12. Qur'an, 2:256.

13. Qur'an, 11:28.

14. Qur'an, 7:123.

15. Sa'di, *Kolliat-e Sa'di*, elegy 323.

16. The author relies on the familiarity of the readers with Islamic mysticism where these concepts are developed and used as a matter of course (*Ed*).

17. Rumi's magnum opus.

18. Here the author relies on the familiarity of the readers with Islamic mysticism where these concepts are developed and used as a matter of course (*Ed*).

19. Sadr al-Din Shirazi (1571–1640), known as Mulla Sadra, was a renowned and highly original Islamic philosopher.

20. "The Lord of Time" (*Imam-e Zaman*) is one of the titles of the living but occulted last Imam of the Twelver Shi'a Muslims.

21. This doctrine was first unleashed by Marxist intellectuals, who ended up as its first victims.

22. Qur'an, 20:68.

23. The author is referring to the well-known Qur'anic verse, "Those who listen to the Word and follow the best (meaning) in it: those are the ones whom Allah has guided, and those are the ones endowed with understanding" Qur'an, 39:18 (*Ed*).

24. *Mathnavi*, Book III, verse 1109.

25. Qur'an, 28:83.

26. The author is boldly using the politically loaded term *velayat* (guardianship) that is a keystone of the late Ayatollah Khomeini's theory of the "guardianship of the jurisconsult" (*velayat-e faqih*). This idea was later molded into the main axis of the political theory of the Islamic Republic and enshrined in the constitution of the Islamic Republic of Iran (*Ed*).

27. *Mathnavi*, Book II, verse 290.

28. *Ibid.*, Book I, verse 2892.
29. Qur'an, 13:29.
30. *Mathnavi*, Book I, verses 1373–4, 1389.
31. *Ibid.*, Book III, verse 2435.
32. Only then can we sing with Rumi (*Mathnavi*, Book I, verses 2311–14, 1810): "Give us a hand, buy us back from ourselves, Lift the veil, but cover our hidden selves. Buy us back from the sordid desires of the flesh. Whose bland torments the bone through the flesh. And then we may take pride: I heaved a sigh in the shape of a rope. A rope hanging in my well a hope. I climbed up the rope and emerged from the well. And became happy, ample and well. I was at the bottom of a well, gloomy. Now the world is too narrow for me. Praises are due to you O Almighty. Suddenly you relieved sorrows so mighty. Your blessing, keeps me in such good cheer, How can a cup of wine compete as its peer?"

Index